CYCLING'S GREATEST MISADVENTURES

# Cycling's Greatest Misadventures

EDITED BY ERICH SCHWEIKHER AND PAUL DIAMOND

Casagrande Press • Solana Beach, California

Published by Casagrande Press
Solana Beach, California

www.casagrandepress.com
casagrandepress@aol.com

Copy Editor: Katherine Spielmann
Book Design: Steve Connell / Transgraphic Services
Cover Design: www.liminalspaces.co.uk
Front and back cover photo illustrations: Kirstin Prisk

Printed in Canada

Library of Congress Cataloging-in-Publication Data

Cycling's greatest misadventures / edited by Erich Schweikher and Paul Diamond. -- 1st ed.
    p. cm.
  Includes bibliographical references.
  ISBN 978-0-9769516-2-9
1. Cycling--Anecdotes. 2. Cycling--Miscellanea.  I. Schweikher, Erich, 1978- II. Diamond,
Paul, 1970- III. Title.

  GV1043.C93 2007
  796.6--dc22

                                                    2007009280

Ever bike? Now that's something that makes life worth living! I take exercise every afternoon that way. Oh, to just grip your handlebars and lay down to it, and go ripping and tearing through streets and road, over railroad tracks and bridges, threading crowds, avoiding collisions, at twenty miles or more an hour, and wondering all the time when you're going to smash up. Well now, that's something! And then go home again after three hours of it, into the tub, rub down well, then into a soft shirt and down to the dinner table, with the evening paper and a glass of wine in prospect—and then to think that tomorrow I can do it all over again!

—Jack London

# Contents

## Revolutionary Ideas

## BIKE CRASH PHOTO GALLERY

## Turns for the Worse

## A World Away

# Introduction

## ERICH SCHWEIKHER

My first real kiss was on a bike.

Sarah and I were stopped at an intersection of Highway 101 and a beach access road outside the quaint town of Yachats, Oregon. The sun had just broken through the clouds, offering a majestic, rayed panorama of the ocean out past the basalt headlands. We were waiting to relay a change in the day's itinerary to the slower members of our group. I was 15 years old, and riding on a six-week, unsupported bike trek across the Pacific Northwest. The route began in Seattle and wound its way down the coast, following Highway 101 through Washington and Oregon until it turned northeast at Coos Bay toward the Cascades, eventually looping back to Seattle.

I'd flirted with Sarah over the first two weeks of the trip. I liked her and the way she rode a bike: her back straight, her chest out and her head high. No matter how difficult the terrain, she always had perfect posture. She laughed at my ridiculous behavior, like when I sprayed her with my water bottle as I passed her or deflated her tires at a rest stop only to help her pump them up. As adolescents sometimes do, I thought mischief was the best way to a girl's heart.

Two weeks into the trip, as our group sat around the campfire exchanging stories about our lives at home, Sarah's friend whispered to me: "Sarah thinks you're cute!" I decided it was time to make a move. Sabotage and water bottles could only take me so far. I needed to rise to the occasion. That night I couldn't sleep. My mind was racing with various scenarios.

The next morning I found myself at the intersection with her. The two of us alone, waiting for the stragglers, in awkward silence. We had just passed the Yachats Chamber of Commerce and its plaque that read: "[Yachats] is the ideal place for rest, relaxation, renewal, discovery, and romance." *Discovery* and *romance*, I thought. *Why not kiss her here, with only the ocean in view?* With one foot on my pedal and the other barely touching the ground, I gingerly leaned across the small space between Sarah's bike and mine. I was happily surprised when our lips met. (In my head I had begun composing a letter to my friends back home in Phoenix describing my exploits in detail.) Then my balance faltered. Unable to pull my foot loose from the toe clip, my fully loaded Diamondback Topanga and I toppled, crushing Sarah and her bike under 230 pounds of flesh and bone, metal, assorted camping gear, and supplies.

Not able to look one another in the eye, we clumsily untangled ourselves from each other and our bikes to the applause and jeers of a pick-up truck bed full of college students.

Other than the devastating effect the incident had on a 15-year-old's self-confidence, I escaped with only a bruised thigh and a cracked water bottle cage. Sarah suffered worse. As we fell to the ground I bit down hard on her bottom lip. Blood gushed out and she began to cry. Three days later her lip was still swollen.

Sarah and I managed to overcome the incident. For another week we held hands, stared into each other's eyes, and even snuck into each other's tents. However, by the time we made it to Crater Lake, Sarah was sneaking into my friend Nick's tent. Though I was upset, and maybe felt a little betrayed, I understood her change of heart: Nick was two years older than me, and he was a stronger cyclist. In the Seattle airport, right before she boarded her plane to Greenwich, Connecticut, she gave me a hug, and we exchanged a kiss on the cheek. "Now, that's a little better," she said. From both my six-week cycling trip and from her, I was left wanting more, and so my passion for the fairer sex and cycling was twinborn. In psychological terms, I guess you could say that my adolescent excitement for girls and the worlds of possibilities held within them fused itself to cycling.

With the exception of my first-kiss fiasco, my career as a recreational cyclist has been relatively disaster-free. That's not to say I haven't had my fair share of crashes, meltdowns, blow-ups, minor injuries, and mechanical problems, but every cyclist who spends a good part of his or her life on a bike knows that he or she will face the inevitable incident or accident. The inevitable, in its many forms and possibilities, is collected here in the book you are holding. Usually the inevitable is entertaining, sometimes it's tragic, always it is individual.

Cycling is the rare sport in which accomplishment is truly personal—we judge ourselves against ourselves. How fast can I make it there and back? Will this modification drop those few necessary seconds from my next time trial? Can I finally climb that 11-percent-grade fire road without walking? Even us recreational cyclists and commuters will lapse into fierce competitiveness: racing a bus to the next stop; trying to beat a light; or catching and then drafting "that guy" on the five-thousand-dollar bike decked out in full US Postal kit, before blowing by him in a pedal-mashing sprint, only to get passed back moments later. Each rider has his or her own criteria for what makes (and ruins) the perfect ride.

As cyclists, when we are not pushing ourselves, we are expanding ourselves—exploring a new trail, finding the most scenic ride to work, or devising a route that passes the best happy hours in town. And for some, cycling is a spiritual experience or a rolling, cathartic meditation. The comforting rhythms of each pedal stroke combined with the familiar feel of the pavement or dirt beneath the wheels puts a rider at ease and reacquaints him with his surroundings and, to a greater extent, himself.

Thumbing through the final selection in this book, I'm struck by how all of these nonfiction stories reiterate similar themes. Some themes are unequivocal, such as these: 1) The aspirations of cyclists—to ride, eat, and ride some more—are clear, yet determined mostly by uncontrolled forces (weather, mechanical issues, spouses or kids, etc.). 2) The trail, or the road, is at once a blissful escape and a fickle, merciless master. And 3) cyclists, more than others, are intent upon vagabonding through vast ranges of land. Other themes that repeat among the stories are not so self-evident: 4) Though much interfered with, the privilege of riding is almost always taken for granted and treated more as an entitlement. 5) Cyclists hold little nostalgia for a bygone era; as a collective entity we are obsessed with what is new. And 6) arising often is the question of what is authentic cycling culture, and does it exist independent from spandex advertisements and commercial culture? Lastly, the stories are all interwoven with the portrayal of the cyclist as a resilient personality or psychological type. And while in these stories the riders don't accomplish what they intended, they are nonetheless engaged in an internal battle between their body's capabilities and their mind's expectations. This nonstop war of self-improvement is a tendency, evinced by the pages that follow, which extends to the broader aspects of cyclists' lives.

# Twenty-Five Count

## CLAUS PALLE

### Costa Blanca, Spain—April 11, 1999

Everything was black. And then I could hear faint sounds. My head felt as though it had just been released from a vise. There was a stinging pain in my elbow. *Something's wrong*, I thought as I came to out of the blackness. *What happened?*

I opened my eyes and stared at a blue sky. As my vision adjusted, I focused on Frank, another triathlete on my training team. "Lie still," he said. He looked worried. Frank had extensive first-aid training, and from his expression I knew something serious must have happened. I was lying on my back on the pavement. I knew I had been involved in a crash. I had probably been riding too tight on someone's wheel, or maybe my front tire blow out; in either case, it had been a high-speed accident. Frank placed a finger on my neck and checked my pulse. His eyes met mine with catastrophic seriousness. I raised my right arm to check my elbow. There was just a tiny scratch. I checked my hands, they too were fine, not a palm or knuckle scratched. I could not feel my legs. *My legs!* I thought as I slowly bent one, and then the other. They both worked just fine, not a scratch on them. Clearly my back was not broken. *What a relief!*

My thoughts turned to my final exams at law school, only a month from now. I would probably have to spend a few weeks in bed, or at least a few weeks not exercising, and that would give me a lot of time to study for my finals. What concerned me was my August Ironman race, four short months away. *Would there be enough time to recuperate and get back in shape?*

I had spent the last three years training hard for the Ironman. In high school I played basketball, and in college I was a long-distance runner. Somewhere along the way, I became a triathlete. Last year, I made a premature attempt at an Ironman in Roth, Germany. Plagued by overtraining, the flu, bad weather, back problems, and stomach pain, I exited 16 kilometers short of the finish line. With three hours to go within the time limit, simply walking the remainder of the race would have allowed me to cross the finish line in time, but dehydration and stomach cramps made my completion of the race impossible. I collapsed and spent two horrible hours in the medical tent, shivering under three blankets with an IV stuck in my arm. To the attending doctor, I vowed to sell my bike and give up the sport. The doctor gave me a warm smile and said, "That's what everyone in here is saying." A week later I hired a personal coach, and began training harder than ever.

And now I was splayed out on the pavement, waiting for the ambulance, wondering if I still had a shot at the Ironman. At least the feeling in my legs had returned. I turned my head slightly and put on a brave smile for the spandex-clad riders surrounding me. As I scanned the crowd of familiar faces, I noticed that I was lying in a parking lot. *Is it possible to have a high-speed crash in a parking lot?*

I thought back to what I remembered. I had been riding with my training team, a mixed bag of triathletes and road racers, on a relatively short 85-kilometer ride. We were in sunny Spain, just south of Girona—I knew that. Last week, we had left the wet Danish spring behind and taken the 1,800-kilometer bus ride south. Not only does Spain have better weather than Denmark, but it also has mountains. Back home our highest "peak" is 173 meters. In Spain, we could climb mountains as high as 1,700 meters on a regular basis.

My recollection was interrupted as Betina, the lone female in our training group, rode into the parking lot. "Claus," she yelled in a parent-scolding-child kind of tone, "What are you doing there?" She and I are from the same town of Aarhus, Denmark. She raced the Ironman Germany with me. After my exit, she had looked at me with a serious face and said, "Why didn't you just puke to relieve the stomach pain and keep going?" Betina is no quitter.

The sharp tone of her question triggered my memory. I burst into laughter as it came back to me. The expressions on the faces of the guys around me turned from concern to serious concern. One of them closed in on me, ready to empty the contents of his water bottle on my face, probably thinking he could shock me into sanity. I motioned for him to stop. Then I grabbed my handlebars and awkwardly stood up. At this point it came back to me.

When my group had come upon the first and only serious climb of the day, a 500-meter knoll along the coast, we were quick to put a little heat under our kettles. The rivalry between the roadies and the triathletes had started earlier in the ride when a roadie said, "You guys can ride at 30 kph for six hours, but you can't do 50 kph for two seconds." So when we reached the bottom of the hill, we triathletes considered it an opportunity to show the roadies what we were made of. I was feverishly spinning my smallest gears, attacking the eight- to ten-percent grade with all my power, relying on my overall aerobic fitness to compensate for my lack of leg strength. With my relatively large 190-centimeter, 84-kilogram frame, I was suffering under the quick tempo. As I struggled to stay near the front, I noticed my pulse was pushing 173—five beats into my "red zone." The last thing I wanted to do was slip off the pace. I managed to keep my position all the way to the top.

Those who completed the climb congregated in the parking lot to wait for the remaining riders—Betina among them. As we waited, our team captain suggested a test to see who was *really* in top form. He began to explain that we should hold our breath for 15 seconds and . . . I took a deep breath while he finished his explanation. We all stood in silence, painfully watching the seconds tick away on our heart-rate monitors.

My body screamed for oxygen, and my lungs felt as small as two pecans. I was counting on my hypoxic training from swimming—holding my breath for three, then five, then seven strokes at a time. As the rest exhaled after their fifteen seconds, I was running on twenty-five seconds. For once I was outperforming the roadies. Finally I opened my mouth to inhale, but it was too late. My pulse dropped quickly from 126 to 109 beats per minute. My legs went weak. Then a black-velvet curtain decorated with purple sparks drew over my eyes. Exit me!

Robert, one of my teammates, recounted what happened next. He told me that I sat down on the top tube of my bike, slumped slightly forward, and released the brakes. My bicycle and I rolled with the slope of the parking lot, picking up speed with each rotation of the wheels, until I collided with an unsuspecting teammate. It all happened in a few seconds. As I fell, I head-butted his fancy Fondriest bike, bending his front bottle cage in the process. Then I hit the ground.

# Spin Cycle

**BOB MINA**

One of the perks of my new job as an IT Engineer was the employee gym downstairs from my office. It wasn't just a locker room stocked with second-hand equipment. This was the real deal: weights, treadmills, showers—it even offered an assortment of interesting classes. When I went to explore the state-of-the-art facility, I passed the front desk, where a sign-up sheet with bold lettering caught my attention:

SPIN CLASS
30 Minutes
Wednesday, November 6, 2002

I'd never taken a spin class. A couple of empty sign-in spaces suggested there were bikes available. Why not start with something I know? While it wasn't exactly "cycling," I felt comfortable with the concept. I scribbled my name in an available slot.

On the way out the door I asked a staff member, "Can I bring my own pedals?" He seemed surprised, "Sure! You'd be the first." Excellent. That night I unscrewed the pedals from my road bike and eagerly packed a bag of cycling gear. I was like a kid going to camp for the first time. As I went to sleep that night I thought, *This is going to be great—better than riding alone, good music, and it'll break up the day nicely.*

The next day, I was the 31-year-old dork who showed up first for class.

I replaced the traditional flat spin-pedals with my own clipless pedals and in true tri-geek form I unpacked measuring tape to set the saddle height, bar length, and pedal to seat distance so that the stationary bike's geometry would be equivalent to that of my road bike. I filled my bottle, got on the adjusted saddle, and waited for the other participants to show up.

As my classmates trickled in I began to feel a little out of place. It became apparent that spin cycling is a female-dominated activity. Not only was I the sole representative of my gender, I was also the only one clothed in Lycra shorts, a sleeveless jersey, and loud yellow cycling shoes. I also had no clue how to ride a spin bike with a 30-pound flywheel fixed to the cranks. I turned the resistance knob to its lowest setting, hoping to get the most out of this experience.

Enter our leader: a motivational speaker/hyperactive aerobics instructor who had DJ access to a selection of 120-beats-per-minute music.

"Okay, let's get going!" she yelled. I clipped in. Her head turned in my direction, eyes fixed on my feet. "First class?" she asked loudly. I nodded.

"Great! Enjoy it!" She yelled over the music. After two minutes of easy spinning, she ramped us into a furious cadence by screaming, "Ready, ladies . . . *Thirty-second sprint! Go! Go! Go!*"

*Boom!* Just like in a criterium from my roadie days, I'm off like a cow hit on the ass by a bottle rocket. With no resistance on my wheel, I spun like Marty Nothstein as I tried to catch up with the music. Taking a deep breath, I wondered just how hard these next thirty minutes were going to be.

"*Stop!*" the instructor yelled.

Like a good roadie finishing a sprint, I put the cranks to the three- and nine-o'clock position, then pushed all my body weight forward as if I were giving that last push over the finish line of an actual race—a remarkably stupid thing to do with a 30-pound flywheel hurtling around at 29 miles per hour.

My left foot snapped out first as my cleat was whipped clean from the pedal, leaving my leg dangling in space like Wile E. Coyote when he's missed a turn. The fly-wheel drove my right foot upwards, which forced my torso forward and downward onto the handlebars. With all my weight on the front of the bike, its rear end lifted a foot off the floor. At the front base of the bike there are two small plastic wheels that allow it to be easily moved. For perhaps the first time in history, these rollers now took an active part in the spin class as I performed a one-legged-nose-wheelie, thinking, *So help me God, I'm really going to crash a stationary bike—and I'm not even wearing a helmet!*

I had traveled about a foot towards the front of the class, when suddenly the back of the bike slammed back down, shocking the instructor, who spun her head so fast, she ripped her headset microphone wires from her DJ station. When she caught my glance I was regaining my balance, pedaling with my right leg while my left leg hung awkwardly.

The woman directly in front of me looked back with an expression of shock, probably wondering how she would have explained a collision that involved two non-moving bicycles to her insurance company.

I clipped my left foot back in, pedaled up to speed, and made a mental note about what not to do on a stationary bike. Then it was damage-control time. I thought, *What would Lance Armstrong do if he'd screwed up like this? I know . . . he'd take a drink and act cool.*

I reached for my water bottle, opened the nozzle with my teeth, and squeezed the bottle for a sip. But my near wipeout had loosened the cap, and now the entire contents of the bottle dumped onto my face. The liquid cascaded down my torso, into my Lycra shorts, all over my bike, and then pooled on the wood floor beneath me. I was only three minutes into the class.

# Divided on the Basin

## MICHAEL McCANN

As I opened my eyes on the morning in question, my body was wrapped in a feeling of contented joy. The sky was clear, the birds were chirping, and the air was clean and dry. A light breeze rolled by and kissed my face as I wrestled a leg out of my sleeping bag. I was warm, cozy, and just a bit stiff, but I felt pretty good . . . or so I thought. As I gazed upward at a lone cloud in the middle of the sky, my eyes started to focus properly. A thought jumped into my head, and as it arrived my stomach instantly knotted up.

"Where in the fuck am I?"

In a panic, my jaw locked and my brain hastily started piecing together the facts. I was lying mostly inside of a tent, my tent. I was on my back, looking up, and my face stung from sunburn. I was in an arid place, my head hurt, and—judging by the taste—a cat had apparently taken a crap in my mouth.

I rolled over and surveyed the land. Empty cans and bottles lay scattered around the picnic table in front of me. On top of the table lay a filthy, long-haired guy wearing only sunglasses and a pair of shorts. To my right was another tent, with the lower half of a body poking out of the door. Three bicycles had been dropped haphazardly around the camp, and each of them had a small, single-wheeled trailer attached to the back.

The body on top of the table let out a painful moan as I fiddled with the small bicycle computer in the palm of my hand. The inch-wide screen told me that it was 7 A.M., and the reflexive push of a button changed the time into mileage: 1,206 miles. That's when the haze started to clear.

A couple of weeks before, I had set off alone from Banff, Alberta, on the Great Divide Mountain Bike Route (GDMBR). Day after day I had pedaled up and down mountain passes, crisscrossing the watershed that separates North America along the spine of the Rocky Mountains. My trusty old Schwinn had towed a BOB trailer full of camping gear through some of the most magnificent scenery imaginable. And day after day, my body was getting stronger and stronger.

Not too many days before the morning in question, I had broken from the trail to spend some time floating the Madison River with my fly-fishing obsessed uncle. And shortly thereafter I had spent my 30th birthday alone, pedaling through Yellowstone and Grand Teton National Parks in cathartic bliss while storms chased me down and humbled my epic ego.

The night before the amnesiac morning, I had reacquainted myself with two riders I'd met before my detour off the GDMBR. Justin and Eric hailed from Portland, Oregon. They had never been on a bike trip before, so it seemed a little suspicious to me that they had decided on such a challenging route for their initiation to the world of bike travel. They had started off with an ambitious amount of equipment, but after our initial meeting they had begun to second-guess the need for much of their paraphernalia.

After storming into Pinedale, Wyoming, population 1,402, I found them sitting in a Mexican restaurant, demanding yet another basket of tortilla chips long after they had finished their plates of food. They were stoked to see me, yet not really that surprised. Our days apart had left them enough time to reconsider the need for much of their gear, and they were eager to show me their new plan.

We rolled to their camp where they proudly showed off the massive box of supplies they were mailing back home. Stoves and fuel and cook sets were wrapped in unworn articles of clothing. Small trinkets of luck and comfort filled the box to the rim. They placed their load of deadweight on the picnic table and asked me if I would be willing to continue riding with them in their newly slimmed-down mode.

For the first time in three summers of long-distance bike trips, I shook the hands of two people I welcomed as my companions, and we set off to paint that one-road town red.

We charged back into town like men possessed with a purpose. In a dark tavern, we swarmed over a small table, covering it with maps and pitchers of beer. Together, we looked ahead at the next few days while comparing stories from the previous few. Our bodies were toned and sunburned in ways that only 10 hours of daily off-road abuse can create. The locals shunned us at first, but our insatiable thirst eventually drew them closer, mostly out of curiosity. We were the circus sideshow of their summer, though our initial welcome hadn't been overly warm.

As the hours drifted by, the crowd thinned to an eclectic mix of cowboys, truck drivers, and us. People who had openly made fun of us early in the evening sat around and carefully listened to our tales from the trails. Some of the locals had spent time hunting on the U.S. Forest Service roads we'd been pedaling up and down. More than once, we had to recall specific sections of mountains and trails in order to prove to them that we weren't full of crap. Before long, the three of us were sitting in disbelief as the hardened roughnecks of rural Wyoming started producing pitcher after pitcher just to hear more of our stories.

By the early morning hours, the crowd had thinned, and things began to fragment around the time the barkeep gave us a tour of the back room. Wyoming, it seems, has a law that dictates: "If you sell liquor to be served, you must also sell liquor 'to-go.'" Our bleary eyes opened wide in the "office" of the smoky pub as the proprietor flaunted his extensive collection of bottles. Eric and I gazed around with a bewildered look. Justin just cackled like a parrot.

I went back to the saloon for my final pint of the evening, but found the place totally deserted. With no one behind the bar, I took the liberty of serving myself. As I fiddled with the tap, I glanced under the railing and noticed a shotgun stowed at waist level. I looked up and assessed the scene, tried to take note of the absurdity of my situation, and realized that it was high time for our hero to bow out gracefully. Without the slightest hint of pomp, or even so much as saying goodbye to my friends, I put a five-dollar bill on the bar and split.

I was well beyond halfway back to camp before I realized I still had the full pint glass in my hand.

And this is where I found myself. I had pledged my allegiance to these two individuals as they were setting forth on a new chapter of their odyssey. In a social sense we were compatible, but there's no predicting how well people will get along when pedaling 80 miles of up-and-down dirt every day. I had become accustomed to traveling without a stove or water filter, but how would they do? I gazed out of my tent at the two motionless bodies in front of me and wondered what in the hell I might be getting these guys into.

Then, as if on cue, Justin sat up. He scratched a bare shoulder and resumed chewing the piece of gum that had spent the night somewhere in his mouth. There was plenty of confusion in his tone as he mumbled something that sounded like the final piece of the sentence he was working on when he'd lost consciousness a few hours earlier. I peeked over at Eric and discovered that while only his torso was lying in the tent, he was dutifully awake, and looking at a map of the day's ride. *Buckle your seatbelts, boys*, I thought, *this is gonna be fun!*

We gathered our respective items and were astonished to find that three unopened bottles of booze had somehow made it home with us. Each of us had taken his own hazy path to camp that night, but only Justin refused to retrace his steps or share with us the time he'd arrived on the picnic table. There was an admission to having witnessed the sunrise, and then he openly deliberated if he should get in a shower while one was still accessible. We told him he should, yet somehow in the muddle of packing up and riding to breakfast this detail was unfortunately overlooked.

Over eggs and pancakes we revisited our notes from the night before. Ahead of us was a flat day of riding to get to South Pass City. After that there was the town of Atlantic City (sans casinos and slot machines), followed by the infamous Great Basin.

The Great Basin is an unrivaled section of the GDMBR. Earlier in the trip, almost every northbound rider had ranted and vented and warned me of this formidable obstacle. The Basin, I'd been told, is "a 134-mile stretch of desolation without trees, drinkable water, or resources of any kind. No one even lives out there, so getting help from locals is out of the question." It's a High Plains desert, its name derived from the fact that the Continental Divide eludes this area. Water that does manage to find its way into this highly elevated saddle just dries up—it never makes it to either the Pacific or the Atlantic Ocean.

Excited and well fed, we rolled out of Pinedale as the town was just coming alive.

The travel and the heat and the debauchery should have slowed us down considerably, but one thing that the GDMBR had provided for us was strength. The three of us were unbelievably resilient by this point. We were eating many times more than our usual intake. Our metabolisms were so jacked up that wounds healed quickly, food was processed at an alarming rate, and alcohol could be imbibed in Herculean binges. We functioned more like machines than cyclists. There were plenty of jokes about how we'd devolved into mere engines for our bicycles.

The morning's ride was fun and playful and warm. The sky loomed far bigger than any I'd ever seen in Montana, and the dirt road we commanded was visible miles ahead on the horizon. A rain cloud tried to dampen the day, but as it moved around us it only managed to mist the road. We could clearly see that torrents of rain were coming out of the cloud, but by the time the water had passed through all of that dry air, it was like vertically falling steam. Everything moved well for much of the day, with the exception of a few frustrating sections of washboard.

Late in the afternoon, we happened upon two other riders who were obviously on the same route (you can tell by the amount of gear they carry, the condition of their bikes, the alarming level of their sunburns, and the generally rough look of their bodies). Jelle was a Dutch rider heading north. His set-up was efficient and classic in the cycling community: front and rear panniers with a little extra gear bungeed above his rear wheel. The other rider was much more of an enigma to us. Gary Samano was a middle-aged guy heading south who, like myself, preferred the comfort and style of regular clothing to cycling gear. He sported normal shorts and sneakers, and would hardly be noticed as a cyclist if he stepped off of his bike and into a grocery store. In all honesty, he and I looked more like homeless vagabonds than serious cyclists. Gary, however, had the exact opposite idea from mine regarding "what to bring." He stood over a loaded rig that sagged under the weight. He had fully loaded front and rear panniers, a totally stuffed BOB trailer, and many additional baskets, bags, and containers strapped all over his bike.

We stopped and chatted with each of them in turn, and found that Gary had crossed paths with Jelle just a few minutes earlier. We marveled at the amount of gear he had with him. As we discussed certain benefits and riding styles versus others, he took photos of everyone's different set-ups. He was jovial and calm, even when we guffawed at how some tubing on his trailer had snapped under the pressure. It was soothing to chat with someone who shared a similar, humble profile of cycle touring. It's never anyone's place to state that one method is superior to any other, so we were glad to see that Gary, too, celebrated the fact that not all things work for all people—he was actually documenting the eclectic methods he encountered.

When we moved on ahead we felt charmed by having met Gary, but none of us were the least bit envious of his haul-as-much-as-possible system. The Portland boys were on their first day of slimmed-down riding—going for more miles per day largely thanks to having less weight. The three of us chatted at length about how long a ride like the 2,500-mile GDMBR would take Gary with his load.

About an hour or so later, Justin's rear wheel, a source of unending entertainment for anyone riding behind him, made itself noticed. It had become more and more warped and out of true as we'd gone along. The swerve and waggle (of arguably the most important aspect of any bicycle) caused his body to jostle with each rotation. Even a mild pedaling pace gave him the look of a cowboy on horseback, yet he rode on, insisting that it'd be fine. Alas, an interminable set of washboard roads had taken their toll on the crippled wheel. Spokes started popping like firecrackers, and the rim bent so awkwardly and quickly that the bike practically skidded to a stop. Even with the brakes undone, the tire was still abrasively rubbing against the frame. He immediately popped off the wheel and started mercilessly beating it against a post in an attempt to return it to a more circular shape. With snapped spokes however, this proved futile. We noticed a rare rest area ahead, and Justin managed to manipulate his crippled bike slowly over to the shelter.

I had some extra spokes with me, but they were the wrong size. To make matters worse, he'd managed to break most of the ones on the "drive" side of his wheel. Since they were sandwiched between the hub and the rear cassette, we would need a chain whip to replace the spokes, and none of us was carrying one. We scrolled through our options and realized this was suddenly a major issue. Catastrophic breakdowns can take days to fix, and we were hundreds of miles away from the nearest town that might have the tool we needed. We circled around and began crafting a hitchhiking scenario.

Suddenly, like a Western hero riding in on a white horse, the great Gary Samano rolled back into our lives. We showed him the victim and begged access to his extensive tool collection. Shockingly, he too lacked the necessary tool. He did, however, happen to have a few extra lengths of chain, spokes of every imaginable size, and the tenacity to fix anything even remotely related to a bicycle. Within minutes, Justin and Eric were securing the wheel, while Gary focused his mass on the chain to keep it from moving. With the wheel and cassette stabilized, I clamped a wrench onto a skewer that gripped the inside of the hub. The wrench handle was a mere three inches long—a few slips, bangs, and bloody knuckles, and I was ready to scatter the operation all over the rest area. But Gary, calm as a Buddhist diplomat, simply produced a small pipe and slid it over the handle, thereby extending its length enough to provide the torque needed. Our four-man effort was rewarded with a "pop," as the cassette slid lightly across the threads and started to unscrew.

And there we had it. That was exactly what we deserved for pooh-pooh-ing someone else's style. Gary's methods were nowhere near any kind of madness. His Boy Scout approach to travel saved us days of inconvenience. We were happy to travel lightly, relying on luck and occasional assistance from others, whereas he plodded along with deference to the world—knowing that at the end of the story, the tortoise beats the hare.

When the thank-yous and handshakes were done, we rolled off into the distance, lauding Gary as a guardian angel in disguise and humming the theme to the TV show *Different Strokes*. That night, as we cruised through a paved section, we somehow managed to miss our turnoff. Frequent reevaluations of the map gave us no assurance that we would be able to find a decent cut-off, and our stubbornness wouldn't let us backtrack for 10 wasted miles. So after a minor amount of consideration, we set off on a small dirt track that pointed in what we assumed to be the right direction. As our little track dwindled into nothing just two minutes into our new adventure, we guessed that the road we should be on was five miles due east of us. We rolled on and soon found ourselves bouncing through a field of small shrubs, praying under our breaths that the area wasn't infested with cacti.

Five minutes later we found our path obstructed by a barbed wire fence. There was absolutely no hesitation as we dismounted from the bikes, separated them from our trailers, and started haphazardly tossing them over the fence. Once assembled on the other side, we continued to blaze a trail through the fields. The land plodded along, then sloped into a hill with a small clump of trees (rare in this area) on top. We determined that we were only a mile or two away from being back on track, but the sun was quickly setting. The security of the trees would do for the night, so camp was immediately set up. Thirty minutes later, we were sleeping soundly under a blanket of stars so bright that even without the moon there was no need for headlamps.

The next morning I awoke to dreams of a grand breakfast. We would obviously go without such a luxury in the Basin, so I was greatly looking forward to whatever order of eggs I could wrestle up in either South Pass or Atlantic City. Living without a cook-set meant that I willingly starved myself of certain luxuries—which made it all the more sweet when I got the chance to indulge in something like a hot breakfast.

We tore down camp quickly and rolled out of our little patch of trees. Before the crisp chunks of the previous night's dreams had been wiped from the corners of our eyes, we were bouncing down a decent hill, plowing through yet another open field of shrubs, tall grasses, and cake-dried soil. We knew we were heading in the right direction by the lay of the land and the rising sun. Within thirty minutes, we were scurrying onto a well-graded dirt road.

With hearty souls and happy hearts we screamed up and down the rolling hills into South Pass City. We found it was a quaint little ghost town with nothing to offer aside from a tiny grocery store that appeared to be permanently closed. We rolled on, in the certainty that Atlantic City would be bustling with far more activity. It was, after all, depicted on our map by a beer mug and a plate with silverware. Any town with a tavern and restaurant was worth its weight in gold, as long as I could get some eggs with my Irish coffee.

It is with earth-crushing sadness that I have to report: Atlantic City has no such breakfast place. What it has is a bar that opens at noon and a souvenir shop that sells the following food items: Gatorade, coffee, salt-and-vinegar potato chips, ice cream sandwiches, peanuts, mixed fruit in a can, Snickers bars, and squeeze mayonnaise. Take away the squeeze mayonnaise and you have the well-balanced breakfast I wish I hadn't eaten.

The next half-hour was spent trying to glean more info from the locals about this Great Basin. Everyone agreed that the biggest gamble in getting to the next town with resources (in a timely fashion) was the wind. As one guy commented, "the gales on this plain rule the land without question, hesitation, or mercy." Granted, this is a town that welcomes visitors with a sign stating: *Welcome to Atlantic City. We really don't give a rotund rodent's rectum how you did it back home.* So you can imagine that the locals have a flair for the dramatic. But after a handful of tales about cattle being blown away and remarkable changes in wind direction, our confidence was beginning to sag.

After another hour we simply had to get going—it was time to roll off into the wild dry yonder. Our dejected hearts and uneasy stomachs motivated the push. We filled our water bottles to their brims and started our defiant charge out of town. We chugged straight up a large hill, as our map had described, and kept plugging along, knowing that it would be our last real climb for days. When we summitted, however, we found ourselves standing on a blacktop road.

Pavement? We weren't supposed to be anywhere *near* pavement! A mutual sigh was followed by a three-way chorus of "yougottabefuckingkiddingme." What better way to start the "hardest" challenge of the GDMBR than to get lost straight out of the gates?

I had been lost so many times in my travels that it was almost a perverse pleasure to share the experience with others. It is a universal custom, practiced around the world by every major culture and class: curse, look at the map, turn the map over and look again, point at the map, curse, put the map away, and start heading back in the direction from which you just came.

Gravity dragged us the three miles back toward town. As we leveled out it was quite clear which road we were supposed to be taking out of town—that would be the only other road in town that we hadn't come in on—and it clearly went straight back up another hill. But, since we'd broken a sweat and we happened to be back in town, we might as well take advantage of having another ice-cream sandwich, right?

Thankfully, it was still relatively early in the day—though the pounding sun would have had us believe otherwise—so up the "correct" hill we climbed. We reached the top to find a scenic vista of the open, flat dryness we'd be sampling for the next 134 miles. It wasn't quite picture-worthy, though it did feel rather ominous.

Ten miles later we crossed a bridge over the Sweetwater River. It was rumored to be the last decent water for what could potentially be a very long stretch of road. We arrogantly skipped the opportunity to refill our bottles, rationalizing that we'd hardly even sipped from them so far, and continued on. We pushed ahead without reservations. Why would we have any? With what we'd covered, we were obviously more than ready to tackle a stretch of road that's "hostile" because it's hot and dry! Puh-lease. Weeks earlier I had gleefully plunged headfirst down a 35-degree graded trail, while fighting with all my might to keep the trailer from bouncing *over the bike and onto my head*. Hot and dry? Wah!

About an hour beyond the bridge, we came upon a scene that truly opened our eyes to the fragility of our situation. Three riders were coming north, having just crossed the Basin. Steve, Kurt, and Karen were pretty travel-worn, but they seemed happy and positive. They were moving a little slowly, but it was just noon and they could have been late risers, maybe early into their day of pedaling. We stopped and chatted for a while. As soon as we got beyond the pleasantries, we moved on to the requisite "information sharing," and our eyes widened as they told us about their last week on the trail.

It had been five days since they left the town of Rawlins, which would be our next supplier of any resources or signs of life. Five days? Holy crap! Our plan had been to skirt that 134-mile section in *two* days—and our rations demanded it. Two of the three had come down with giardia, which had obviously slowed their pace a bit. Water had been very scarce, and the total lack of shade had given them a bit of the crazies. The route was apparently hard to follow, and under such circumstances—especially without any traffic in the area—the thought of getting lost was a complete mindfucker. As it turned out, their upbeat manner was due simply to the fact that they knew there was a tavern waiting for them before the end of the day. Or, as one of them so eloquently described it, "the place that's going to serve me the greatest steak dinner and beers of my life!"

But the sun was only getting higher and the day was only getting hotter, so we said our farewells and moved on. In fairness, I had reached my own threshold of self-doubt, and the best way to restore faith was to crank out some miles. As we parted ways, one of the guys told us to "enjoy the antelope, but realize that they will always win." I looked to Eric and Justin for clarification, while Karen called out quite cheerily, "and horse poop. For god's sake keep an eye out for the horse poop."

I guess one could have called this "advice," but really it felt more like we were hearing the punch lines to some inside jokes we were not yet privy to.

And on we rolled. We took turns out in the lead and our natural paces left some desired distance between us. Without any serious elevation gains I frequently drifted to the middle position. Most riders would label me a "climber"—and climbing hills is seemingly one of the things I was brought into this world for. I love to do it and it feels disturbingly comfortable for me to drag a trailer full of goods up a long hill. I'm not a fast rider by any means, but it damn near takes an act of Congress to get me out of the big ring up front. Longer strokes make for faster movement . . . even if it's up an 8% grade.

By nature, Justin is a "masher" as well, preferring larger gears and forceful grinding of the knees. He tends to move fast and his riding style is described by most as haphazard, erratic, and just plain unsafe. Outwardly, it appears that he's never paying the least bit of attention, even as he barrels through potholes and ditches at full speed. What most observers can't comprehend is that his apparent carelessness is actually an expression of what some would call a Zen state. He is the only person I have ever met who can chew tobacco, gum, and sunflower seeds *all at the same time,* while riding . . . and still carry on a conversation. He is capable, as he'd shown, of riding 60-plus miles a day on a wheel so out of true that most people would consider it unrideable. And under all the long hair and the shirtlessness is a guy who truly loves bow hunting and Jack Daniels. What's not to love?

Eric's position appeared to be that of the caboose, but that was a ruse as well. He is a "spinner" by nature—preferring high gears and a fast-paced cadence of the pedals both for climbing hills and cruising the flats—and a damn fine one at that. One might call it a matter of preference, but it can also be an indication of one's persona. Eric is cleaner and more calculated than Justin or myself. His attitude is solidly positive and his persistence in pedaling is practically unrivaled. His wise ways and "together" appearance evoke the things parents look for in a guy they'd want to be dating their daughter. I always felt that he lent a certain clout to our convoy of stooges.

When by happenstance I did drift out in front—when one of the others had a mechanical issue or needed to take a break—we all reveled in the agony of my misguided bike computer. Early in the trip I had neglected to recalculate the little gadget to accommodate the new tires I put on the bike. Therefore, my stats were always one tenth of a mile off. Normally this was not a serious issue, but when our directions were specific to the unmarked miles and so many roads and trails crossed our path at random intervals, it became fodder for the aforementioned mindfuck (at the possibility of getting lost in the place where you were strictly not allowed to do so). The ongoing joke was that I only did 90% of the work the others had to do.

We were over halfway into the day when we spotted our first group of antelope, standing motionless on a hill to our right. Together the three of us pointed and stared at the tiny little pronghorns as they reexamined us from a mile or so away. They were petite and cute and looked like they carried next to no meat on their bones. We rolled along without stopping and giggled at the way they focused on us. We could see their tiny heads shift a bit as we moved across their horizon. Then suddenly, and without any provocation on our part, they started running.

Having seen spiral-horned antelope on the Discovery Channel, I naturally assumed that these hoofed creatures all moved in a "leaping and bounding" fashion. Negative. These little buggers use their legs in a synchronized manner that leaves their bodies motionless as they run. Actually, these animals do not so much "run" as *fly!* I was shocked and awed to witness a small herd of them go from attentively staring to a 50-mph sprint directly at us. We yelped and shook and proceeded to haul untold amounts of ass as we tried to get in front of their trajectory. Within seconds it was obvious that these 3-foot, 50-pound creatures had us seriously outgunned. They easily dashed across the road in front of us, amidst our exhausting sprint to get in front of them.

The thought suddenly crossed our minds as Eric verbalized it: "The antelope always win."

The day brought more such run-ins and at times, spurred by sunstroke bouts of insanity, it was entertaining to try and outrun the little four-legged freaks. Weeks later, a chance to look at the *Encyclopedia Britannica* would reveal that they can actually run at 60 mph for long distances.

Late in the day, at a junction so utterly confusing that the final decision had to be made by flipping a lucky quarter, we took note of an accurate bike computer and noticed that we'd covered some serious miles during the hours we'd been active. As I strained to figure out exactly where on the godforsaken map we were, I realized that the wind was constantly trying to rip it out of my hands. "The breeze is crazy in this spot," I declared, as they looked up from the mileage indicator. You could almost hear the gears turning in our brains as we realized that the wind we had suddenly noticed had actually been blowing strong at our backs for hours. We were being granted the greatest gift of all: a tailwind through the roughest portion of the GDMBR. Dame Fortune was smiling upon us . . . and her smile was far brighter than the oppressive sun.

Our progress was blissful, confirmed by odd landmarks referred to on the map. At times our speed was breakneck and hindered only slightly by massive piles of horse crap littering the road. There were sparse viewings of wild horses cavorting in the distance, and we were forced to contemplate why these majestic animals would always leave their offerings in the middle of the road. Sometimes the piles would go unnoticed until they were unavoidably situated directly in the path of our tires. They were impressive not just in height (the largest around knee-high) but also in diameter, with one pile covering almost half of the road. Nothing polishes up a road-weary and unholy funk of unshowered bodies in the heat quite like a fine spraying of horseshit.

We were wretchedly filthy and parched when the sun finally neared the horizon. Just before dark, we found ourselves at a crucial turnoff leading us in a new direction. The intersection was as good a place as any to set up camp. As we surveyed the best spots, Eric did the math and rejoiced at the news that we had traveled 92 miles across the desert plain. We were low on water and exhausted, but our spirits were high. Our tents were erected amidst a fading wind, and we had the brilliant luck to get a mind-boggling sunset to match our mood.

A lone meteorological sign in the distance gave us some perspective, as clouds raged around the edges of the Great Basin. Storms brewed and dumped rain in all directions, but none of it dared to break the ring of mountains that stood guard around the place where water goes nowhere. Lightning flashed and thunder roared as we dined on beef jerky, peanut butter, non-refrigerated jelly, and hubris. Ninety-two miles was an unspeakably grand total for such a place. We were kings of the desert, gods among the sagebrush, and we basked in our greatness.

That evening we laid heavily into all three of the bottles of booze we were carrying. Two of these soldiers fell dry during our stories and recollections of the day's events. We passed around our food caches and our bottles intermittently for a while, then with more precision. The rules of bravado dictated that a cap removed from a bottle of whiskey had to be thrown into the trash, while rotgut rum could be re-corked at will. Finally, the efforts of the day left us fatigued and numb. We each fell into our tents amid cheerful congratulations and back-patting. Nothing could even come close to stopping us, it seemed.

The next morning, however, a menacing sun brought the three of us into the new day. I first noticed that my tent was facing a different direction from how I'd set it up the night before. I glanced over to see that Justin's tent had also been readjusted, and it was listing badly to one side. I rolled backwards out of my shelter to find that the wind had picked up again, and it was pushing vigorously to the south. I was confused for a minute as to what was going on. Separate from my amnesia two mornings before, I was coherent and remembered everything right away. Facts, however, were facts, and in the end I had to conclude that in a sleepwalking delirium I had re-staked my tent to accommodate the shifting maelstrom. Justin had done the same, but Eric's tent defied the gale force throughout the night. As his face poked slightly out of the tent, I noticed a small dried spot by the door. He slowly lifted his head and opened his swollen eyes. I gazed at him—the face of death stared back at me.

He'd managed to get a couple of hours of sleep in before stomach seizures interrupted his evening. The poor sonofabitch had awoken many times throughout the night to puke his guts out, without actually leaving the tent. Justin and I felt fine, leading us to believe that it was Eric's Little Smokies from the night before that had left him in such a condition.

Dinner between the three of us was spent sharing what gifts we had to offer: peanut butter, candy bars, chips, etc. In Pinedale, Eric had received a care package from a well-intentioned aunt. Along with all the cards and notes and chocolates was a bag of jerky snacks that looked remarkably similar to dog treats. Justin and I had fortunately shunned the greasy little wieners all night long. The proof of their effect had been evident in the oily sheen that had covered Eric's face before bedtime—just as the last of the bottles was being passed around.

We thought it funny at first—until we saw how much pain he was in. It was disheartening to watch him fumble around the campsite. I was suddenly plagued by the notion that our arrogance was about to foil us in the form of a package of spoiled Little Smokies.

We slowly packed up our things in a formidable wind that seemed determined to spread our gear all over the desert. Trying to roll up a tent properly in the equivalent of a violent wind tunnel virtually defines frustration. In the end, I opted for simply wrapping my tent into a ball and fastening it to the trailer with a bungee cord. Eric was taking many times longer to get his act together, so I wasted some time climbing around on a water tanker truck that had been abandoned at the intersection. It protruded from the horizon like it had once tried to defy the waterless wasteland. Now it was just collecting sand like a dinosaur skeleton. As I paced the top of the rusted cylinder I thought about the potential fiasco that faced us . . . and how badly we could have used some of that water.

We had 14 miles of dirt road left before we hit a paved section. From there it was just 40 miles to Rawlins. This was doable—easily doable by our standards—but an ill crew member was an x-factor. How long would we be able to hold up if he was unable to ride? Exactly two days after pledging to ride with others, and I was already hearing a voice in my head telling me to cut the cord and split. *Not yet,* I told myself.

As we eased back into our saddles, we found the changing wind was actually working in our favor. Strongly at our backs again, the gusts propelled us through sandy patches at dangerous speeds for much of the morning. Eric brought up the rear, but while he was still able to ride, he was pushing twice as hard to go about half as fast. Justin and I had each given him half of our water rations for the day, but after watching him get sick again just before we left, I knew it wouldn't be nearly enough to get him to Rawlins.

A few miles into the ride, a pack of wild horses appeared about a half mile off the trail. They instantly launched into the same game of chicken that the antelope had destroyed us in. But one straggler held to a slightly different course that must have beckoned Justin to a challenge. He pedaled ahead at full bore and forced the horse to continually readjust its trajectory. I dashed ahead to be close to the action, and from my viewpoint it looked like they were dead set to collide. But when the two sprinters crossed paths, the horse managed to lurch about three feet in front of him. As they simultaneously crossed the imaginary finish line, both the horse and Justin gave up their dash and slowed almost to a stop, as if to congratulate one another on a race well run. Justin was covered in the dust kicked up by the stomping hooves—and he was cackling like a parrot, while muttering something under his breath about a glue factory.

By the time we reached the pavement, the wind was absolutely relentless. The last couple of miles had been spent fighting the strength of the gusts at our backs. There were moments when the force was so strong that we actually had to brake to avoid fishtailing through some patches of sand. But now the real dangers presented themselves: Eric was lagging far behind and he seemed to be getting slower by the minute. Forty more miles would take absolutely everything he had . . . if he could make it at all. What's more, the wind was blowing hard, and the turn in our route meant it was now pushing into our faces.

We waited for Eric to catch up so we could examine his condition. He looked terrible, but we lied and tried to make him feel better. Justin and I gave him half of our water again, and he grudgingly accepted. He was heaving up anything that he swallowed, so baby sips were his key to staying hydrated. Food was pretty much out of the question. We knew we had to either get to civilization, or find more water quickly.

We pushed on and found ourselves struggling to hold a straight line on the road. The gusts tossed us from one side of the pavement to the other. Had there been any traffic at all, we would have been hood ornaments. Justin and I drifted well ahead of Eric, who plugged along as best he could. The steady noise of the wind, and our numb faces, began to drive us mad. I found myself screaming in order to be heard, and while the constant spray of sand had cleaned my teeth, it had also sheared several layers of skin from my face.

Soon it became obvious that we needed a barrier from the relentless wind—just a little break from it to give us a chance to readjust our attitudes. But only sagebrush and a barbed-wire fence even dared to stand up in this landscape. With no real options in sight we just continued to plod along and dream of better times we had spent on the ride. I tried to stay sane by singing songs to myself, but I couldn't even hear my own voice over the noise. With each mile, I was growing ever so slightly more crazy.

Then, a small blip appeared on the horizon. A mile later it took the shape of a small shack. Closer still and it appeared to be near the edge of the road. Ten minutes later, it was finally discernible . . . and it looked a lot like a small horse trailer. *Thank the gods!!!!* Justin and I dashed ahead and hopped off our bikes with zealous optimism. A quick survey showed that the trailer was concealing a deep well with hoses poking out of it. A pump was chugging along heartily, but the water was nowhere to be found. It must have been re-routed through another set of pipes to be used elsewhere. We looked around and marveled at where in the hell "elsewhere" might be. Nothing was visible for an eternity in any direction. We peeked into the trailer to find four huge trashcan-sized barrels of diesel fuel, uncapped and filled to the rims.

How strange, we thought, that someone would leave a pump like this, with all that fuel next to it, just raging alone like that in the middle of nowhere. That had to be dangerous amid an ocean of sagebrush, right? But who were we to judge the random? We were the least likely things to be traveling through the area, and besides, the tiny structure was at least enough of a windbreak to allow us to enjoy a snack and some sanity. There was no water to be had, but a break would at least liven our spirits a bit.

Eric was still barely a speck on the horizon when we noticed the vehicle coming up the road.

By the time we could tell it was a truck that was coming toward us, Justin and I had already unloaded most of our food. Many things could be expected from this vehicle: a lonely passerby, a curious local, a lost tourist, maybe a friendly mailman. Of the many things that the approaching truck might provide, we were most hopeful that it would bring some water with it. But as it lurched off the road and skidded up next to us, our prayers were spun around, turned over a bare knee, and beaten beyond recognition.

At the wheel of the truck was a male character whose outward appearance greatly resembled that of famed country crooner Willie Nelson—only this guy had eyes that were both sunken and glowing red. Two-week-old stubble covered his face, and thick reading glasses gave him a cross-eyed look. The wheels of the truck had barely slowed to a stop when the first of a litany of verbal assaults spewed forth from his mouth.

"What in the name of Sam Hell are you sonsofbitches . . . garble, garble, garble. Ever seen a brush fire?!?!?! You better get the hell out of here before I fucking load you full of . . . garble, garble, garble. Git yer goddamn . . . garble, garble, garble."

Justin and I just stood there frozen—half from fear and half in disbelief. Evil Willie was absolutely frothing at the mouth in a blind rage. The words came out of him in an uninterrupted discharge of hatred, like Yosemite Sam on a drinking binge. This man was pissed. Wicked pissed. And Justin and I were quite obviously the sand in his ointment.

Yet there we stood, transfixed like Lot's wife, still processing what in the hell was going on. It was almost like he was speaking a foreign language, and we were just trying to understand the gist of what he was saying. He continued berating us, but we remained in place, dumbfounded and hypnotized—until a solitary word popped into my head—"gun." "Holy Jesus", I thought, "if ever there was a paranoid and heavily armed fanatic, this is the guy." I spun my head towards Justin and motioned towards the bikes.

We immediately jumped into action and started packing up the things we'd laid out. Evil Willie was starting to slow his words down a bit, but only due to a lack of breath. He started taking little pauses to *almost* think about the insults before he hurled them. In one tirade, he managed to threaten us with the wrath of God, the government, the military, multiple firearms, and his right foot . . . all in one.

On and on he went, and his words got crazier and crazier. As he gifted us his last few nuggets of racist wisdom, Justin and I scooped up the last of our things and hopped onto our bikes. With perfect timing, Eric finally arrived upon the scene. He was pale, drenched in sweat, and totally out of breath. "Does that guy have any water for us?" he asked. We glanced back at the still babbling tweaker, snickered, and pedaled on.

For the next few miles, I thought long and hard about our little run-in with Evil Willie. Trying to find the silver lining led me to think that maybe he was actually a road-weary sage in disguise. Maybe these were more coded secrets of the High Plains. I could write a book about it called *Philosophies of a Methamphetamine Enthusiast*, and include little tidbits like: Brush fires are bad. Yankees are bad. Hippies and commies . . . also bad. Don't call someone "sir" if he was only a corporal in the Marine Corps. Never set foot upon a stranger's property unless you're willing to have creative things done with said foot. And so on, and so forth.

As we rolled on, Eric moved slower and slower. We were getting more worried, so we started coming up with alternate plans if he couldn't continue. Our buddy was in need of all the water we could spare, but Justin and I were starting to crash from a lack of food and good humor. We gave Eric the rest of our water minus a fourth of a liter between the two of us, and moved on towards Rawlins. We knew from the map that we would eventually take a south turn onto a highway, and that would put the wind mostly to our backs again. From there it would be an easy coast of fifteen miles into Rawlins, but if needed there was a spring off the road about halfway there. We'd figure it out ... but for now we just needed to get through this wicked deserted stretch.

Justin and I plugged along in lethargic fashion and finally determined there was no break to be found from the mind-numbing wind anytime in the near future. We pulled over next to a fence post. Yes, a fence post was the only thing that we could find protruding from the ground to prop the bikes up against. The best part was that there was no actual fence in the area, just some old posts left over from back when someone felt the need to actually have the area sectioned off with barbed wire. Judging from the post, that was a millennium ago. We were probably a good mile ahead of Eric, so we figured we might be able to get some food ready for him in case he could get it down. We propped up our rigs and started digging out the goods. We procured the necessary ingredients and started assembling things, as Justin commented on some strange new noise. I was so hungry that I would have guessed it to be my stomach growling. I listened, but didn't hear anything, and my eyes were glued to the road in case Willie decided to track us down.

But after another minute I did hear something a little different. I looked over the open wasteland surrounding us, and I noticed a cow that had been way off in the distance was now a bit closer. "Hey," I screamed at Justin, "that cow thinks she's getting some lunch." We laughed and continued with the food assembly. But the noise persisted, and after another minute I looked up to see the cow even closer. I couldn't explain it—even to myself—but the intruding bovine looked a little agitated. I wondered for a moment if this apocalyptic wind just drove all living creatures in the area totally bat-shit crazy.

Another minute passed and Justin piped up: "Hey man, doesn't that cow look pretty pissed off? I mean, she keeps digging her hooves into the dust like that, and thrashing her head around."

"Yeah, she's angry with the wind gods, like we are," I replied. But the new noises from our guest whipped both of our heads up. There we stood, sand-wiches now at the ready, with the "cow" moving ever closer. It was heaving and wailing and digging up massive chunks of dirt with its curved horns. Yup. Big ... fucking ... horns. He would rev himself up by pawing at the ground, charge forward in a short sprint for a few paces, then stop and start tearing at the ground again. For the second time in as many hours, we'd managed to totally infuriate one of the locals.

We looked down at the lack of barbed wire between the fence posts, then back up at the charging bull, then back at the vacant gap. *You must be kidding me,* I thought. *I mean, this kind of stuff only happens in cartoons.* But fear was instantly overcome by apathy, as hunger gnawed at my stomach lining. In my hand was a mish-mash of peanut butter and Nutella, and I was convinced that it could possibly save my life. We were seconds away from being mauled by a bull, and all I could think of was how incredible my sandwich was going to taste.

When we looked up again, the snorting beast was close enough to decimate the both of us in one hard charge. In place of tears or screaming or yelling or praying, all we could manage to do was laugh. The wind had swept our sanity across the plains, leaving a punch-drunk lunacy to hold sway over the sinking ships that were our bodies. We kept the food in our hands, left our bags wide open, eased back into the saddles, and slowly started pedaling on as El Toro closed in on the scene. By the time my bike was righted on the road, I could have spat on his fat back. We looked back to see Eric getting closer, then slowly veer to the other side of the road and pick up the pace just a bit. He was so spent that his chin hovered around his breastbone. He plodded passed the bull with all the enthusiasm of a sloth, hardly even acknowledging the 600 pounds of anger just a few yards away from him.

We continued riding on, as the road took us in a direct line towards the highway. The wind continued to pummel us, and toss us back and forth across the road as it pleased. Eventually, we started spotting houses out on the horizon. They seemed odd and heavily fortified. Each house had multiple satellite dishes and antennae and there was at least a mile separating each of them. This was obviously where people came to get away from civilization. The structures themselves emitted a strong presence of paranoia. *This,* I thought, *is exactly how people say "stay away."* I wondered which stronghold belonged to Willie.

A few hours later, we finally noticed some texture to the horizon. A turn in the road ahead of us led to a small hill. From the top of it we could see the slightest flashes of light in the distance. Minute by minute they got the tiniest bit brighter, until we realized it was sunlight reflecting off of car windshields on the highway.

I had already left Eric behind, and at the mirage of civilization I scooted well out in front of Justin. I pushed all the way to the entrance ramp, then coasted off onto the dirt shoulder with my chest poking forward—crossing an imaginary finish line. I dropped my bike and trailer and lay on the dirt as cars cruised just 40 feet from me. I lay there and watched Justin arrive with similar pageantry. The shoulder of the highway wasn't the end of the line for us that day, but it symbolized our return to civilization—our return to a place where we could get help if we really needed it. Without discussing it, we both stared back at the vacant space we'd come across and waited.

By that time Eric was so far behind that we couldn't even see him on a flat road lacking landmarks. Even though his body should have shut down hours earlier, our guts told us he was still plugging along. Granted, if night-fall were to come without him, we'd surely go back and find him, but that was an afterthought. We knew it would take more than food poisoning, dehydration, and heat stroke to bring him down. There might be lots of breaks. There might be lots of self-motivational monologues. There might be nothing left in his engine but spirit, but we knew that it was still running.

When our sickly soldier finally appeared down the road, my stomach eased a bit. We still had 15 miles left to town, but it was enough that he'd made it this far. He too, collapsed upon arrival at the highway. As the three of us lay there on our backs, the sun painted a few more layers on our chests. We shared stories of our individual dementias over the last stretch of road. Needles to say, Eric had fared the worst. It turned out the poor bastard had stopped more than a few times to catch his breath. Once he even stretched out in the middle of the road and rested, wondering if a car would grace the abandoned road and stop to help him out . . . or just run him over and put him out of his misery.

All our water rations combined to about half a liter. Dangerously low under normal conditions, but we were thrilled to find that we even had that much. Six miles away there was a turnoff with access to a fresh-water spring. And nine miles beyond that was the city of Rawlins, Wyoming, home to 8,538 people, and, as one of those riders we'd met outside Atlantic City had put it, "the place that would serve me the greatest steak dinner and beers of my life!"

With Eric in such dire straits, Justin and I decided to push on ahead, get water from the spring, and meet Eric back on the road with new reserves. Emotions were running high, as we rightfully assumed that the worst was now behind us. With the wind pushing hard at our backs, Justin and I made it to the turnoff to the spring in record time. We carefully followed the directions, but there was no water to be found. We retraced our route and tried again, but still turned up empty-handed. We examined every feature of the land for a square mile, desperately searching for anything even slightly resembling a spring.

In the end, we were left with no other option but to head back out to the highway and wait for Eric to arrive, *sin agua*. Having let him down at such a crucial time, we felt obliged to give him our last few thimbles of water. If he'd known it was the last we were carrying, he certainly would have refused it. The three of us sat down atop a small hill on the edge of the highway and stared at the cars flying by in front of us. We were dejected and pouting.

The map claimed that we were straddling the Continental Divide for the thirteenth time on our trip. Granted, the road sloped downward in both directions away from us, but there was no such sign demarcating the area. I rolled over a few times and made certain that my body was on the other side of the invisible line that expresses the water-flow bisection of our continent. If I'd had a drop of moisture left in my mouth, I would have spat over my shoulder (back into the Great Basin) where it would have gone . . . nowhere. Instead, I just stared at the traffic.

We knew that we had won. We had beaten the odds and triumphed over the toughest obstacle of the GDMBR. We had proven ourselves to be bumbling warriors of the adventure-cycling world. Yet we still weren't quite finished. It was close to an hour's ride to Rawlins proper, and then we still had to find a place to stay for the night.

My mind was starting to drift, and I was losing reasonable control over my motor skills. While thinking about what it would take to motivate my next steps, I realized that I was already getting back on the bike. Justin looked over and asked, "What did you just say?" I was surprised to realize that I had been talking, and shocked to notice that I had no idea what I'd said. But it was too late to second-guess anything; I was already bounding on down the road. I left my puzzled friends on the hill and rolled on towards town.

Less than an hour later, they found me sitting under the first bit of shade I had seen in as long as I could remember. The evidence of my guilt lay all around me in the convenience-store parking lot. Three empty bottles of Gatorade, two ice cream–bar wrappers and a spent water bottle lay right where I'd dropped them after the last of what they had to offer had entered my mouth. My stomach was swollen to the size of a basketball, and a half-empty Schlitz tallboy can rested on top of it like the star on a Christmas tree.

Jose, the clerk, had come outside to give me my change. Apparently I'd walked in, placed a twenty-dollar bill on the counter, grabbed the items that now littered the parking lot, and walked outside feverishly attempting to consume them all at once. He was a kind young man who was more concerned with my condition than angered by my lack of etiquette. He was even giving me directions to a nearby campground as Justin and Eric pulled up. Jose simply surveyed them in a non-judgmental manner, and then opened the door to welcome them inside.

Now that we had the spoils of victory, our success seemed more genuine. We laughed at our despicableness and at how magical a Strawberry Shortcake Ice Cream Bar could taste. Justin and Eric were beaming with joy, and I was the happiest person in the world ever to relax amid the dried remnants of motor oil and antifreeze.

The rest of the details were inconsequential. The campground offered us a small cabin for two dollars more than a camp spot would have cost. Sleeping in actual beds was a marvelous taste of decadence. The showers were coin-operated, and I wasn't the only one who had to make a visit to the ATM to be certain that I had sufficient funds for the job. The calls to family and loved ones were short and sweet. "Yup, we made it. Yup, very tired."

When the time came to paint the town red, Eric opted to stay in the cabin and get some rest. Good thing too, as he would end up being far from peak condition for the next week. By sunrise he would have consumed over three gallons of Gatorade. Justin and I exalted in the options available in town. We twice pedaled the length of the city while considering what we wanted and what was offered. In the end we settled for a steakhouse that served B-grade steak and C-grade beer for A-grade prices, but I could have cared less. It was still the greatest steak dinner and beers of my life!

# The Shock and Numbness Are Starting to Set In

**HEATHER ANDERSEN**

## Part 1

**Williamsburg, Virginia, 5 May 2005.** I sat at the introductory meeting with two lightweight cutting boards in my hands, and asked again, "Who hasn't gotten any group gear yet?" There was no response. I'd carefully counted out fifteen piles, one for each rider in the group. So why, I wondered, did I have an extra one? I looked around the crowded hotel room. Fifteen faces looked back at me.

Bill, an older man with reddish hair and a matching mustache, asked, "Don't you have a tool kit?"

"Yes," I said. "I'll carry it and the first-aid kit as my portion of group gear."

"I'd like to carry the tool kit," he said, happily volunteering to carry the heavy tools, and also (as is the rule with the tool holder) to fix bikes when they broke.

Before the trip started, I had sent an e-mail to the group introducing myself. Many of the participants replied, warning me they were both the oldest and the slowest rider. Bill, at age 69, proved to be the oldest, though seven others were also in their sixties. And Bill, I would soon find out, was also the slowest, partly because he rode slowly, but also because he took his time exploring areas. Having ridden the original Bikecentennial on the TransAmerica route in 1976, Bill was rarely in a hurry.

Since retiring in 1999 from Lockheed Martin, where he worked as an aeronautical engineer, Bill had done numerous long-distance rides: from Montana to Alaska, the southern tier cross-country route, the Great Divide Mountain Bike Route, and every inch of the Odyssey 2000 around-the-world ride. Now, 29 years after his first continental crossing, Bill joined our group to ride the TransAmerica at the urging of his friend and former co-worker Russ. On his first cross-country ride, Russ had wanted Bill's company.

**Yorktown, Virginia, 6 May 2005.** To test all our equipment and make sure everyone really could carry the gear they'd brought along, the group went on a "shakedown ride" along the Colonial Parkway from Williamsburg to Yorktown, the official beginning of the TransAmerica route. The route was created as part of our country's bicentennial celebration; it begins at the site of the last major battle of the Revolutionary War.

A church group in Yorktown volunteered to host a lunch for us. They provided not only wonderful food but also shelter from a bitter, windy, rainy day that would prove to be our worst weather of the trip, an ominous beginning to our ride. The church group took an interest in our journey, so the riders introduced themselves one by one and explained why they were riding across the country.

I told them my short history: After my first long ride in Maine in 1987, I went on more rides which led to an interest in improved conditions for cyclists, and then to work in bike advocacy. I left that career to go to Africa. I came back recently wanting to lead trips, to share my love of bike touring and my love of getting to know places by traveling at human speed. My first two cross-country bike trips had been on southern routes, and I was eager to ride the historic route that had helped bike touring grow exponentially in the US over the past 30 years. After our introductions were finished, the church group offered each of us the gift of a scallop shell on a string. They explained that historically scallop shells were worn on pilgrimages, and that they would bring good luck on our cross-country trip.

This lunch was typical of the way bike touring brings out the kindness and curiosity of strangers. People seem to enjoy helping long-distance riders, especially those traveling self-contained (carrying all their gear without the help of any motor vehicles) as we were. I have cycled on five continents, and I find that bike touring always reaffirms my faith in the basic goodness of people. Even here in the States, where people tend to be more self-absorbed, I have found much kindness in my travels.

**Williamsburg to Troutville, Virginia, 7-14 May 2005.** The trip started out like lots of other bike trips—a happy bunch looking forward to the adventure of cycling across the country. The group shared laughter and seemed compatible. But when my scallop shell broke, I wondered: *Does a broken good-luck charm bring bad luck?*

**Whytheville, Virginia, 16 May 2005.** One group member arrived in camp screaming at me about bad planning and a hard day's ride. I'd rearranged the itinerary slightly so that we could stay at a group member's brother's house the previous night. It had meant ten more miles today in exchange for a catered feast, a soft green lawn to camp on, hot showers, and laundry. She was upset because this made today's ride more difficult. Bill heard the exchange, and later that evening he told me quietly, "They don't pay you enough."

**Damascus, Virginia, 18 May 2005.** Today was a rest day. Bill and Russ bought, cut, and shaped metal windscreens to fit around the outsides of our stoves. Our resident rocket scientists had made outdoor cooking easier and faster.

**Damascus, Virginia to Rosedale, Virginia, 19 May 2005.** In the morning, one group member looked pale and uncomfortable, as he had the previous day. He lost his breath quickly and needed many breaks. I decided to wait at the top of a three-mile climb to make sure he was okay. Bill crested the hill and gave me a report. The man was stopping every 50 feet. I waited for an hour, and then stayed behind him on the easy remaining part of that day's ride.

After we arrived at camp in Rosedale, I persuaded him to go to the emergency room. The doctors more than confirmed my suspicions: at some point in the previous two days he had suffered a small heart attack and was now suffering from the effects. His tour was over.

**Pippa Passes, Kentucky, 21 May 2005.** I arrived at camp and found out another group member had gone to the emergency room with chest pains. His tour was over, too.

**Booneville to Berea, Kentucky, 22-23 May.** I woke up to find a group member shivering uncontrollably. She had slept in her flooded tent and got hypothermia. Warm tea and two dry sleeping bags eventually warmed her up.

That afternoon, another group member crashed, cracking his helmet, but he was able to continue the ride.

The next day, before dinner, a man in the group told me he was leaving the tour because he wasn't enjoying the experience. He had been under the impression that the tour would be camping in towns that afforded restaurants and exploration. He complained about staying "in the middle of nowhere," mentioning a campground that was five miles from the closest store as an example. I realized that my perspective was different, especially after returning from Africa, where I'd volunteered for the Peace Corps in the tiny country of Lesotho. After finishing my volunteer service, I'd spent more than six months bicycling through southern Africa. After cycling through the Namibian desert and northern Botswana, carrying gallons of water and food for days, I didn't think anywhere in Virginia could be considered "the middle of nowhere."

**Bardstown, Kentucky, 24 May 2005.** A woman in the group with a Palm Pilot got an e-mail message from the man who had dropped out first. His cardiologist told him he would have succumbed to a major heart attack if he had continued with us. His message also said that he followed our daily progress on the maps and checked our weather forecasts. He was reluctant to let go of his dream, a trip he'd wanted to complete for 30 years. He'd pushed himself hard even with shortness of breath, because the alternative—not finishing the trip—was unthinkable.

**Harrodsburg, Kentucky, 25 May 2005.** I called the office to give them a trip update. The tours director knew Bill from previous rides and asked to speak with him on my next call. I mentioned the call to Bill, and he joked that he was going to report me, claiming: "Heather has failed to establish a beer economy." That was the short way of saying that I hadn't encouraged a practice whereby the cook of the day buys beer for the group.

**Fordsville, Kentucky, 28-29 May 2005.** Just when I thought the group was settling into a groove, there was a freak accident outside Fordsville. Five group members had stopped, and moved well off the road to fix a bike. Then two cars crashed on the road near them, and one of the cars careened into their parked bikes, sending them flying into the group. It happened so quickly that the riders didn't initially know what hit them. I arrived at the crash scene to find that two women in the group had been taken to the hospital by ambulance, and three bicycles were damaged.

With two more riders in the hospital, someone remarked, "I guess the trip's over now." Bill responded by telling us that two cyclists had been hit and killed by cars on the original TransAmerica ride, but that ride went on. "You do not abort the ride," he said.

Each day of the trip, Bill sent postcards to his wife and grown daughters. On this day, his postcards simply diagrammed the crash scene.

It turned out one of riders in the hospital couldn't walk well, but she could hobble around. Both were traumatized but determined to continue the ride. So the next day, those two, along with the owners of the damaged bikes, arranged to be driven to the next town along our route that had a good bike shop, a four-day bike ride for the rest of us.

At this point, three weeks into a three-month trip, I started to wonder what was going on. How could so much bad stuff happen to one group? Was it karma? Were we jinxed? Was this tour a test of my leadership ability? Was it preparing me for something? That evening the group members told me that they were glad they didn't have my job. Bill just said that I was a great leader.

**Missouri and Kansas, 4-20 June 2005.** Our flexible, inexpensive, cross-country, camping, participatory bicycle tour began to wear on some in the group. The reality of adventure travel was less exciting than the idea of it. They complained about the hills, the heat, and the cold. They complained about hose showers, about the tap water not tasting good, about the quality of city park bathrooms. They complained that Missouri was too hilly and that Kansas was too flat. They complained about a group member who couldn't prepare meals on time and another who was rude. Some days I arrived at camp wondering what the complaint of the day was going was to be. Through it all, Bill never complained. He just said to me, "They don't pay you enough to deal with all this." And he kept fixing bikes.

If I were doing it for the money, he'd be right. But I do it because I'm a nomad. I'm addicted to waking up in new places each day, not knowing what each afternoon might bring; riding my bike in deserts and mountains, meeting the strangers along the way. My traveling lifestyle tends to elicit two types of responses from people. Either they think it's wonderful that I do what I love, or they think I'm crazy and question whether it's safe. In response to the latter, I find it appropriate to paraphrase Ben Franklin, who said that to sacrifice liberty for safety is to get neither. I sensed that Bill and I shared a similar spirit with regard to bike travel.

Bill and I were frequently the last to leave camp in the morning. When he left before me, his last words were usually, "Off to the post office," and he rode away on his 24-speed Bike Friday folding bike to mail his daily post-cards. I frequently passed him stopped in towns along the way looking for postcards, or sometimes I'd see his bike outside a restaurant and know he was having a second breakfast.

Kansas was boring for some of the group, but for me it was great for meditative cycling. I could ride for hours without having to focus on the upcoming terrain. I knew it had been a tough trip for everyone, but as we neared the Kansas-Colorado state line, the midpoint of the trip, I planned to refocus the group on the adventure to come. The rewards of getting through Kansas and into Colorado were a rafting trip and the majestic Rockies.

**Ordway, Colorado, 22 June 2005.** The forecast for this day was similar to yesterday's: 102 degrees. The group voted to have breakfast at 5:45 a.m. Walking in the early morning to the breakfast spread, Bill tripped and tumbled. When he got up and dusted himself off, I joked that it was a "breakfast-too-early injury." Bill sipped coffee quietly, but didn't eat any breakfast.

**Pueblo, Colorado, 23 June 2005.** Our group had planned to camp at the city park in Pueblo. The first rider arrived to find a prison chain gang doing work in the designated camping area. By the time I arrived, the chain gang had left but most of the group sat fuming in anger. The only area in which the park authorities would allow us to pitch our tents was gravel (there was lots of soft grass in the park, but we were not allowed to camp on it because of timed sprinklers), and the restroom was deemed far from acceptable by the group. The problem solved itself when a park neighbor invited us to camp in her yard and offered her bathroom. Predictably, there was a rush for the shower. While I set up my tent, I looked at Bill sitting on his camp stool, patiently waiting for one of the last showers, after others had already gone out for a drink. He embodied the spirit of adventure cycling, accepting that things do not always work out as planned, but that patience and a willingness to be flexible frequently lead to new opportunities.

**Pueblo to Canon City, Colorado, 24 June 2005.** As I turned onto Colorado Highway 67 in Wetmore, I heard a voice yell from a car, "Heather, stop!" It was

Russ's wife. She had been visiting and driving the route for a few days. "Bill's been hit," she said. "They're doing CPR." She offered to drive me to the crash scene, only a few miles away. I grabbed my leader journal with emergency contact info out of a front pannier, and I quickly locked my bike to a post and watched as it slid into the adjacent ditch. I knew the sight of my bike lying alongside the road would worry the riders behind me, but under the circumstances, leaving a "don't worry" note seemed inappropriate.

I had been trained in CPR and bike safety, so I understood how futile CPR was following a violent, high-speed collision. At the scene, four group members stood forlornly on the shoulder of the road. Further down, paramedics stood around an ambulance, seemingly in no hurry. I didn't see Bill anywhere. As I approached, the police tried to shoo me away from their "crime scene investigation." But I would not be deterred; we'd been bicycling across the country together for the past seven weeks and had become like family. I demanded to know his medical condition. A policeman then told me what a part of me already knew: Bill was dead. My first thoughts were of his wife, Bonnie, and my second thoughts were of the group. I went into crisis-management mode. I couldn't think about my personal grief; I had to focus on what to do as a leader. Handling a death was not covered in leadership training, and I was on my own in the worst possible position a tour leader could be in. I called the office, answered the policemen's many questions, and arranged rides for group members who didn't want to continue that day's ride. I didn't have any time to think about myself.

That evening our group gathered with a retired pastor for a grief counseling session that turned into a memorial service of sorts as we shared memories of Bill—the time he comforted another group member whose niece had just died, his Cheshire cat–like grin, the way he sat on his camp stool by his tent and relaxed, how he was such a slowpoke. At one point, I looked around the room and saw that all the women were crying. I couldn't cry—I knew that if I started, I might not be able to stop. If I collapsed, the whole trip could fall apart. And I had a meeting to run, a group to take care of, so I didn't let myself cry. I no longer cared about riding across the country, but I cared more than ever about their dreams of completing the journey. I didn't want their dreams to go unfulfilled. We recalled Bill saying, "You do not abort the trip," and we knew it was what he would want of us.

The police had trouble notifying Bonnie, because she was traveling at the time of the crash, but after our meeting I got a message that she'd been reached. Before I called her, I sat for a while trying to think of something to say. I couldn't think of a single thing. What do you say to a woman who has just found out that her husband of 41 years is never coming home? Finally, I dialed. When she said, "Hi, Heather, how are you?" I knew the reality of her husband's death had not sunk in yet. She wanted to talk with me before she collapsed. The police had told her about the crash, that Bill had been riding alone and was hit from behind by an off-duty police officer who didn't see him until it was too late. The man claimed Bill was riding in the middle of the road. The only witness was the driver's wife who was following him in another car. It was a bright sunny day. Bill was riding on a wide-open road without much traffic.

I told Bonnie about Bill's last day alive, about how relaxed and at peace he was in the backyard of a stranger's house in Pueblo. I also told her how happy he was when he received her recent package that included his "second-half cycling jerseys."

After talking with Bonnie, my dorm room in the abbey where we were staying felt too confining. I wandered around outside, then sat alone on a bench until I started to get chills. I went inside and wrote in my journal, "I'm numbish. And perhaps still a bit in denial. I keep seeing Bill's face flash in front of my eyes. As his death is starting to sink in, the feeling of unreality is changing to anger at the driver who killed him." From my bike advocacy work, I knew that more than eight hundred cyclists are killed every year in the United States. But now the statistics suddenly had a face, Bill's face. I'd spent years advocating an increased emphasis on crash prevention, rather than helmet usage, exactly because of crashes like this one. Bill's helmet could not save his life; crash prevention might have. I was angry that after all the work I'd done, Bill was killed on a trip I was leading. This anger, along with the realization that I'd never had to deal with a sudden death before and I didn't really know how to, kept me awake long after I'd put down my pen and turned out the light.

**Canon City/Royal Gorge, Colorado, 25 June 2005**. Most of the group went rafting as scheduled. It was a somber occasion. After dinner I read Bill's autopsy report to the group.

**Canon City to Hartsel, Colorado, 26 June 2005.** I woke up with tears in my eyes, lacking an appetite, and wishing that this had all been a nightmare. I woke up with no desire to ride my bike—something that I had never felt in eighty-thousand-plus miles. I'd ridden through physical exhaustion, extreme sleepiness, pain, lack of motivation, and dehydration, and I'd always pushed on. I watched each rider leave camp then finally got on my bike and began to pedal. I was surprised when I caught up to some group members who were finishing a round of miniature golf—in smiles. They seemed to be handling the death better than I.

Later in the day, I rode along thinking about fate and destiny. Two days ago, I would have said I didn't believe in destiny, but now I wondered if it had been Bill's time. Where else could Bill have died other than on the TransAm route? While riding, I crested a summit that gave me a sudden and expansive view of snow-capped mountains. As I looked around, I felt Bill's presence and knew that he had become our guardian angel, keeping us safe for the rest of our trip. And indeed we were safe, not free of tension and squabbles, but safe for the rest of the trip.

**Wyoming, 1-12 July 2005.** Following my suggestion that we honor Bill's postcard tradition, the group sent cards with messages from each of us to Bonnie and her daughters. I wrote a longer letter to Bonnie and enclosed it with the cards. The letter began: "Not a day goes by when I don't think about Bill—and what he would be saying or doing if he were still with us. Where he might set up his tent and camp stool, the restaurant he might stop at for a second breakfast, when he might choose to try to persuade us of his theory to have breakfast on sun time—moving our breakfast time in 15 minute intervals as we cycle across each time zone."

**Darby, Montana, 17 July 2005.** The group had our official TransAmerica group photo taken, with Russ holding a photo of Bill.

**Florence, Oregon, 4 August 2005.** We went out to dinner to celebrate the end of our journey. I gave everyone a group photo and a photo of Bill. A week later I began a solo trip down the coast from Astoria, Oregon to Los Angeles.

# Part 2

On January 5, 2006, the driver who hit and killed Bill was convicted of "careless driving with a fatality," but found innocent of speeding. Sentencing was scheduled for March 7, which turned out to be the same day I would arrive in San Diego to lead my next cross-country tour.

**San Diego, California, 7-8 March 2006.** I arrived in San Diego with two days to prepare for another cross-country cycling tour. I was working for a different touring company this time, and the trip would be different from any of the previous tours I had led: it was for women only, and vehicle-supported. We would have our own cook and be staying in hotels every night. The company president joined the group for the first few days of the tour. She told me that one of the riders, Marlene, had called her earlier in the winter to say she was afraid of dying on the trip. She had called back another time to say that she'd put her will in order. Marlene had made the president promise not to tell anyone about her fears. When the president told me this, I responded, "Don't worry, I've handled a death on a trip before, and I can do it again if I need to."

The day before the tour started, I found out that the sentencing of the man who killed Bill had been postponed.

**San Diego to Alpine, California, 9-11 March 2006**. The first thing Marlene said to me when I met her in San Diego was that she was afraid of dying on this trip. We discussed her fear of traffic and of riding on the interstate. Then I went over the cycling days ahead of us, and basic safety precautions, but I never reassured her that she was not going to die.

After only one day of cycling, we got snowed in when a seven-year storm closed the road near Alpine.

**Brawley to Blythe, California, 13 March 2006.** Our third cycling day was a 90-miler. The women were concerned about being able to ride such a distance. Because of the lack of services along the way, our cook prepared a lunch out of our van and trailer. I biked to the lunch stop and waited for the last few riders. The cook gave me the van keys, and left to bike to our hotel. I would drive the remainder of the day. Marlene was one of the last two to arrive. She told me she was petrified of the upcoming series of steep hills on a shoulderless highway with bad sightlines. I suggested she ride in the van with me over the hills, then I would drop her off to bike the last 20 miles of flat ground. When Marlene arrived at the hotel, she exclaimed enthusiastically what a great ride it had been and thanked me for my idea. It was "perfect" for her. So began her pattern of needing a lot of support, then being appreciative of getting it.

**Globe, Arizona, 19 March 2006.** As the ride continued, I enjoyed fostering a supportive atmosphere and watching the women bond and gain self-confidence as they learned to fix flats and ride more miles each day. Rest days became bike-cleaning and repair days, and Marlene joined the other women in the morning ritual.

As for myself, I found the transition from having my own tent to sharing a hotel room difficult. Exchanging the privacy of a tent for a bed and a hot shower wasn't always a good trade.

After dinner, I asked the group for funny stories from the day. Marlene told us that in the bathroom she'd noticed that she was accidentally wearing underwear under her bike shorts. She said, "This is not right," and took off her underwear and tossed them behind her. When she turned around to pick them up, she couldn't find them anywhere. They'd gone down the toilet, which was still flushing.

As she got to know the group, Marlene gradually opened up and shared her fear of dying on the trip.

**Silver City, New Mexico, 23 March 2006.** Instead of cycling, Marlene rented a car and drove to the City of Rocks. She'd visited there many years ago and found it to be a very spiritual place. When she returned, she chattered excitedly about how wonderful it was and how she felt at home out there.

**Kingston, New Mexico, 24 March 2006.** We stayed at a historic stone lodge. Marlene approached me at dinner and told me she couldn't possibly sleep in her bed because she had just found a cat in her room and is allergic to cats. Our group had taken over the entire lodge and its annex across the street, so there weren't any extra rooms to move her into. I offered her the only free bed, an empty top bunk in a room with three other women. She didn't want this because she was afraid someone would snore and keep her awake. I suggested an upstairs sofa, but she didn't like sleeping on sofas. One woman offered to switch beds with her, and I thought about doing so myself, but both our beds were in the musty basement of the annex, an area Marlene rejected because she was also allergic to mold. I offered her the futon in the annex living room. She didn't like this because there were no doors to close and she thought others would inadvertently keep her awake. I was out of options and told her so. I asked her what she wanted to do. After some contemplation, she decided the cat was not so bad after all and returned to her room. When I asked her the next morning if she was able to sleep okay, she said, "Yes, thank you. I guess I just needed to know someone cared."

**Kingston to Las Cruces, New Mexico, 25 March 2006.** Our second longest ride of the tour, 89 miles, had lots of early downhill balanced by some later headwind. Shortly after she completed the ride and arrived at our hotel, I asked Marlene how she did. "Great," she screamed, "I did the whole ride. It was great!" Shining with the joy of a child, she grabbed me and hugged me. I congratulated her on setting a new personal best for miles ridden in a day.

**Fort Hancock, Texas, 27-28 March 2006.** In the evening, Marlene surprised me when she told me our modest hotel in this small town was her favorite of the places we'd stayed thus far. She liked the view of the mountains from her door. In the morning, she told me privately that she and another woman were interested in being permanent roommates for the rest of the trip rather than rotating through the group. Not wanting to insult anyone, she asked if I could quietly arrange for the two of them to room together frequently. I told her not to worry, that other people had permanent roommates, too. Once she had her permanent roommate, she had a new concern—her roommate, being a faster rider, would always get the better bed. "Which bed is the best?" her roommate asked.

"The one closest to the bathroom." Marlene said. Her roommate promised to leave that bed for her.

**Kerrville, Texas, 7 April 2006.** On our non-cycling days, our cook had the day off and the women were on their own for dinner. The majority of the group decided to eat at the lodge's beef-centered restaurant; I went out for Chinese food with Marlene and two other women. At dinner Marlene asked, "Did the trip work out well for you?" I told her that the trip was not over yet, and to ask me again at the end.

On our way back to the lodge, we passed a street festival and stopped to listen to some music. We heard that the museums were open and free for the evening. Marlene and I both wanted to stay out for a little longer to take advantage of the opportunity to enjoy the local flavor, but the other women we were with wanted to get back to the lodge and get to bed early. Marlene exclaimed, "Come on, you guys. This is great. We have to stay out." They could not be convinced, so we returned to the lodge.

**Bastrop, Texas, 9 April 2006.** At the midpoint of the trip, we got a new cook and a new SAG (support and gear) driver, as planned by the touring company. Our calm, laid back, and supportive crew was replaced by two talkative, highly-strung, chaotic women.

**Bastrop to LaGrange, Texas, 10 April 2006.** On their way out of town in the morning, a few of the women stopped to explore Bastrop. Marlene picked up a brochure from a bed & breakfast that was for sale. She later gushed about how she loved Bastrop and wanted to buy the bed & breakfast.

**Navasota, Texas, 12 April 2006.** On a rest day, Marlene had her first ever pedicure at a spa. She happily raved about it at dinner.

**Navasota to Cleveland, Texas, 13 April 2006.** A heavy morning fog led to a delayed start. Marlene didn't want to ride, even after most of the fog lifted and the other women had departed. Instead she rode in the SAG vehicle for the first twenty miles. Later in the day, I saw her bent over a lost puppy; she was so absorbed that she didn't even notice me pass.

When I arrived at the hotel, a local reporter was interviewing two group members. The reporter asked me questions about bike touring, our trip, and the tour company. When the interview finished, I got my key from the registration desk and wheeled my bike to my room. With free time before the rest of the riders arrived, I decided to take a shower.

I stepped out of the shower to the simultaneous ringing of both my cell phone and the room phone. I knew something was wrong. I answered the hotel phone. It was a group member, there had been a crash just down the road and the police needed me there. I quickly got dressed and grabbed my emergency contact info. As I walked through the lobby, someone asked me who it was, and I said I didn't know. I walked out of the hotel. In surreal ways, strangers pointed me towards the crash. Once I reached the emergency vehicles, I saw the yellow cloth over what could only be a body on the road. A police captain came and took me aside. He told me he thought the victim's name was Marlene—he had found a scrap of paper in her pocket with her name and emergency contact information on it. But she didn't have a photo ID, so I was asked to identify her.

I'd never seen a dead human body, and I'd never imagined that my first would be under such sudden, drastic circumstances. The police officer put his arm around me for support. I looked down at the body only briefly. I saw Marlene's face, as I knew I would. It was hard to look at. Hours before she had been so full of life. I nodded and turned away.

I knew what to do next. Put my grief aside and attempt to assuage the sorrow of the group. A pastor came to talk to the group and offered a prayer. I said a few words about Marlene. A police officer came and answered questions about the crash.

Marlene had missed the hotel where we were staying. She had turned around and was heading back to it. She had just passed a parking lot exit. An SUV driver looked only to his left for oncoming traffic, but neglected to look right. He ran Marlene over from behind. She was killed less than a quarter of a mile from the hotel.

All of our options—staying near the site of her death, cycling out of town, or shuttling in the van—were depressing, but we concluded that not cycling would be like giving in to Marlene's fears. If any of the other cyclists in our group had been killed, Marlene's trip would have been over; she would have been paralyzed with fear and unable to get back on her bicycle.

Late that night, after I'd talked with the president of the company, I returned to the site of Marlene's death to have a quiet moment alone. Later, I sat in my room with my journal and wrote, "The shock and numbness are starting to set in. How could it have happened again?"

**Cleveland to Kountze, Texas, 14 April 2006**. In honor of Marlene, we held a private, early-morning roadside memorial service at the site of her death. A few of us talked about her, then we laid down roses and said a prayer. Again, I couldn't let myself cry because I had work to do. The group did not want to bike past the site of her death, and I needed to arrange a new route out of town. After breakfast, we cycled out of town through fog and tears behind a police escort.

I tried to focus on the scenery, but yesterday's image was seared into my memory. I saw Marlene lying lifeless on the pavement, with her twisted bicycle, crushed helmet, and duct-taped shoes. She had duct-taped the cleats on her cycling shoes as a first step to clipping in. Afraid to ride clipped into pedals, she'd cycled most of the way wearing tennis shoes. I'd recently encouraged her to wear her cycling shoes with duct tape, in order to have the advantage of hard-soled shoes.

**Kountze, Texas to Crestview, Florida, 15-26 April 2006.** Every day I watched the group gain back a bit of its lost confidence and slowly recover from the shock. At the end of the first day after Marlene's death, there was a feeling of relief that nothing else had happened. The next day, we rode from Texas into Louisiana. It was good to leave Texas behind.

But I didn't feel like I was leaving anything behind. I felt I was still carrying it with me. Mostly, I couldn't come to terms with the eerie symmetries of the two deaths. Both Bill and Marlene were hit and killed from behind by drivers who didn't see them. Both died instantly at the scene. Both crashes occurred a little more than halfway into our trips—late enough that they'd formed strong bonds within the groups, but early enough that the groups still had weeks of cycling left to reach the coast. Both were kind people and integral parts of the groups—Bill, our wise uncle who lived each moment in the fullness of time, and Marlene, our fearful, exuberant child, hesitant about embracing life yet joyful when she did.

I felt an overwhelming need to write about the two deaths, but whenever I might have had time to write, something else went wrong—problems with our new SAG driver, a broken trailer hitch, wrong cue sheets, another serious crash that required an overnight hospital stay, and numerous other episodes. I had no time, and no energy. I couldn't fully grieve for Marlene as well as keep the trip going, so I kept the trip going. That way, this group of cyclists could accomplish their dream of cycling across the country.

**Wakulla Springs, Florida, 29 April 2006.** A group member told me that her daughter is a clairvoyant, who can stage intrusions into the spirit world and communicate with the departed. Her daughter, who had never met Marlene, said she had communicated with her spirit twice. The first time, two days after her death, she described Marlene as very frightened, darting out of sight, extremely nervous, anxious, and weary—just the way she had acted many times on the trip when her fears overtook her. Their second meeting was a week later, and the spirit of Marlene said that she was "at peace and looking forward to her new work." She said that Marlene told her she had known she would die on the trip, but she was thankful nonetheless that she got to do it, and was relieved that her death had not ended the trip.

**St. Augustine, Florida, 4 May 2006.** With black armbands on our cycling jerseys and rose petals from our roadside memorial service in our handlebar bags, our group completed our cross-country journey.

Marlene's best friend greeted us on the beach. She asked us all to send her copies of any photos we had of Marlene on the trip. She would later comment that Marlene was smiling in all the photos, and that she hadn't seen her smile much in the past few years. She said it was as if she was watching Marlene come alive again before it was all over.

**St. Augustine, Florida, 5 May 2006.** Exactly one year after Bill's group met in Williamsburg, Marlene's closest friends and family (minus her parents, who were both infirm) gathered for a memorial service on the beach and scattered her ashes into the ocean. Her journey with us was over, as was our journey together.

## Epilogue

I spent the summer of 2006 working on a series of shorter bicycle tours. The need to write never went away, so finally I sat and wrote this story about Bill and Marlene, two people who did not sacrifice liberty for safety. After writing out all the words, I came to believe that, as sad as both of their deaths were, it was their time.

Editor's Note: *The driver who killed Bill was sentenced to two years' formal probation, two hundred hours of useful public service, traffic safety school, a $1,000 donation to Bicycle Colorado, and $2,401 in court costs.*

*At the time of publication, the district attorney's office was pursuing a manslaughter charge against the driver who killed Marlene. The case has not yet come to trial.*

# Resisting the Inevitable in the French Alps

## RANDALL STAFFORD

I almost didn't make the trip at all. Just two days before I was to leave, my kidney specialist, the humorless Dr. Yang, told me in an emphatic monotone that it was just too risky. He even phoned me that evening to repeat his warning. As I already knew, the problem was being so far away from home and possibly needing dialysis if my transplanted kidney of 21 years finally failed. I considered his earnest, logical advice as I cleaned and packed my 1996 24-speed DeRosa, carefully polishing the shimmering royal and sky blues of its steel frame.

It wasn't that my kidney function had declined without notice. Over the past year, I was increasingly nauseous after eating, often unusually fatigued, had to get up repeatedly to pee at night, and had frequent cramping in my hands and legs. My thinking wasn't as clear as it once was, either. But the most concrete and disconcerting measure of my kidney function was provided by blood tests. The most recent, taken by Dr. Yang only ten days ago, indicated that my creatinine and potassium had reached dangerous levels. A year ago, I shifted to a low-potassium diet, all but eliminating fruits and vegetables. In the last few months, I'd started three new medications, including the twice-a-day Kayaxelate, a slurry of gritty powder I reluctantly swallowed to soak up excess potassium in my body. These extra measures bought me some time, but now declining kidney function seemed inevitable. With unconscious, almost reflexive arrogance triumphing over my better judgment, I stepped on to the France-bound Lufthansa 747. The DeRosa, securely packaged in a bike box, was riding along with the luggage.

My plane landed in Lyon, where I spent a week working with other medical researchers to finalize our draft of a World Health Organization book on the influence of estrogen on cancer. Work ended, and with swollen ankles from too many lavish, high-salt, hard-on-the-kidney meals, I hopped a train to Annecy and the foothills of the French Alps.

In my life, calamity is only a few bananas away. Trying to restrict my diet in France was a losing proposition. I should have limited myself to one liter of fluids a day, and a diet centered on white rice and vegetable oil. Instead, I strayed from my intended gastronomical course and ate too many fresh fruits and vegetables and other high-potassium foods in the restaurants of Lyon. Fruits and vegetables had always been among my favorite foods. Avoiding them seemed at odds with my conception of a healthy diet. For more than a third of my life I pushed my kidney disease into the background, but now it was in the forefront—a source of disruption in my daily routine.

My wife didn't like the idea of my bike trip. She thought I was taking unnecessary risks in my attempts to avoid change. And maybe for this reason I did not always tell her everything. For example, I had told her about the bicycle tour, but hadn't mentioned that my plan was to climb over two of the highest passes in the French Alps. If I had been completely honest with her, she might have asked, "Why, when you can ride anywhere in France— through vineyards or along the Mediterranean—why would you choose to ride over these two passes?" After a long pause of uncertainty, my reply would have likely changed the subject.

Before I left for France, my wife and I watched an episode of *ER* in which a teenage transplant patient is rushed to the emergency room after losing consciousness while driving. While the doctors evaluate her failing transplanted kidney, she has cardiac arrest due to high potassium levels. The TV stars, of course, heroically rescue her. My wife and I watched this episode together in silent tension. Afterwards, she was off-balance and upset by the show, persistently questioning whether the events it depicted were realistic.

My first day of warm June cycling began like a dream, rolling along the lakeside roads of the Annecy Valley, but the ride quickly turned into a breathless affair as I climbed 2,000 feet to the Col du Tamie. The small country road wound its way up into the increasingly clearer air of a steep side-valley.

Out of wind, and with my legs burning, I mused about the ironic nature of my fixation on exercise. While intense physical activity was vital to keep me functional in muscle and mood, the risks were far greater than for the average person. With my heart more susceptible to developing an abnormal rhythm, lungs more vulnerable to filling up with excess fluid, and muscles more likely to cramp, it was difficult to regard any ride as routine. Normally, on a climb like this, I would focus on my rhythm, my breathing, and all the tasks that go into getting myself and 15 pounds of gear up the mountain, but I was distracted by the palpable fear that I shouldn't be out here to begin with. My mind drifted far from the present into ruminations on life's strange events and my reckless resolve not to let them slow me down. I found myself pushing the pedals too hard, becoming more and more out of breath, and developing an odd twinge in my left outer quad. I stopped at the side of the road to catch my breath. Back on the bike, somehow I relaxed, helped by the brief, but amazing views over my shoulder to the green valley below. My pedaling found a tolerable tempo, my breathing became more regular, and I continued up the steep hill.

Once over the pass, I descended 1,900 feet to Albertville. The speed was fantastic, though I felt clumsy and slow on the sharp hairpin turns. In Albertville, I bought lunch from a small grocery store. My selections were a bag of jelly candy (high in sugar and low in about everything else), a large bar of dark chocolate, a 500 ml container of vanilla yogurt (high in protein, containing less potassium than fruit yogurt) and a liter of lemonade drink (mostly water and sugar).

Like the Tour de France racers who eat massive platefuls of pasta and vegetables to match their immense caloric output while on their bikes, I too struggled to take in enough food. The extra 2,500 calories I was burning each day should have translated into the pleasure of larger meals, but my dietary restrictions forced me to be selective. Fortunately, cycling did provide me with some latitude, because of the salt loss from sweating.

I was born with only one small kidney, and this went undiscovered until 1982, when I was 23. Within six months, my kidney failed and dialysis began. A year and a half later, in 1984, I received a successful kidney transplant from my younger brother, Derek. His kidney worked perfectly for an amazing two decades, dramatically transforming my life. Following the transplant, I returned to work with an altered attitude: at once serious and expansive. I decided to pursue medical school. Seven years later, I had graduated. I remained in academia, teaching public health, seeing primary-care patients, but mostly conducting research on heart-disease prevention. Eventually, I received tenure at Stanford University. Thanks to my brother's kidney, I had realized many goals. But his kidney, now part of me, was failing.

Ten miles past Albertville and its drab outskirts, I started looking for a hotel. I passed through a series of quaint towns, reaching the turnoff to Col du Madeleine at 2 P.M., perplexed at still not having located a place to stay. Several signs advertised lodging further ahead, so I reluctantly pressed on. The first couple of hotels advertised were several miles down steep side roads, but I wasn't keen on doubling back to the main road the next morning. I plodded along up a series of tight switchbacks followed by a pair of white-haired, French brothers heading, I later learned, to a late-afternoon picnic at Col du Madeleine. The younger drove a white minivan and stopped at every other turn to shout encouraging words to his 60-year-old brother as he climbed. Often caught between the two of them, I was able to make out descriptions of the delicious feast that waited at the top. Eventually, I had to rest and the two moved ahead, leaving me alone again on the mountain road. After an exhausting ascent of nearly 3,000 feet, and the arrival of a cool late afternoon breeze, I pedaled into the mountainside village of Celliers with its single rustic hotel.

I checked in and ate a dinner of pasta with olive oil and herbs, a green salad, and crusty bread—high on the glycemic index and low in protein, but not likely to put much strain on the kidney. I went up to the room, stood under a steaming, muscle-soothing shower, took a handful of routine medications, and promptly fell asleep. I slept peacefully, until a tearing cramp in my left hamstring threw me out of bed. It was a grim reminder of kidney disease and electrolyte imbalance. Eventually, by stretching my legs, walking in stiff-legged circles around the room, and massaging the spasming muscles, the pain subsided. I slept the rest of the night, and awoke to the tinny sound of bells as goats were herded up the road by barking sheepdogs.

At breakfast, I fortified myself with sugary coffee and a large array of French pastries, as well as yogurt and bread with cheese—more salt than I should have been consuming, but at least reasonable in terms of potassium. Lastly, I swallowed a handful of pharmaceuticals. I got back in the saddle and continued the panting, first-gear climb up to Col du Madeleine; an additional 2,300 feet above the hotel. On the way up the mountain, I stopped only once and even passed another cyclist riding uphill. A few miles from the top, the road was painted with words of encouragement for various current and past Tour de France riders: Lance (Armstrong), (Richard) Virenque,

Ja Ja (Laurent Jalabert), Christophe (Moreau) and others. Just before the Col, the road flattened slightly and I sprinted breathlessly for the last 500 feet, as though I were racing in the 11th stage of the 2005 Tour de France, which was just a month away.

At the top of the Col, I relaxed on the bright sun deck of a large but empty restaurant. I sipped a glass of cold orange juice while taking in a brilliant eye-level panorama of mountains, rocks, and bright ice. The lower slopes were soothing green pastures and forests. Having reached this promontory, I made a pledge to call my wife that evening and finally tell her about my bicycle journey so far and my plans for the coming days.

Back on the DeRosa, the descent was an incremental rush of speed, braking hard before steep corners only to accelerate out of them ready to lean into the next curve. I lacked the killer instinct of the Italian cyclist Mario Cipollini, who had boasted "If you brake, you don't win." I was more concerned about riding off the road while taking a turn too fast.

As I wound down the road I saw large groups of cyclists, dozens at a time, ascending. We exchanged small half-waves from hands still gripping the handlebars. My fingers were achingly tired when I reached the valley floor a vertical mile below the Col. I cycled slowly through the flat Maurienne Valley and stopped for pizza in St. Jean, worrying afterwards about my excessive intake of salt.

In St. Michel, I waited out the hottest hour of the day, putting off further riding until the Supercasino mega-market opened again at 2:30 P.M. after its typically French midday closing. I bought a supply of yogurt and dark chocolate and looked up to the top of the Col du Telegraphe—the main climb of the 8th stage of the 2003 Tour de France. Iban Mayo won the stage, but Lance Armstrong's third-place finish put him in the overall leader's yellow jersey for the first time that year. The antennae that give the pass its name were visible directly above the town, like a bird's nest clinging to a rock wall. It was hard to imagine how the road would possibly reach the apex of the rocky cliff. I clipped in and began spinning my way up. After a long series of 10-percent-grade switchbacks that tested my compulsion to make the top without stopping, the road took a sneaky, wide arc through deep forest, emerging with even more switchbacks to head up a steep rock face. I took simple pleasure in looking straight down between turns to the road below, realizing that my own body, despite its defects and vulnerabilities, had been responsible for lifting me up the mountain. I made the 8-mile, 2,800-foot climb without stopping. It was a small success, indicating that at least the hills weren't, as I feared, wearing me down.

From Col du Telegraphe, the road descended a short few miles into the resort town of Valloire. I circled through the small town before selecting the Hotel de Poste for the night. The room's flower-rimmed balcony offered a magnificent view of the mountains to the South, including several peaks directly above the next day's route. As dusk came, the evening was punctuated by the vague murmuring of the town's river. At a restaurant across the street from the hotel, I ate a simple pasta dinner with bread (a food surprisingly high in salt). At least I had the fortitude to avoid the cherry tart, which I had my eye on. If not for my thorough exhaustion, I would have worried more about how far I was from the nearest full-service hospital. With the day's accomplishments tempering my worry about the consequences of cycling, I called my wife. She was happy and relieved to hear my involved description of the day's highlights, glad that all had gone so well so far. After reviewing the events of each other's lives over the last week, she ended the conversation with her typical admonition: "Make sure you don't overdo it, no matter how well you feel."

Over the last couple of years, my kidney disease had progressed to the point where I couldn't make enough red blood cells, greatly reducing my ability to exercise. My hematocrit—the portion of the blood taken up by the oxygen-carrying red cells—was well under the normal range. To boost production of red cells, I now injected the hormone Epogen (EPO), into the subcutaneous fat on my belly every ten days. This is the same performance-enhancing drug assumed to be widely—and illegally—used by endurance athletes, particularly cyclists, to raise their red cell counts. Lance Armstrong was accused many times of using it to improve his cycling, charges he denied yet never convincingly refuted. For me, the drug's benefits went well beyond raising my blood count: It increased my stamina, bolstered my ability to strain my muscles harder, and improved recovery after hard rides. Touring through the French Alps provided an insight into Epogen's irresistible attractiveness. With this drug, I could climb the toughest mountains in the footsteps of famous Tour de France riders, albeit at a much slower pace.

The next morning started with a bright, cloudless blue sky. The peaks above Valloire were particularly sharp and dazzling, half sparkling gray granite and half bright ice. After a large, relatively kidney-friendly breakfast of two bowls of granola, a dozen pastries, three slices of cheese, a couple of cups of strong coffee, and more drugs, I began the 4,000-foot climb to the Col du Galibier. The route started with a few miles of steep nine-percent hills passing through forest, but then ascended more gently through a wide mountain valley, a treeless expanse of bright emerald green. With no more valley left, the road swung in a steep arc into a series of hairpin turns winding up the mountain in earnest. I now had the pacing down, somehow tolerated the burning in my quads, and continued on without stopping. A multitude of switchbacks climbed up the steep, bare, rocky gray mountainside. For more than half the year, snow covered this barren landscape.

Near the top of the Col du Galibier, fatigue set in—I felt like an awkward buzzard working hard to hover above the great valley I had just ascended. I rode close to the remnants of a low snowbank that jutted out into the roadway. I grabbed a large, icy handful and massaged the crumbling, watery ice into my overheating legs. The thought that the 2005 Tour's 11th stage would ascend this same mountain in another month gave me enough motivation for the last steep miles of climbing. Hill-climbing provided a deep and intriguing contentment, just as it required meditative, inward concentration. It was a revelation to travel upward along a single roadway as it connected the changing landscape, transitioning gradually from green valley farms to desolated mountain passes.

At times, I drifted from contentment to brief thoughts of a worst-case-scenario health meltdown. I figured this would entail falling off my bicycle as I climbed. My problem would be misconstrued as a downhill crash by passersby, who would transport me to the nearest clinic. After more confusion, including my own, the clinic doctors would at last recognize fluid overload and the fuzzy thinking associated with end-stage kidney failure. There would then be a long ambulance ride to Grenoble, where I would begin emergency dialysis to clear the toxins and excess fluid from my body. All the while I would be worrying about what had happened to my beloved DeRosa.

Reaching the 8,700-foot pass without having stopped, I joined the summit-top festivities of arriving bicyclists and motorcyclists. There was a cacophony of German, French, and Italian voices, as groups posed near the sign announcing the summit. I was the lone American. The view was unreal, with the whole panorama to the north filled with looming mountains and glaciers. To the south lay a more remote vista of a dozen high peaks, including the snowy white shoulders of Mont Blanc.

The descent to Col du Lauterat was smooth and short, quickly dropping 2,100 feet to a landscape of bright green foliage. I felt comfortable gripping the handlebars lightly enough to relax, but tightly enough to retain control over unexpected bumps in the smooth and well-maintained pavement. I soon passed into La Grave, a mountain resort just to the north of the huge peak of La Meije, with its half-dozen north-facing glaciers. At La Meijette, the largest restaurant in town, I ate a salt- and potassium-heavy lunch on the sun deck, gazing directly up at the mountain and its formidable display of ice and rock, a view unbearably bright without my dark cycling glasses. Perhaps this wasn't the best meal for me, but I felt I deserved it after the morning's climb up the Galibier.

Back on the bike, it was mostly downhill to Bourg d'Oisans. On the route I rode through six narrow tunnels, before a strong, warm headwind flowed up the valley. It was hardly noticeable when descending the steep hills, but became quite intense whenever the roadway flattened or turned upward, as it did for two miles in skirting a deep gorge. In Bourg d'Oisans, the destination for the day, I delighted in having bicycled up all of the passes on my route so far without mechanical mishap or medical catastrophe.

In 2003, before my kidney went south, I traveled to France for the World Transplant Games, an international athletic competition held every two years. While I did well, I enjoyed more the stories of other transplant recipients, which so often revealed hardships and struggles far beyond my own. On the last day of the trip, I finally experienced the Tour de France in person, after following it for 14 years from Greg LeMond's first win in 1989. I stood on the Champs-Élysées in a howling crowd at the edge of the barricaded avenue watching Lance Armstrong, in the yellow jersey, leading the huge peloton in the final 20 local laps. The peloton of 170 of the world's best riders would pass, only a few feet away, with an overwhelming whoosh of sound, wind, and bright colors, so fast that it was impossible to identify anyone other than the yellow-clad Armstrong.

Riding even a small portion of the Tour at my slow pace gave me a glimpse of what an incredible feat it is to ride 2,300 miles of flat plains and steep mountains in the course of only 23 days. I, too, wanted to achieve something that few others could: to take satisfaction in the irony of an accomplishment achieved as my health declined.

On the fourth day of the ride I deliberately ate a small breakfast in anticipation of a big lunch at the summit, and headed out early to the base of the Alpe d'Huez. Unlike the previous days' rides, I cycled without my backpack, thankfully leaving it behind at the hotel. I took only essential tools and extra clothing, shoving them into the small pack beneath my seat. Bourg d'Oisans was filled with other cyclists there for the same ascent. The town had a Mecca-like atmosphere, drawing an extraordinary number of cyclists to climb this mountain with its 21 numbered hairpin turns.

Without a pack, the climb at first seemed easy, especially after I passed another cyclist struggling to continue. The ascent turned more difficult after a few more turns when a small group of cyclists passed me. I considered speeding up to stay with the slowest among them, but quickly returned to my previous pace. It was better to keep in my comfort zone than to risk blowing up near the top. With kidney disease, I was especially wary of pushing myself to that extreme.

Each hairpin turn up Alpe d'Huez was numbered in descending order starting with number 21. On the prominent signs, the elevation was listed, as well as the names of Tour de France riders who won this brutal stage. This stage was the site of Lance Armstrong's decisive time-trial victory in the 16th stage of the 2004 Tour in a time of just 39:41, beating Jan Ullrich by a full minute. The upper portion of the climb became steeper again, but perhaps psychologically easier, because of the large cluster of resort buildings filling the skyline, indicating the end was near. Approaching the village at turn 3, a photographer snapped a short series of shots, and handed me his business card and a sales pitch. I continued up another mile past the resort across the same finish line used in the Tour de France.

A party-like atmosphere greeted me when I returned to the cliff-top village of Alpe d'Huez. There was a congratulatory camaraderie among all the successful ascenders, punctuated by several photo-posing, color-coordinated cycling groups. On the descent back to Bourg d'Oisans, I finally mastered the hairpin turns, taking them fast with the DeRosa angled deep into the curves. After the quick downhill rush, I picked up my pack at the hotel and continued down the road towards Vizille, my last night before Grenoble.

Twenty miles later, I was out of the mountains and nearing the flat, expansive valley of Grenoble. I spent a pleasant late afternoon in Vizille's main park, complete with fountains and an 800-foot-long reflecting pool. Many people were out enjoying their Saturday afternoon, wedding parties were in full swing, and children rode on the backs of ponies, led along by parents. After a couple of hours in the park, I found a hotel and took a long shower before a meal of a thin-crust pizza covered with roasted vegetables and an additional side of eggs—as usual, more sodium and potassium than I should have been eating. Not much later, I floated into the deep sleep of physical fatigue.

The next warm morning, I had only a short, flat 12-mile ride to the

Grenoble train station. On the way to Grenoble, I passed two hospitals, wondering if this was where I might have ended up had my worst-case scenario proved true.

I arrived at the Grenoble train station with 45 minutes to spare. There was a friendly bustle, as animated hawkers and shoppers overflowed the market square. The air was alive with the scents of garlic, fresh bread, olives, and roasting chicken, but for me there were also pangs of longing, because I wasn't able to fully indulge my desire for these culinary delights. Instead of sticking to kidney-friendly foods for lunch, I ate several pastries, and then on impulse added a pound of cherries for the train ride. *I shouldn't eat all these cherries*, I thought as the train headed west, but it was hopeless once my teeth had bitten through the lustrous, firm surface of the first cherry and tasted its sweet, bleeding juice.

Postscript: *Five months after I returned from France, my wife and I were lying next to each other in separate hospital beds awaiting my second kidney transplant. Early the next morning, the surgeons removed her left kidney and placed it in my lower abdomen on the opposite side from my brother's kidney. Within three days I was returning to a normal life, and at this point I'm back to bicycling hard and enjoying large meals, although I'm also more responsive to my wife's worries, now that part of her is working within me. But her worries and my own have themselves dissipated, as if we had found shelter together just as the rain poured down.*

# To Become a Cyclist

## LUKE BAUER

After graduating high school I moved to Phoenix, Arizona. Shortly after arriving, I went through a phase in which I really wanted to be a cyclist. Initially, I don't think I actually cared so much about being a cyclist as about finding some sort of community in a new city. But I didn't have a car, and already rode my bike every day, so becoming a cyclist wasn't much of a leap. The *American Heritage Dictionary* defines a cyclist rather simplistically as "one who rides or races a bicycle." According to this logic, any drunk college student who steals an unlocked bike and rides home from a frat party is a cyclist. I beg to differ. To me, cyclists are people who ride lengthy distances wearing garish spandex outfits. Cyclists shave their limbs in an attempt to cut milliseconds off their time-trial results. Cyclists are physically fit, they train, they argue over gear ratios and pedal float, and they measure things like their VO2 Max.

    I wanted to be my definition of a cyclist. There were a number of factors that stood in the way of this, however: 1) I'm as lazy as I am competitive, so while I could handle the in-race pressures, I had little use for the training necessary to achieve "racer" status. 2) Phoenix is an incredibly hot and unpleasant place to ride a bike. There are few bike lanes, a lot of exhaust-spewing traffic, and not much in terms of scenery to take one's mind off the ride, just mile after mile of strip-malls and sub-divisions. 3) I was a grossly underpaid and under-appreciated Assistant Production Manager at a professional hair care products manufacturing facility. My position, which led my friends to call me "the gay chemist," left me with no money to buy a nice bike or cool gear, and no time off to train or tour. 4) I smoke like a chimney. I was really in no position to be a "cyclist."

I needed a loophole into the cyclist's world. I decided a self-supported cycle tour would provide the quickest, most accessible entrance. While one does not ride particularly fast or compete against other cyclists, one does have the option of wearing tight spandex in grotesque color combinations, carrying stupidly heavy amounts of gear, and riding absurdly long distances. And a cycle tourist does not need to know technical things like "degrees of float," nor does he need to shave his body. If I could successfully plan, implement, and complete a bike tour—preferably with friends—I would then be a "cyclist."

First, I needed a bike. I started hanging out at my local bike shop. I think I ended up being "that guy" fairly quickly. Apparently, being "that guy"—if you're pleasant enough—can get you a honorary position on the cycling team, which means a 20 percent discount on everything in the store.

In the spring I received a fairly substantial tax refund (one of the few benefits of being poor). I decided to blow it all on a bike and some touring gear. Twenty minutes after walking into the bike shop, I was the proud owner of a shiny new Trek 520 (in Pearl Sparkle or some other idiotically named color), a pair of nifty panniers, and some garish spandex outfits. The acquisition of this new gear demanded that I use it, so I planned a mini-tour, a sort of orientation to prefigure a larger tour that would make official my becoming a "cyclist."

I visualized my overnight trip: I would ride out of the city in a few short minutes, then spend most of my day leisurely riding through the beautiful Sonoran Desert. In the evening, I would pitch my tent in the shade of a cottonwood tree and be lulled to sleep by the sound of the breeze and the gurgling of a nearby brook. The return trip would be an easy downhill coast back into Phoenix.

This vision was, of course, idiotic.

I began my ride at 5:30 A.M. My panniers were loaded with a tent, clothing, water purification tablets, a pulpy vampire novel, energy bars, and a space blanket (one of those shiny backed tarps that trap heat). By late spring, it is more than warm enough to camp in the Sonoran Desert without a sleeping bag.

I rode the first 30 miles, out of Tempe and into Mesa, in mortal dread. I was convinced that a car or truck was going to clip one of the panniers and send me spinning into traffic. On I went—fearful, but in surprisingly good form—eastward toward Apache Junction and the Superstition Mountains.

Fifty miles after leaving my house, I realized I had no real idea where I was going. This was right around the time that the city petered out and the desert began in earnest. I looked at my maps.

"I guess I'll ride to around, uh . . . there," I told myself, pointing to a light-green patch adjacent to a reservoir.

I continued riding. It became exceptionally hot. Then it drizzled. Then it became hot again. As I neared the Superstition Mountains, I no longer enjoyed the sensation of extended cycling. At mile 78, I found that patch of green I had pointed to on my map. National Forest? No, it was not. It was a scenic overlook above the reservoir, with a few parking spots, a picnic shelter, and no marked hiking trails. I shouldered my bike, and in my rigid, uncomfortable biking shoes hiked a good half-mile or so into the desert. I found a spot near a creek, shielded on all sides by short, scrubby mesquite trees, and pitched my tent. It was three in the afternoon.

I spent the next four hours sweating and reading my book. I finished my book. I spent the next three hours reading the contents of my bags—the nutrition information of every piece of food, as well as their ingredients. Later, balancing awkwardly on a slick bolder in rigid cycling shoes while trying to fill my water bottles, I discovered a half-rotten piece of a *US Weekly* magazine in the creek. I read the wet page several times.

By 10:30, I passed out under a blanket of stars. I awoke before six to bright beams of sun. Bleary-eyed and irritated, I stuck my head out of my tent, reluctantly willing to face the day. To my astonishment the desert ground was covered in hundreds of small plastic eggs, some within arm's reach of my tent door.

Why in the hell were these eggs so close to me? That question I couldn't answer. Who had made the early morning mile trek from the road to scatter them quietly around my tent? Methamphetamine addicts are rampant in the Southwest, but even if this prank was benign or childish at heart, I was becoming increasingly uncomfortable with the situation. Plus, I was not interested in meeting the perpetrators, assuming they would return.

I paused for a second to take in the scene, then I started throwing my gear into my panniers. I was getting out of there as quickly as I could. I hoisted my bike over my shoulder and jogged as fast as my cleated shoes could carry me back to the road.

On the ride back to Phoenix, three things occurred to me, in this order:

1) I had encountered the uncomfortable truth that many people do not share my view of wilderness as a place that should be kept free of the bizarre trappings of contemporary society. 2) A cycling tour, due to its dependence on roads, will always contain at least a small element of, well, other people and their devious behavior. 3) It was Easter Sunday.

I moved back into my parent's house in Madison, Wisconsin (free rent, right?) and got a job as a bicycle courier. By most people's definitions, I was now a cyclist. But other people's opinions have a tendency to drift through my mind without taking a firm hold. I still believed I needed to complete a bicycle tour (one more substantial than the Easter Egg Fiasco), in order to become a cyclist. So I set about planning the next tour.

First, I needed some friends to bike with (no more reading labels to pass the time). These I obtained very quickly—my childhood chums, Lou and XT. They had just as little to do as I did, meaning they were up for whatever half-assed scheme was presented to them.

Second, I needed a destination. Why not go big? Madison, Wisconsin to Olympia, Washington—to visit our friend Tyler, who was studying at Evergreen State University.

First *real* bike tour? No problem. Little to no experience? No problem. 2,400 miles in 56 days? No problem.

We're idiots. But we think big.

We decided to let the autumn and winter pass, and take the trip in May. This would leave us ample time to train, sort out the logistics, and obtain gear and maps. XT and I rode bikes and rock-climbed almost daily. Meanwhile, Lou was doing—well, nothing, as far as I could tell.

As the streets of Madison froze, XT returned to Oshkosh to continue his college education, leaving me without a training partner. Lou decided, more or less, that training was for sissies. This left me out in the increasing cold, riding around in mountaineering clothing and ski goggles a few times a week, trying to pretend that I was offsetting the rapid atrophying of my muscles. Spring arrived, and instead of springing back into my training regimen, I got in my car and took off on a ridiculous spur of the moment road trip to Olympia, by way of New Orleans, Austin, Phoenix, Los Angeles, and Fresno.

I returned exhausted from punishing my liver. I was in poor shape and I only had eight days to gear up, organize, and plan the tour. I threw everything I was taking on the trip in a pile on my parent's garage floor. I stared at it with little motivation to organize the gear—then I picked up the phone.

Me: What's happening? All set?"

XT: "I need a new bike."

Me: "Jesus. Uh . . . Let's go to the bike expo tomorrow."

Next I called Lou.

Me: "Lou, been riding at all?"

Lou: "No."

Me "Got all your gear?"

Lou: "Not really."

Me: "Well let's go shopping then, huh?"

A few days and a few thousand dollars later, the pile on the garage floor was much bigger and significantly more organized.

**Tour Day 1.** It should not take almost 11 hours to ride 66 miles. And Reedsburg is only 44 miles from Madison, so it shouldn't have taken us 66 miles to get there, but it did. Our grossly incompetent navigation skills ("Oh, we don't need maps for this section, it's close to home!"), combined with Lou's excessively frequent rest breaks, made for a dubious beginning to our trip. XT's and my attempt to quit smoking lasted about four hours—just as long as it took us to find a rural bar that was both open and willing to sell me smokes in spite of my mohawk and bright yellow spandex. That first cigarette tasted amazing.

**Tour Day 2.** The second day was beautiful and uneventful. We rode along a series of decommissioned railroads, part of the Rails to Trails network, from Elroy to LaCrosse. The riding was wonderful, aside from the headwinds: no significant hills, just enough terrain variation to keep us interested, nice scenery, and the occasional tunnel to ride through. It was a day that seemed to fit within my vision of cycle touring. We stayed at Lou's girlfriend's house. She had beers and an excellent meal waiting for us, which would turn out to be a rarity on this trip.

**Tour Day 3.** I carried with me a little gizmo that allowed me to compose text-only e-mails and send them via pay phone. Both my mother and XT's mother were convinced that we were going to die in a bear attack or some other nature-related episode, and they had pleaded that we keep in frequent contact.

*Most of you know that XT and Lou and I are riding our bicycles across the country, from Wisconsin to Washington. We're currently on day 3. We've ridden 175-odd miles in the last three days, 84 of which (day 2) were directly into a 20-mph headwind. Not much fun. Unfortunately, Lou has a possible MCL tear in his knee and was forced by both pain and the possibility of lifelong disability to drop out of the tour. And then there were two.*

**Tour Day 4.** The previous night, sitting around our campsite, XT and I had decided that our next day would be a relatively low-mileage "rest day." I pulled our maps—photocopied pages from a *Wisconsin Gazeteer*—out of their two layers of plastic-bag storage and spread them on the picnic table. It seemed that we could easily ride the forty miles to Bay City, Wisconsin to link up with the Adventure Cycling route. What we didn't realize was that I had failed to photocopy one of the pages—a crucial page, as it turned out.

*Well, 73.48 miles into our 40-mile "rest day", spirits are low. At mile 68, we climbed the longest incline I've ever climbed, 1.2 miles of straight climbing. Yippee. Now we're camped in wet tents, on some god-awful spit of land jutting into a backwater of the Mississippi, at the tail end of a trailer park swept by gale-force winds. And I have frostbite on the two small toes of my left foot. XT would like to add that we are, quote, "having a riot." Good night.*

**Tour Day 5.** In what quickly became a common experience for us, the campground attendant looked at us like we were insane when we rode past her in the morning with cigarettes dangling from our mouths. Our five-day beards, coupled with my mohawk and XT's severe military crew cut, probably didn't help. And yes, we rode without helmets.

*There's no better way to start a day than with a 620-calorie cream-cheese muffin from a convenience store, a cup of black coffee, and a cigarette. The sun has come out, the wind has died down, and we are 24 miles into today. Spirits are high.*

**Tour Days 6, 7 and 8.** For a few days after our so-called rest day, we stopped planning anything and just rode. This took us across the St. Croix River into Central Minnesota with little fanfare or excitement, other than what I detailed in my message home:

*We've finally started reaching country a little bit wilder than our home area. Admittedly, it's still rolling farmland, but XT and I have seen a bald eagle, a fox, an osprey, and a skunk in the last two days, which, for me at least, is fairly exciting. We got some free gear from a bike shop in Hudson, Wisconsin while en route to our destination, Stillwater, Minnesota. Once we got there, we realized it was Memorial Day weekend, and all camp-sites and hotels within an 80-mile ride were full. So we decided to ride all the way to Fargo, North Dakota—300 miles—in one Red Bull–fueled push. This failed. After 94 miles, we eventually found a hotel, though XT did have to sweet talk the receptionist to get us a room. While eating a burger at lunch, we were invited to a "mud run" by the youths of Morrill, Minnesota (pop. 50). Neither XT nor I has any idea what a mud run is. We declined, but that decision is plaguing me now. What is a mud run? What local customs are we missing out on by sticking to our schedule? In any event, we are currently in a campsite near Long Prairie, Minnesota. We intend to be in Fargo soon. Further bulletins as events warrant.*

**Tour Day 9.** At no point was riding 150 miles from Long Prairie to Fargo a good idea. Again: we're idiots, but we think big.

XT and I hammered our pedals into a strong headwind for the last 40 miles into Fargo. It was painful, and the scenery was not interesting enough for us to forget how painful it was. For the last several miles, we rode on a major highway, with cars blasting by us at 70 mph. So by the time we rolled into Fargo proper, we were not particularly happy.

"Hotel?"

"Hotel."

The first hotel over the bridge connecting Moorhead, Minnesota to Fargo, North Dakota was a Day's Inn. This should not be construed as a plug for that hotel chain; I point it out more as a warning concerning this particular Day's Inn's hotel bar.

Why did we go to the bar at all? Well, at the time, we thought we deserved a break from hard riding and convenience-store meals. We had accomplished a lot in the last 10 days (700 miles, if one was generous about rounding up), our knees hurt, we were bored, etc. Nothing a few beers couldn't remedy.

XT and I paid for a room, showered, primped, and put on our most presentable outfits, which, realistically, were not even vaguely presentable. We both had untrimmed, scruffy facial hair that only charitably could be called beards. Because I hadn't thought to bring hair products to make it stick up, my mohawk, which had started out as a neatly trimmed haircut, had turned into a matted, wild shock of hair that resembled a dead animal glued to my scalp. Our "presentable outfits" consisted of nylon-blend, quick-drying "travel pants" with legs that zipped off, and flip-flops. I'd had the presence of mind to pack a long-sleeved, button-down shirt, but it was wrinkled and stained, with a few holes in it. XT was wearing an equally stained and battered Army issue workout T-shirt. We trotted on down to the hotel bar around seven in the evening and each ordered a beer. We quickly met a young local whose name I forgot within seconds of meeting him. I shall refer to him as "Dawg," since that's the name he elected to use with reference to almost everyone he addressed, male or female.

XT, Dawg, and I had a fairly lengthy conversation about politics, snowboard and ski photography, movie making, the economic difficulties of the "extreme sports" cinematographer, religion, and all the topics one is supposed to avoid while talking to strangers in bars. As we became more intoxicated, our stories, as men's often do, turned to girls, explosives, sexual deviance, cars, etc.

Concurrent with our conversation's escalating level of personal revelation, the bar's populace increased dramatically. For a Wednesday night at a hotel bar in Fargo, I thought there were an astounding number of people, from varied social and economic groups: Goth kids in black leather and heavy eyeliner; punk rockers with safety-pin piercings; frat boys and sorority girls right out of the pages of an Abercrombie ad; hippie folk in tie-dye, hemp jewelry, and patchouli; and plenty of astonishingly beautiful women from all social strata. Wait—we're in Fargo, North Dakota, right?

"Is this normal?" I said, looking around at all the women.

"Oh, Dawg, totally. These chicks are always here. I'd caution you, though."

"About . . . ?"

"Well, they've all been in some of my films."

"I thought you made snowboard films, how is that bad? Snowboarding chicks are hot."

"Yeah, Dawg, but . . ."

It turned out that Dawg, in order to supplement his income, was also an adult entertainment cinematographer. To put it more clearly, Dawg made porn films. And, according to him at least, all of the women in the bar were his, uh, actresses.

"Hey, you guys ever made any movies?"

This story, thankfully, does not devolve into a sordid account of my introduction to the adult entertainment industry. Dawg did offer both XT and I a fairly large sum of money for "one-time appearances" in his films, guaranteeing us the hottest of the women. This, shockingly, did not appeal to me. I won't speak for XT's perception of the whole experience, as I have no idea whether he considered it or not. I will say though, that we quickly began searching the bar for other people to converse with. This led to my second introduction to Fargo, in which I learned that if a restroom contains a urinal, a toilet, and a sink, with no dividing walls between these fixtures, it is not, as one might expect, a "one-holer," or even a "two-holer"—it is actually a "three-holer."

We were soon both pretty intoxicated. I elected to go back to our room and pass out. XT, on the other hand, made the acquaintance of some folks who took him to their apartment, fed him a lot of wine, and may or may not have tried to recruit him into some unrelated, perhaps more personal, adult film. He is unclear on that. Whatever the case may be, he staggered back to our room much later, with a confused look on his face.

**Tour Day 10.** We stayed a second day in Fargo, to rest off our hangovers and allow the experiences of the previous night to sink in. In the morning and all through the day, XT remained vague about what had happened at the apartment. We avoided the hotel bar that night, in favor of a good night's sleep.

**Tour Day 11.** The following morning in Fargo did not start well. The Weather Channel's *Local on the Eights* forecast rain with 40 mph winds, gusting to 60 mph (these would be headwinds for us).

"Feel hard?" I asked XT.

"Oh yeah. We can ride in that."

We checked out and started riding. We rode for precisely one-half mile before we stopped for breakfast. It took us precisely 10 minutes of standing outside the convenience store to decide that riding into 60-mph wind and rain would not make for the most enjoyable day.

"Still feeling hard?" I asked XT.

"Hell no."

We rode another half mile and checked back into the same room in the same Day's Inn. It hadn't even been cleaned yet. Waiting out the unplanned day in Fargo, I composed an e-mail about the days leading up to our arrival, leaving out the events of our actual stay in Fargo.

*We're in North Dakota! Fargo, to be specific. The last two days have been one nasty bit of riding. Headwinds the whole way . . . strong headwinds. The riding has all been through rolling hills covered in farms. The scenery hasn't changed much since Wisconsin. Hopefully, North Dakota will be slightly more interesting. We did, however, see some bison. They were in a fenced-in field, so I assume they're not wild. In addition, we've begun seeing quite a few birds I don't recognize . . . and weird cattle (see how I'm scraping the bottom of the barrel). We are currently 654 miles into the trip, which is roughly a quarter of the way there.*

**Tour Day 12.** We rode off from the hotel in surprisingly favorable conditions. It was sunny, the breeze was actually coming from behind us, which was shocking, and the temperature was in the mid-60s. As the day progressed, the temperature stayed pleasant, the breeze stayed pleasant, and the sun stayed out. It was, well, pleasant. "Pleasant" was probably the most positive word we could use to describe our first riding day in North Dakota; all the other words would have been disparaging. These include: flat, level, horizontal, smooth, even, uniform, regular, and mind-numbingly boring.

**Tour Day 13.** North Dakota was, well, North Dakota. We began to doubt ourselves.

*Sixty-seven flat land miles. Almost zero terrain variation. Not even rolling hills. I got actively depressed riding today. This state is hell. Could never live here. Dear god . . . the insanity and boredom sets in. My knees feel weird. If you go to a store in Hope, North Dakota and expect that you can use your debit or credit card to pay for various sundries, you are wrong. Yes, they have a little credit-card reader machine, but that machine will only read food-stamp cards. "Oh yeah, we take out of state checks with no driver's license though." Where are we? Rural North Dakota.*

**Tour Day 14.** In Tolna, where I composed my next e-mail, we decided there was no way in hell we were going to ride all the way to Washington state. Not only would we have had to ride through the remainder of North Dakota, we would have had to ride through about six hundred miles of flat prairie in eastern Montana. Forget it.

*Otherwise titled: "On the Oregon Trail . . . Johnny Has Dysentery." The wagon seems to have broken an axle, we can shoot nothing but rabbits, and Johnny has come down with dysentery. For those of you who know what I'm talking about, you're welcome. Have your chuckle.[1] North Dakota is exceptionally flat, and there is nothing but neatly plowed farmland in all directions. In any event, both XT and I are experiencing trouble. Though it is not pain, per se, it is a worrisome feeling. We intend to stop again in Minot, ND (three easy days) to assess the situation. As far as riding conditions are concerned, aside from the mind-numbingly boring scenery, riding through ND is fairly "pleasant." There are no hills, winds (surprisingly) have been favorable, and the weather has been sunny and pleasant (mid-70s). Wildlife sightings are almost non-existent, with the exception of many unidentifiable colorful birds, and one unknown animal that may have been either an immense jackrabbit, or a very small and fleet-footed cow. Again . . . the Plains madness.*

I called Tyler from a pay phone in Tolna.

"You mind if we show up early?"

"No. When?"

"In a few days."

"What? Where are you?"

"North Dakota. Find us a plane, train, or balloon station somewhere near Tolna."

A couple minutes later I called him back and he said, "Minot. There's an Amtrak station with daily service direct to Portland, leaving at 8:05, then a spur to Olympia. Two hundred bucks. And you'll be here for my college graduation. Sweet!"

Now we had to break the news to our parents, who were partially bank-rolling the trip. And by "partially", I mean, I hadn't had a job in six months. We couldn't simply say, "This is really boring. Sorry, Pops, we're off to go drinking in the Northwest." That's what we did, but we couldn't *say* that. Thankfully, our knees actually did hurt, in a truly horrific fashion. They had been acting weird before, but now they really started to burn and ache. We could abandon the tour guilt-free, but first we had to get to the train station in Minot.

---

[1]The author is referencing *The Oregon Trail,* an educational video game used in public schools since the early 1980s.

**Tour Day 15.** Our enthusiasm for getting to Minot was met with strong head-winds. Twenty-five miles and three car-beaver altercations later, we rolled into the town of Esmond. Esmond is a populous burg of 156 people. We rode along the street (note the singular) and parked our bikes outside the town's cafe/restaurant/post office/community hall, which seemed to have last been painted during the Carter administration. The inside was, like so much seems to be in North Dakota, pleasant. We sat down and ordered sandwiches and pie. The food was pleasant, too. For the past two weeks we'd mostly been eating Snickers bars and Lipton chicken-flavored instant noodles. Between bites of sandwich I composed my final e-mail:

> As we had feared, knee damage reared its ugly head today. After North Dakota's hellish flat plains became rolling hills, and our favorable winds became 25 mph headwinds, our knees became upset. Today in Esmond, ND, we decided that to continue would be to require surgery. Unfortunately, Esmond has a population of 156 people. Not too many non-bicycle forms of transportation available. Or so we thought . . . Conveniently enough, as XT and I sat in the local diner, discussing our options, our waitress offered to drive us and our gear to Minot, ND . . . some 100 miles away. I suppose one shouldn't doubt the kindness of small town folk . . . or, as we discovered, their abject boredom and desire to do anything other than be in small towns—reap the whirlwind.

**Tour Day 16.** We spent the night at a hotel a few blocks from the train station. Not wanting to relive the Day's Inn experience, we opted to ride to a local establishment whose name escapes me. We made quick work of a few celebratory pitchers and the occasional shot bought by a good-natured local.

The following morning we awoke hung over, exhausted, irate at the early hour, and with barely enough time to scramble and make our train. After struggling to get our bikes into Amtrak's mandatory bike boxes, we collapsed into our seats, sweaty, stinking, and irritable. After 900 miles of biking, 16 days of the "American Experience," and one too many encounters with America's marginalia, we were on our way to Washington. As the train pulled away from the station, XT turned to me, "Hey, does this mean we're cyclists now?"

I watched the flatlands fly by at a speed I wasn't used to. I didn't know which way the wind was blowing, and I wasn't in pain. I felt like I was cheating. "I don't know, XT. I just really don't know."

# Riding Tandem with Rodent

**AMY NEVALA**

In Washington, D.C., where I lived for a year, rats were as much a part of the urban landscape as politicians and lawyers. So it was no real surprise to see a dirt-colored foot-long rodent one warm summer evening as I headed to a friend's home for dinner. The rat and I were both in a hurry, me pedaling my mountain bike, the rodent scurrying along a low cement wall adjacent to the sidewalk that paralleled the road.

I was impressed with its size, and that it kept pace with me. I imagined telling my dinner companions, "You'll never guess what I raced on my way to your apartment." But amusement turned to nervousness when it showed no sign of veering from its track, and when the wall ended we were still moving side by side. I turned right, assuming the rat would also take a right turn into some bushes.

Instead, it leaped—high and straight—into my path.

I can still see the rat's front paws extended and whiskers spread back as it flew up, Superman-style, before gravity sent it sailing down into the spokes of my front wheel. I recall a sickening thud as fur and bone hit moving metal. Seconds later came the squealing. Around and around it circled, trapped near the hub in a rat-sized Ferris wheel. As it twirled, its long, hairless tail whipped my bare shin, five, six, seven times.

Shocked, I could do nothing but continue to pedal. Soon my own squeals joined my companion's now high-pitched screeches. I feared that braking might give the rat a chance to attack. I feared that not braking might lead to something worse. How long could we go on in tandem through the nation's capital, squealing and screeching at each other?

I started hyperventilating. After what probably was only a moment but felt like an eternity, I coasted to a stop. Wheezing and dazed, I watched the rat untangle itself and stagger away. I was clearly in no shape to eat a peaceful dinner with friends, so I bolted home. Even several hours later, after a long shower and meditative breathing, I still couldn't shake the snap of the rodent's solid tail against my shin. People had warned me about the rats I might meet in Washington. Until that evening, I assumed they meant the variety in business suits.

# Hazard on the Trail

## ROLAND GOITY

It all started innocuously enough. Jeff Glass and Paul Bryant—both mid-pack, sport-level racers—had ridden Henry Coe State Park's challenging singletracks and fire roads numerous times in the past, covering every inch of the park's more than one hundred miles of quad-burning climbs and technical descents. The 24-mile loop they planned that day—designated as "epic" by the International Mountain Bicycling Association—was one of their regular rides. As serious riders, they'd suffered broken bones, deep gashes, and painful falls—motivation to learn advanced first aid. A month before, Jeff had wedged his fingers into the mouth of an unconscious friend to clear his air passage after he'd taken a devastating, high speed tumble over his handlebars.

But today, as Jeff put on booties and gloves to keep out the chill, disaster wasn't on his mind. "We're going to have to forego post-ride beers," Jeff said, "The wife's made dinner plans for tonight."

Paul looked up from adjusting his cables. "Not if we make good time!"

"We'll have to drink fast, then. I've flaked on her too much recently."

They slipped their cleated shoes into clipless pedals and began spinning up a series of steep fire roads. Steam rose from their backs in the cold morning and was reflected in the light of the rising sun. They traversed the hills and mashed up to ridges that afforded views of 87,000 acres of northern California wild open space. They cut across high grassy meadows, rode through gullies and creek beds, past a variety of oak, sycamore, and bay trees.

Deer scampered through tall grass, rabbits watched from under manzanita bushes, turkey vultures wobbled overhead, and red-tailed hawks watched everything that moved.

By mid-afternoon, Jeff and Paul were nearing the end of the ride. At this point, the road was overgrown with weeds and brush—virtually a single-track trail. The road paralleled a trickling creek that ran through a landscape dotted with cattle. Two miles of screaming downhill, custom-made for ungodly speeds, was all that remained between them and the trailhead at the entrance to the park.

After closing the first gate at the top of the ridge, they hopped on their bikes and quickly picked up speed, careening down the trail at over 30 mph. In moments they were bearing down on a herd of cattle, which dispersed into the hillside on both sides of the road. A few stragglers stopped on the road and glared at Jeff and Paul, forcing them into a dirt-kicking skid. Then a red Angus bull, the size of a minivan, sauntered onto the trail only a dozen yards in front of them and began trotting downhill. The two followed the bull, though they knew that if the bull turned threatening, they would have no real escape route—the path now butted against a canyon wall on one side, while there was a steep drop-off to the trickling creek below on the other.

Suddenly the bull halted and turned toward Jeff and Paul. They squeezed their brakes hard. Jeff looked in its eyes and knew they were in trouble. The bull was the largest, most pissed-off animal he had ever seen.

Jeff, who was riding in the lead, was about to get an optometrist's view of those eyes, as the bull lowered its head and charged. It happened fast. Instinctively, Jeff picked his bike up by the handlebars and balanced it on its back wheel. This effort to shield himself against the charging bull was actually a recommended defense against a cougar attack, but it was the first thing Jeff thought to do when he saw the lowered head and the horns coming at him. Just before impact, he decided to bounce the bike up and down to make his 6' 2" physique appear larger.

Jeff's tactic lasted less than two seconds. The bull blasted him flat on his back, knocking him out, as his bike soared many feet overhead.

From Paul's vantage point, "It seemed that the bull had run right through Jeff."

In a moment Jeff came to. He saw the bull near his bike and became gravely concerned, such is the reverence Ellsworth owners hold for their bikes. He struggled to his feet, gasping for wind. But he collapsed on the first step he took toward his bike, as horrific pain emanated from his ankle and shot up his leg.

The beast turned to look uphill at Paul, tucked its head in, and charged. Paul ran behind a sizable sycamore tree that stood on the ledge over the drop-off to the creek. As the bull charged, it lost its footing and rolled itself down the embankment in a spray of dirt and dust. Paul seized the moment, ran down the road to Jeff, and dragged him off the trail into the creek bed. As they hunkered down they heard a noise: pppfsssssssssss. It was air escaping from a punctured tire on Jeff's bike.

The big bull had recovered now and stood only 20 feet away. It hovered over Paul's bike, grunting, snorting, and stomping. "Drool poured out of its mouth, and its eyes were wide open," recounted Jeff. Seeing his bike threatened, Paul burst from behind the embankment with a piercing scream, throwing rocks at the bull as he moved forward. But the bull froze Paul in his tracks with a series of stop and start charges. Paul countered the bluffs by throwing more rocks. Aware that this scenario wasn't playing in his favor, Paul listened to Jeff when he shouted, "Stop throwing shit at it!" and retreated.

After a few deep, calming breaths, Paul and Jeff came up with a quick plan: Jeff, whose bike was well away from the bull, would hobble to his ride and with the help of gravity make it to the lower cattle gate. There he would wait for Paul and attend to his ankle, which he now realized had been stomped on when the bull knocked him flat. Meanwhile, Paul would attempt to retrieve his bike by circling around behind the bull.

Jeff made like Lance Armstrong on steroids, albeit Lance Armstrong with a swollen ankle and a flat tire, to the lower gate. Then with sneaky moves and quiet feet Paul circumnavigated the canyon wall. After five minutes of climbing and descending he got to the other side of the bull, only to find that it stood massively between him and his beloved bike. Without a Plan B, Paul retraced his steps back over and down the canyon to where he started. When he got back down to the road he saw his bike unattended, beckoning him. He ran towards it, stopped, then ran back as he realized the angry, vindictive two-thousand-pound bull might still be nearby. But nothing stirred, so he rushed forward again, got on the bike, and rode.

Late that afternoon, as Jeff iced his swollen ankle in the comfort of his San Jose home, he called his wife to inquire about the possibility of forgoing their dinner plans.

"What's your excuse this time?" she asked. "You're tired from the ride? A few too many post-ride beers?"

"Honey, I was run over by a bull," Jeff replied, as he examined the cloven-hoof mark imprinted on his neoprene bootie.

Monday morning, in his boss's office, Jeff enthusiastically recounted his weekend adventure. His boss reached into a drawer with a smile, then tossed Jeff a copy of *Worst Case Scenarios: Ultimate Survival Guide,* saying, "There's something on bulls in there."

Jeff flipped through the pages until he came across the section which read: For bull encounters, slowly vacate the area with a wary eye. However, when faced with a charge, quickly sidestep the animal like a venerable matador, as bulls aren't the most nimble of creatures.

What the book strongly advised against, was trying to look big and confrontational.

"Thanks," Jeff said to his boss. "This would've come in handy . . . *two days ago.*"

# Rambo

## MIKE HAINSWORTH

### April 1984, Greenville, NC

My cousin owned the local bike shop in Greenville, North Carolina, the little college town where I grew up. One day I was hanging out in the shop after school and met Phil, a psychology PhD student. He was freckled-faced, bloated, and had a large round head topped with thinning red hair. His physical appearance and his pompous speaking tone combined to give him a likeness to Kelsey Grammer's TV character, Frasier. Phil and I started talking about Greg LeMond's chances in the upcoming Tour de France. At the end of the conversation Phil mentioned that he took part in a Sunday group ride. But he told me not to try the ride—I would never be able to keep pace. He hit my 15-year-old's pride hard, so I hit back by going on the ride anyway. I only wished he had warned me about the dogs.

On the back roads outside of town, the dogs flew off farmhouse porches and bounded through the tobacco fields. Because I was behind the peloton, struggling to keep pace, the dogs would choose me, the straggling sheep. One after another charged me in a barking rage, and I would sprint as hard as my legs and lungs would take me. If I made it to the end of the dog's territory, then I was safe until the next encounter. To be honest, I liked the adrenaline pumping thrill of having to outrun the dogs—at least, until one caught me.

At the halfway point of the ride, a steep hill rose from the usually flat farmland. Phil and I got dropped from the pack and drifted well off the back of the group. From behind me I heard the rustling of tobacco leaves, and then the clicking sound of claws on pavement. Looking over my shoulder I saw a huge German Shepherd/Doberman mix, ears straight up, froth dripping from its mouth. The dog had me targeted, and Phil was smiling. I thought quickly and grabbed my water bottle. When it got to my back wheel, I sprayed it in the face. It didn't even flinch. Just as its jaws were sinking into my ankle, I gave it two solid blows to the head with my pump. The dog backed off.

Phil smirked in amusement. "Hey, Chickensworth," he said. "If you want to ride in the country, you've got to accept the dogs." I decided then that my best defense was not the pump, but staying in the middle of the pack, where I would be protected by numbers, with larger bodies between me and the dogs.

We took the same route each Sunday and as my fitness and riding improved, I became a fixture in the middle of the peloton. Safely tucked in among other riders, getting pulled along by their draft, I felt unthreatened by the sprinting, barking dogs. But there was one mutt I still did not look forward to seeing—that big German Shepherd/Doberman. It was amazingly fast, it attacked on the uphill, and unlike the other dogs, it didn't stick to its home turf. It just kept chasing. I named it Rambo, after Sylvester Stallone's character in *First Blood*. Like the character, Rambo the dog was what Phil called "not well adjusted." It waged a solo war against the Sunday group riders, much as its namesake took on the entire police force of a small town.

By my fourth ride with the group, Rambo had begun to seek out Phil exclusively. This wasn't that surprising, as Phil was frequently dropped on the long hill. According to Phil, the birth of his first child had "conspired" with his doctoral studies to keep him out of the saddle for some time. His lack of exercise had allowed the pounds, many of them, to gather around his midsection. Though he still had skinny legs, and cranked circles as smooth as a Swiss-made sewing machine, his weight really held him back on the steep inclines. Not only was Phil slow on the climbs, he also drew a lot of attention to himself. He wore an old yellow wool race-leader's jersey with French writing on it that he had won years ago as an amateur cyclist in Europe. Greasy chain marks on the sleeves and scuffs on the back of the jersey revealed a history of his cycling accidents. The jersey should have been framed and put on display to memorialize his past accomplishments. Instead Phil wore it to remind us that at one time he had been faster than any of us. Now, with every pedal stroke, the jersey would creep up his body, exposing the folds of his belly.

Rambo's first series of attacks on Phil were the same. It would leap from the rows of tobacco and run him down from behind. When it caught up to Phil, the dog would hesitate for a moment, searching for an opening among the whirl of wheels, crank arms, and legs. Then, with a quick lunge, Rambo would bite down hard on Phil's ankle and hold on for dear life as its head rotated in sync with the motion of Phil's legs. In response, Phil would deliver a series of whacks to Rambo's skull with his chrome Silca pump. Each attack resulted in a broken pump, but every Sunday Phil would show up for the group ride with a brand new Silca. I took guilty pleasure in watching Phil get abused. Maybe it was because he directed chicken noises at me for riding in the middle of the pack, or maybe it was because he had been so amused the one time I got attacked.

By June it appeared to me that Phil had lost a few pounds; his face was slimmer and he'd gotten noticeably faster. As we rolled up "Rambo's Hill," Phil moved to the middle of the pack. Rider after rider passed me, and soon I found myself alone, far off the back. I prepared myself for the inevitable. From out of nowhere came the dreaded sound of claws rapping on asphalt. Rambo was gaining quickly. With one hand on my frame pump, I waited. Seconds later, Rambo was running even with me. I turned and we made eye contact. But the ferociousness I'd become accustomed to was gone; the dog had a look of utter disappointment. Rambo slowed to a walk, and its head hung low.

At the top of the hill, I asked Phil why Rambo now attacked him exclusively. "I can't speak for the dog," Phil said in his professorial tone. He ran his hand through his wispy red hair. "If canine Rambo were a patient of mine, receiving psychoanalysis, I might say that the dog's ego (the rational, responsible, 'there are consequences' part of the mind) is not checking its id (the 'I want it, I want it now,' immediate gratification part of the mind). And its superego (the moral, ethical part of the mind) simply does not exist. The dog's metaphorical id is literally running me down. Of course one can't anthropomorphize a dog. It's just a dog." Phil looked at me flatly.

I gave Phil a blank look.

"Let me put it in another light. Perhaps, the dog is not really after me; it's after the position of top dog—a total validation of existence. A successful attack on me could elevate its position. Rambo, as you call him, doesn't want me—I just happen to be the pathway for it to relish in the validation of existence."

I nodded in agreement.

"But," continued Phil, "I am the top dog, and I will not hand that distinction over to a mutt. And one other note: it's a wild beast that's been selectively bred, so disregard any comparisons of it to a human."

Two months after I first joined the ride, Phil's form returned, and the yellow jersey, which had barely covered his midsection, actually fit. He rode as if he were back on the amateur race circuit, dancing on his pedals as he led the group up "Rambo's Hill." This Sunday, the group rode without fear. Last week, Rambo had remained sitting by the side of the road, seemingly uninterested in the cyclists as we sped by.

As we rode along, Phil and I exchanged theories. "Maybe," I said, "the dog was caught off guard by your impressive improvement."

"Perhaps," said Phil, "the dog began psychoanalysis this week and is now contemplating the patterns in its life."

Once we reached the hill, Phil led the pack. As I changed gears, I looked up and noticed Rambo waiting at the very top. When Phil was two hundred yards from the crest, Rambo bounded into action and made a beeline straight for him. This looked to me like it was going to end badly, and the rest of the riders seemed to agree. We collectively slowed, and a large gap formed between Phil and us. All the while, Rambo tore down the oncoming lane, fixated on Phil. Phil looked right, then left, and then back at us. There was a hint of terror in his expression when he realized he was alone, far from the safety of the group. With nowhere to go, and no pack to drop back to, Phil increased his cadence, apparently willing to take Rambo on in another battle for "top dog."

At that moment an 18-wheel truck appeared over the hill, approaching with alarming speed. I imagined the worst-case scenario: the truck driver would slam on his breaks to avoid the dog, and this would cause the trailer to jackknife and take us out like bowling pins. The group and I drifted as far on to the shoulder as we could, to give the truck driver extra space on the road. The driver, however, remained committed to his lane, and only applied the brakes slightly. Rambo took a few final strides and then, mouth foaming, leapt from the oncoming lane straight at Phil. As it did so, the truck's grille hit the dog in the hindquarters and rocketed it directly at Phil's torso. Phil and Rambo hit the ground with such force they bounced off the pavement and into the drainage ditch by the side of the road.

We all rode up to Phil. He sat up slowly, dazed. He held his shoulder and grimaced, then rocked back and forth.

"I'll find the closest house and call an ambulance," I volunteered. I felt this was partially my fault, for relishing the times Rambo had attacked Phil earlier in the summer; somehow, I thought, I had wished this upon him.

"No, I can make it back, just get me on my bike," said Phil. "I've had worse. My wife will freak if she and the kid have to come to the hospital. She won't let me ride again. I'll go home and then see a doctor."

His entire body shook as he tried to stand. He sat back down. Blood trickled down his neck. I suspected he was lying about worse accidents. It is not often one gets knocked senseless by a semitrailer-assisted dog. A palm-sized piece of Phil's prized yellow wool jersey had been ripped clean off, exposing a nasty bit of road rash. "Shit," he said as he touched the exposed skin. His facial expression told me this was the yellow jersey's final ride.

"What about the dog?" asked a rider from the group.

"What about the dog?" Phil mimicked.

Rambo was lying in the ditch next to Phil. Blood dripped from its mouth, but the dog appeared calm and serene, and I swear there was the hint of a smile on his face.

Then the yelling began from a nearby house. "Brutus, Brutus!" A skinny, almost malnourished, elderly man came out his screen door. He didn't move too fast. "Brutus! Come here, boy!"

We improvised a sling from a spare inner tube, then steadied Phil as he gingerly mounted his bike. We rode him to within a few blocks of his house, until he said, "I'm stopping here." I grabbed his seat and put on my brakes while he braked with one hand. He winced as he pulled off the sling and handed it to me. "My wife can't see this," he said. He wiped some blood from his body. "Or this."

"Thanks for getting me home, guys," he said, then walked down the sidewalk holding his bike by the stem with his one good hand. I never saw Phil again.

# The Day I Beat Miguel Indurain

## GREG TAYLOR

My colleague, who rather reluctantly agreed to look after my cases for me while I was gone, didn't understand why I was using my vacation time to run off to France to ride in a bicycle race. Most of the attorneys in my office spend their vacations in more time-honored ways, such as relaxing on the beach with a drink in one hand and a Blackberry in the other, obsessively checking e-mail and calling the office to pester the staff.

"Do you speak French?" my colleague asked.

"No."

"Well, that just takes the cake. How will you get around? How will you order food at a restaurant? You might wind up with a very nice sauté of shallots and pig's anus if you aren't careful, bike boy!"

"Just keep an eye on my cases, okay? I'll see you in two weeks."

Since 1993, the organizers of the Tour de France and the publishers of *Vélo Magazine* have run an event known as the Etape du Tour, which translates loosely as "A Stage of the Tour." The premise is simple: during one of the rest days of the Tour de France, the promoters open the roads to riders who want to test their mettle against the clock and get the feel of what a tough day in the Tour de France is like.

The Etape is the real deal: the roads are completely closed to vehicles, gendarmes man each intersection and crossing, Mavic support cars follow the massive peloton, cheering crowds line the brutal course, and there is a broom wagon ready to sweep up those who aren't up to the task. Not everyone finishes the Etape du Tour under their own power. Some simply give up in defeat—sad hulks of human wreckage deposited on the side of the road—and some are involuntarily pulled from the race for failing to make the required average speed. Of the 8,500 riders who started the 2003 edition of the Etape, nearly a quarter (2,112) did not reach the finish line.

At the upper end of the field are the pro and semi-pro riders who show up to stretch their legs and compete for the overall victory. For example, the 1993 Etape winner, Christophe Rinero, went on to have a fine career as a professional, placing fourth in the 1998 Tour de France. The list of past winners of the women's prize is even more impressive; it includes Marion Clignet, a world track cycling champion, and Jeannie Longo, an Olympic gold medalist and woman's world road-race champion.

However, with all due respect to Mr. Rinero and the others, they are relatively small potatoes compared to the mega-celebrities of cycling who frequently make an appearance at the Etape du Tour starting line: Abraham Olano, the winner of the coveted rainbow jersey in 1995 and three-time Tour de France champion Greg LeMond, who took part in the Etape in 2000.

And then of course, there is Miguel Indurain.

Anyone with even a passing interest in cycling has heard of Miguel Indurain. One of the greatest riders of all time, he utterly dominated the sport during the 1990s, becoming the first man to rack up five consecutive victories in the Tour de France, a feat eclipsed only recently by Lance Armstrong's seven wins. Indurain's success came as a result of his being a physical mutant. Massive legs, an eight-liter lung capacity, and a zombie-like resting heart rate of 28 beats per minute, the lowest on record, allowed him to time-trial with the absolute best while holding his own in the mountains. They normally give people pacemakers if they have tickers like that.

And when the 6' 2", 176-pound mutant lined up at the start in the city of Pau for the 2003 edition of the Etape du Tour, he was a marked man. He was a marked man because, you see, I was entered in the race as well, and I had an old score to settle with Senõr Indurain.

This was not the first time that I had gone head-to-head on a bicycle with Miguel Indurain. No, we had met several years earlier in a more social setting—a Lance Armstrong Foundation cancer fundraiser. We chatted briefly, his poor English skills matching my utter lack of fluency in Spanish. Nevertheless he was unfailingly nice, a true gentleman. The highlight of that weekend was a 25-mile group ride with Lance and Miguel and about a hundred other riders over hilly back roads outside Austin, Texas. The wind was horrific, and my main memory of that morning was struggling along hunched over on an uphill section into the teeth of a gale, only to watch in disbelief as Indurain sat up, casually took off his jacket, and calmly spun away from the group while riding with no hands. Okay, I realize that he's a five-time Tour winner, and I'm just an overly competitive attorney who likes to ride my bike, but I can honestly say that on that windy morning in Austin I swore on a stack of *Vélo Magazines* that somehow I would return the favor and put the hurt on Indurain some day.

As fate would have it, the next time that Indurain and I would meet on two wheels would be nearly 4,000 miles from Texas, in the Pyrenees mountains during the 2003 edition of the Etape du Tour. The race organizers were pleased to announce that Indurain would be among the honored guests, along with Abraham Olano and Formula One star Alain Prost. Me? I fancied myself as a dark-horse threat in "Category C"—men aged 40 to 49.

Dark-horse threat? Yes. When I signed up to do the race, I honestly thought I would be a genuine force to be reckoned with over the roads of France. What was the key to my stunning overconfidence? Well, I was able to convince myself early on that the route mapped out by the race organizers actually played to my "strengths" as a rider.

We would be contesting Stage 16 of the Tour, the roads between Pau and Bayonne. It was the same stage that Tyler Hamilton would capture later in the week with an amazing solo ride while nursing a broken collarbone. *Vélo Magazine* reported that Stage 16 featured three categorized climbs: the Col du Soudet, the Col Bagargui, and the relatively minor Côte du Aubertin. The first major effort of the day, the Col du Soudet, was listed by the organizers as a "First Category" climb, 8.75 miles in length with an average grade of 7.5 percent. I'd done climbs with nearly identical average statistics in the United States with little problem. Ditto the other "First Category" climb, the Col Bagargui, 5.5 miles with an average grade of 9.2 percent.

On paper, it didn't look *that* hard. It never does. So sitting there in my coach-class seat on the flight to France, I was confident that the mountains would hold no terrors for me. I was going to kick ass, and the only glimpse that Miguel Indurain would have of me on the road would be of a solitary rider in the distance ahead of him, soaring through the snow-capped peaks like an eagle. Sipping that second glass of Air France merlot, I couldn't think of a better place on the planet than the Pyrenees for a beefy amateur racer who lives hundreds of miles from any actual mountains to drop the hammer on a five-time Tour de France champion.

I should have known I was in for a tough day when I lined up for the start of the Etape in the city of Pau. It was a gorgeous morning, dewy and mild, and there were thousands of riders jammed into side streets around the square, waiting for the start. Somewhere up front, rubbing elbows with the mayor of Pau, was the guest of honor, my bête noire, Miguel Indurain. As befitted his exalted status, Big Mig, or Miguelón, was at the front of the massive pack, ceremonially given race number 1.

Looking over the crowd, I noticed everyone was sitting on a bike equipped to tackle some *serious* hills; bikes fitted with triple cranksets or big-ass mountain cassettes. And when I say "everyone" had a rig like this, I really do mean *everyone*—with the exception of me.

Having convinced myself that the Etape route would be just like my normal Sunday group ride, only a little hillier, I decided bail-out gears and all those other fancy mountain-climbing doo-dads simply were anathema—mechanical artifices that would only detract from the glory of catching and dropping Indurain on his home turf. I didn't need that stuff. I had spent the spring sprinting up any hill I could find, and damned if I didn't think I was ready for whatever France had to throw at me.

I will admit, however, that the contrast in the equipment caused a moment of doubt. It was pretty obvious that *someone* had gotten it wrong here. It's just that sitting on my bike at the start line in Pau, fully occupied with my normal pre-race routine of looking cool and exuding confidence, I was damn sure it wasn't me. I thought, "How hard can these climbs be? How can eight thousand Frenchmen be so wrong?"

Mercifully, there was no time to think about it, because the race soon began. I threw my leg over my bike (a titanium Dean road bike, powder-coated an attention-grabbing shade of canary yellow) and took off with the pack. The first twenty miles or so passed effortlessly for me, riding along in a huge group at a steady 25-plus miles per hour. The massive peloton negotiated innumerable small villages, each gaily decorated in our honor. The entire population of each town we flashed through turned out to greet us, and we all pedaled a little harder with every "*Allez!*" shouted from the crowd. As we received the good wishes of the townspeople, I got the sense that, yes, this was a small taste of what the Tour de France must be like.

With the first climb looming, my pre-race plan of knifing through the pack and rocketing away from Indurain as the road angled up was quickly

Miguel Indurain changes gears as he summits the Col du Colombiere in the 1994 Tour de France.
John Pierce/PhotoSport International

going by the board. My progress through the peloton was more fizzle than fireworks, and I was having trouble making up ground on Indurain. In the criteriums that I used to race in, moving up through 50 or 70 riders is one thing. Moving up through 8,500 riders who are all frantically racing to be at the head of the pack is something altogether different. In addition to trying to pass my competitors, I spent a lot of time and energy dodging water bottles, arm-warmers, and extra clothing that got tossed away as people started peeling off layers on the fly. You could have stocked a pretty nice bike shop with what was left behind.

Twenty-five miles into the race, and Indurain was clearly making good time. Given my starting position at the back of the group, there were still several thousand bug-eyed and flailing riders between Miguel and me. An obvious sign that my plan to avenge my humiliation was about to go horribly wrong was just that: a road sign, warning of the extremely steep gradient ahead. The comfortable delusion that I would fly up the Pyrenees (fostered by the correct-but-amusingly-misleading statistics for the stage provided by *Vélo Magazine)* expired as I pedaled past the road sign and began my climb up to the Col du Soudet.

A relatively benign-sounding "average" grade for a climb can, and often does, mask a complete horror show out on the road. So it was a rookie mistake on my part not to recognize that, although the evil geniuses at *Vélo Magazine* could truthfully say that "statistically" the climb up the Col du Soudet "averages" a reasonable-sounding 7.5-percent grade, big chunks of it were much steeper. Try 15 percent for the first couple of kilometers, leveling off to a ripping 10 percent for the first half of the climb.

Somewhere, off in the distance, I faintly heard those eight thousand Frenchmen snickering.

In hindsight, I can take some comfort in the fact that even some of the pro riders in the Tour were just as surprised as I was by this nasty little shocker. Of course, the ever efficient, always in control Lance Armstrong was completely aware of the road between Pau and Bayonne before the Tour hit the mountains. In the days leading up to the Tour, Lance had targeted this stage as a potential ball-breaker:

> In the Pyrenees they look to the Tourmalet and Luz Ardiden. They look to the legendary stages, but they forget about the stage to Bayonne, which goes over two climbs that are probably the steepest climbs in the Tour de France. So for me, there are the famous climbs, but there are also these ones that nobody thinks about and I'm glad we saw, because they're very difficult, and they could change the results of the race.

Others who were less prepared, like Michael Rogers of the Quickstep-Davitamon team, were flabbergasted by the apparent disconnect between the race-book's description and the actual difficulty of the route:

> I can honestly say I have never, ever climbed up a road as steep as that one—let alone raced up it like we did in today's 16th stage. It felt like we were pedaling up one giant wall forever and ever. . . . We all knew it was a steep climb, but we never expected it to be that steep.

When the pro riders say it sucked, believe them—it sucked.

Back on the Soudet, no one was having an easy time of it. Even with a triple chainring there was no getting around the fact this bad boy was *steep*.

Complicating matters, the change in grade from relatively flat to ungodly steep was abrupt; so abrupt, in fact, that a small traffic jam formed at the foot of the mountain as the entire peloton struggled to find a gear that would allow them to stay upright. For those of us who were bold enough (read "stupid enough") to have come to the Pyrenees with gearing more appropriate for a flat criterium, we were shot out of the back of the pack like we were fired from a cannon. I quickly crunched down into my lowest cog. Finding myself out of gears, there was nothing left to do but try and grunt my way up the mountain with brute strength.

Well, actually there *was* one, less dignified option that I was trying to avoid. I really didn't want to do it, but there was simply no other way. Yes, I got off and pushed my bike for a *short* distance up the Col du Soudet.

Push or no push, I did make it over the Soudet well ahead of the time cut, a moral victory of sorts. I stopped at the feed station near the top of the pass, elbowed my way through the stiff-legged, panting crowd, and downed two or three energy drinks along with handfuls of orange slices. My thighs and calves were twitching like Shakira's hips, just waiting to curl me up into the fetal position if I so much as even thought about getting back on my bike. Worse yet, there was no sign of Indurain.

One mountain pass down, one more to go.

Recovering my strength and a few shreds of my dignity, I tried to make up some time and hopefully catch the ever-elusive Indurain on the descent. Dropping down the Soudet was a complete hoot, but having just been bitch-slapped into reality by the climb, I was concerned about my ability to get over the second First Category climb of the day, the Col Bagargui. My concerns were well founded; if the passage over the Soudet was an undignified interlude in my cycling career, the subsequent ascent of the Bagargui thoroughly eclipsed it in terms of animal suffering. *Everybody* struggled up the Bagargui.

We inched our way up the mountain, kilometer markers passing like kidney stones. Emerging from the tree line I was disheartened to see at least another 3,000 feet of climbing. Neck craned skyward, I saw what appeared to be a slow-moving caterpillar of cyclists strung out over an endless series of switchbacks all the way up to the Col.

The carnage up the Bagargui was unspeakable. The switchbacks were the worst. Riders trying to negotiate the turns were often overcome by the grade and not able to unclip from their pedals. They simply flopped over onto the asphalt. Rows of exhausted riders perched like gaunt crows atop the guardrails. Those who weren't completely blown sucked on water bottles and nervously fiddled with their bikes as they contemplated remounting and completing the climb. Some, catatonic from the effort, sat silent and glassy-eyed, staring vacantly at the endless stream of riders grunting past. A few wept quietly while waiting for the broom wagon to take them back down the mountain.

Somewhere along the climb, I was passed by a petite woman who punctuated each turn of the pedals with an obscenity.

"Shitshitshit . . . shit . . . shit . . . shit . . . shitshitsthitshitshit . . ."

Her rhythm slowed as she negotiated the switchbacks, and then picked back up as the effort eased slightly on the straight runs between corners.

What was even worse than the carnage was that I had no idea how my main competition was doing. I had failed to catch Indurain on the flat section before the mountains. My "Plan B"—hoping that Indurain had gotten fat in retirement eating *tapas* and drinking *sangria* so I could catch him on the climbs—hadn't panned out either.

I eventually crested the Bagargui amid polite applause from the surprisingly large number of spectators parked at the top of the Col. It was time to unleash "Plan C"—hang it out on the descent without killing myself and, if I still had the legs, sprint like hell to Bayonne.

After the mountains, the last third of the race consisted of terrain that is my meat and potatoes: rolling hills. Determined to try and salvage a little pride and glory, I was on a search-and-destroy mission to pick off as many riders as I could. With each rider I passed I received an appreciative *"Allez!"* from the crowd. How cool is that? A cheering crowd for a 42-year-old guy on a bike? Only at the Etape. I felt 10 feet tall and pedaled like mad with every cheer.

As the route entered the city of Bayonne, our final destination, I was in my element and riding strong. There were a few guys stuck to my wheel as I passed underneath the red "1 Kilometer to Go" sign. I decided the only appropriate way to end the ride was a sprint to the finish.

After blowing up in the mountains, I was probably sprinting for five thousandth place, but it didn't matter. I was going to attack right up to the end and, more importantly, I was *not* going to get passed by *anyone* in the last kilometer.

I was suddenly struck by the thought that maybe the reason I hadn't seen Indurain all through the race was because I was looking in the wrong spot. Maybe Indurain had somehow managed to sneak up *behind* me, and was biding his time in my draft before making his move. Yes! There *was* a chance that I had unwittingly caught and passed the five-time Tour de France champion somewhere on the road, and he was now sucking my wheel, poised to settle our grudge match with a final dash to the line!

So up and out of the saddle I went, pushing for all I was worth. I dropped whoever or whatever it was on my wheel and passed a surprised group of racers ahead of me . . . and then over the line! Finished!

I hobbled around the finish line village in Bayonne on two rather sore legs, chewing a sandwich and looking for any sign that Indurain had arrived ahead of me. As the adrenaline rush from the day's events slowly ebbed, I realized it was probably time to admit to myself that Indurain was the better rider, always had been the better rider, and was likely always to remain the better rider. I merely wanted to shake his hand and wish him well, humbled by the fact that yet again I felt his sting.

The road imposes its own truth, as harsh as it may be, on even the most ardent wishful thinker. As I walked among the tired and happy finishers I felt sure the final results of the Etape, when they were announced, would provide all of the participants, me included, with a true and objective measure of ourselves against the unforgiving mountains and the accomplishments of our cycling heroes. Today, it was enough to have ridden the same roads as the champions and finished the race.

Yes, I was willing to concede all this and possibly more—until I walked over to the scoring table where the race results were being posted.

If one were to check the results of the 2003 Etape du Tour, as I did on that fine July day, one would find that Miguel Indurain abandoned the race in the tiny mountain village of Larrau, which is in the shadow of the Col Bagargui.

I had beaten Indurain.

I bought myself the biggest beer I could find, declared victory, and announced my immediate retirement from international competition.

As a postscript to the events of the day, I eventually found out the reason why Indurain stepped off his bike in Larrau. It wasn't because he found the pace too fast or the course too difficult. No, it was because his family and friends threw him a party in the village near the Spanish border. Indurain turned 39 on July 16, 2003, the day of the Etape. In other words, I beat a five-time Tour de France winner because he stopped to eat birthday cake.

Back in the office, I was catching up on my e-mail when my colleague poked his head in my doorway.

"So, bike boy, did you win the Tour de France? That was the race you went to go ride in, wasn't it?"

"Not quite. But I did okay. I beat Miguel Indurain."

"Indurain? I've heard of him. He plays for the Yankees, right?"

"No. He's won the Tour de France five times."

"How did you pull *that* off?"

To paraphrase Marie Antoinette: "I let him eat cake."

# The *Kleedkamer*

**AUSTIN KING**

## Galmaarden, Belgium — May 10, 2004

The Zellik-Galmaarden race is one of Belgium's most prestigious amateur races. I had ridden it for the past three years as a member of the US National Cycling Team. This year, I was hoping to ride strong and not be pulled, as I had been the year before, for being outside the time limit.[1] As usual, just getting to the starting line tested my strength. There were naked Europeans as far as the eye could see in the *kleedkamer* (changing room). Before a bike race in Europe, it is common for the riders to undress in the *kleedkamer*, then hang out and chat, completely naked, before dousing themselves in body spray and putting on their team kits. As an American, in my fourth year of amateur racing in Belgium, I was still acutely uncomfortable in the *kleedkamer*. But the experience awaiting me after the race would disturb not just my comfort, but my psyche.

Before I get to that incident, though, let me timeline the race to give you a feel for what it's like to ride and suffer, and ride and suffer some more, in a typical Belgian race.

---

[1] Time limits are imposed on long races, typically as a percentage of the winner's time. For example, if a race winner finishes with a time of 3 hours and the time limit is 10%, then any riders still on course after 3 hours and 18 minutes would be pulled from the race, classified as *hors delais* (outside the time limit).

12:15 PM. Enter the *kleedkamer,* joining 200 naked European men wielding their cologne and body spray.

12:35. Walk out of the *kleedkamer,* dressed and ready to race, but slightly traumatized.

1:00. Zellik-Galmaarden starts. The Belgian weather is foul as usual, and Mr. Wind shows up immediately with his cousins Rain and Cold in tow. I think they will be joining us for the duration of the race. No matter what direction I ride in, Belgian winds always seem to be headwinds.

1:45. Mr. Wind is in a sour mood today. Only 125 riders left in contention.

2:00. I watch with gratification as 25 more riders get dropped. My lungs burn and I have the slight taste of blood in my mouth. The "taste of blood" is not a metaphor. Really, there is the taste of blood in my mouth.

2:20. Meet Mr. Bosberg, a bastard of a cobbled climb. The cobbles jangle my nerves from my ass to my elbows.

2:50. Meet Mr. Muur, a serious bastard of a cobbled climb. On the way down, while descending at 50 mph and wearing only a thin layer of spandex, I notice my brake pads are already critically worn. I knew I forgot to do something last night.

3:02. Humming along in the peloton, I look at the spectators scattered about the Belgian countryside. They brave the foul weather, a painful endeavor in its own right, to watch us give all that we have. Can't they just go back inside and let me suffer in peace and quiet? I stop thinking and start eating a PowerBar. I'll need the calories to finish this race strong.

3:22. Voice in head says, *Move up, Austin, the peloton will split soon.* My body says, *Sorry, bud, I can't.*

3:28. The peloton splits and I am in the trailing group. I chase the leaders to close the gap. Can't feel my hands, too cold. A rider next to me dry-heaves. Perhaps he ate dairy before the race, or perhaps the chase has depleted his blood sugar. I don't really care. In a race like this everyone faces his own battle.

3:33. I catch the leaders just in time to get reacquainted with Mr. Bosberg. I begin fading toward the back of the peloton, and try desperately not to get dropped as we crest the climb. The effort is so intense that I become stricken with one of the *Seven Degrees of Suffering*, a system I have devised to catego-rize the various ailments associated with bike racing. It's not the "dry heave" or the "upchuck." I bypass those and head right into what I call the "fuzzy navel." My vision becomes distorted and blurry. I ignore the symptoms and push onward. I lose peripheral vision completely, and what little I can see ap-pears as if in a haze. Vision remains impaired until five minutes after clearing Mr. Bosberg's backside.

3:39. Normally, the more I suffer in a race, the better I do. Not true today.

3:48. The peloton is now only 75 riders deep. Mr. Wind is howling, doing his best Jimi Hendrix impersonation, crying "Mary."

4:03. Wonder what the other racers would say if they knew I had no brake pads left? Begin evil laugh.

4:06. End evil laugh, as four riders break away.

4:32. Can't feel left hand due to the cold. I begin waving my left hand vio-lently, slapping it on my leg and handlebars to regain enough feeling to shift into the little chainring. Start wondering how ridiculous I must look to the spectators who are braving the wind, cold, and rain.

4:36. Finally, able to shift to little chain ring. I wonder how far ahead those four riders are by now? I stop wondering—because, honestly, I no longer care.

4:37. Damn, Mr. Bosberg again. I notice one of the breakaway riders climb-ing from the bushes back onto the road. I suspect he must have just expe-rienced another one of the *Seven Degrees of Suffering*. This one I call "The Screen Door at 200 Meters." It begins as a churning bowel surge and rapidly escalates into urgency. A rider can take deep breaths, sip water, and continue riding with as little movement as possible, but he will not avoid having to take immediate action in the form of a rolling dismount into the bushes. Subject will quickly rip off his jersey, tear down his bib, and take care of busi-ness, which will take the form of a violent emission that could penetrate a screen door 200 meters away. As I ride past, I take a closer look at the rider coming out of the bushes. He's wiping his shoes in the grass and he's missing a glove. Bingo.

4:38. I attack Mr. Bosberg for the final time, giving everything I have, I push myself hard enough to hit another degree of suffering, the "dead ringer." First,

I lose hearing in both ears. Silence is quickly replaced by a loud ringing that stays with me through the end of the race.

4:45. I think I've had enough fun for today—too many *Degrees of Suffering* attained in too short a time period.

5:00. With one local lap to go, my group of 15 is pulled. We are scored "outside the time limit." Brain is too cold to produce an emotional response.

5:05. As my hearing slowly returns, I look at the final times posted on the scoreboard: 200 or so starters, 49 finishers, 23 scored "inside the time limit."

5:06. I am excited about taking a hot shower that will restore feeling in my hands and feet, but not so excited to shower with a bunch of naked Europeans. I walk slowly into the *kleedkamer* through the stink of sweat and cologne. I look around. The Europeans casually stroll to the shower, dangling naked and chatting. They are completely comfortable and at ease. I am not.

5:10. With my towel snugly covering my nether regions, I cautiously navigate my way through the water and filth on the floor and around the sweaty bodies to the shower. I maintain at least a one-meter buffer zone between myself and the naked cyclists, while keeping my eyes focused well above their waistlines.

5:11. I exit the shower, clean but not fully warm. Then I teeter back and sit on the bench where I'd placed my bag.

5:15. As I sit on the wood bench, leaning over and digging through my bag, a local rider tries to squeeze by me. His rear end wipes across my face. One cheek—gap—the other cheek. I freeze and mutter, "Oh my Lord!" I get up to confront him, but quickly consider a round of naked arguing to be perhaps more traumatizing than what just happened. I hurry back to the shower muttering the words "butt face." I scrub a layer of skin from my forehead in hopes of removing all memories of the Belgian man's heinie.

5:45. As our team van pulls away, my teammates begin laughing about Bennett, a new addition to our team. We recently discovered that he had been eating dog food every morning for the past three weeks. He thought it was cereal—odd tasting cereal—and that the cartoon on the packaging—a dog in a chef's hat holding a fork—was meant to entice kids to try the cereal. Dog food—that was Bennett's official welcome to Belgium.

All amateur racers who head to Belgium to test their mettle get an official welcome. When I arrived five years ago, I got poached on every training ride I took. Recreational cyclists would see me riding solo and sprint to get on my back wheel, and I wouldn't be able to lose them. I'd bomb hills and take corners fast with no effect; they would stay on my wheel for hours. That was my welcome to Belgium—so much for thinking I had strong legs.

Now, I put my head back against the van seat and try to understand getting ass-wiped as a welcome back to Belgium. But perhaps it was a metaphor for the larger picture of suffering and humiliation that is bike racing. More times than not, a day at the races is a long, hard, cold affair with little or no gratification. Yeah, I pushed my body as hard as it would go, maybe I should be happy with that. But I'm not. I didn't step on the podium today (or last week for that matter). The long van ride back to our team house gives me more than enough time to marinate in the feeling that I might not make it to my lifelong dream of becoming a professional European rider. Sure, I can dominate in plenty of amateur races in the U.S., but I want more.

I've chosen a hard path. My self-absorbed thoughts turn back towards the feeling of the Belgian man's rear wiping across my forehead. The feeling is not dissimilar to getting pulled from a race after riding your guts out for five hours in cold, wind, and rain. I'll get that guy back, somehow, but for now, I just curl up in a fetal position, close my eyes, and let the van gently roll me home.

# Sheepskin Saddles

## EUGÉNE ETSEBETH

### The Poster

The typeface of the poster grabbed my attention immediately. It reminded me of a Western "Wanted" poster, except that it was promoting a bike race in a nearby town. The reward was a substantial sum.

I visited my local bike shop, Coimbra Cycles, in Port Elizabeth, South Africa, more religiously than I attended lectures at the University of Port Elizabeth, and was intimately aware of the bulletin board's comings and goings. The poster was certainly a very recent addition. It was nestled between a dog-eared Bike for Sale sign and a personalized note from Sandy offering post-race massages. All her telephone tentacles had been torn off.

The poster described a 60-mile race starting in Aberdeen, a small sheep-market town, and finishing in Graaf-Reinet, the region's capital. The point-to-point race was set in the arid Karoo desert, with the craggy Camdeboo and Sneeuberg mountains providing the backdrop. The race was to be the center of festivities during the local church fête. Promises of an accordion *boere-orkes* (farmers' music band) as well as a sheep auction filled out the draw card.

I glanced over my shoulder. No one was looking in my direction. I returned my gaze to the race poster and tore it from its green felt backing. A tack came loose and landed on the tiled floor with a plink. I tensed up and looked around slowly. No one had noticed. I shoved the poster into my pocket and darted out of the store. The less competition in this race, I thought, the better. But the distant reprimand of my mother's voice filtered into my mind, "Eugéne, was that the right thing to do?"

As a cash-strapped student with a penchant for all things to do with cycling, including an obsessive need for the grand prize, a Campagnolo groupset, I found the race too much to resist. The Italian bike-parts company had iconic status amongst road cyclists. Their exquisite workmanship and smooth shifting mechanisms were the envy of all cyclists. I desperately wanted these accoutrements on my racing bike, as they almost ensured my path to cycling greatness. But I could not buy them, as my monthly stipend from my family only covered race entries, cheap tires, and occasional beer guzzling. But dreaming was free, and I dreamt for Africa even while I sang Italian opera songs and shaved my legs in the bath, just like Dennis Christopher's character, Dave Stoller, in the cycling film *Breaking Away*.

Cycle racing, and especially European professionals, captured my imagination and transcended my earlier childhood dreams. I dreamt of racing along the Champs-Élysées as South Africa's first finisher in the Tour de France, and hammering through the forest of Arenberg on my way to the velodrome in Roubaix, in a solo display of dominance. Laurent Fignon, with his resplendent blond ponytail, was my cycling hero at the time. My hair flowed in the wind, just like his, but I was a lot taller, 6' 2", and I couldn't speak in his Parisian accent. My ancestry, like a lot of white English-speaking South Africans, is a Viking cocktail of Nordic and Norman. And my blue-grey eyes, dulled from the African sun, were neither myopic nor far-sighted, so there was no way I could sport the oval spectacles that had earned him the sobriquet "Professor," although I certainly considered it.

## Cold Start

The two weeks I needed to fine-tune my fitness for the race were a resounding success. Hill sprints, individual leg training, and four-minute pursuits would pave the way to the podium. My Campagnolo fetish was soon to be satisfied. This period, though, was jotted with a feeling of unease due to my removal of the poster, and my competition, from the race. A number of times I resolved to return to the shop and reinstate the poster to its rightful place. I didn't, though. Instead I concentrated on forgetting my misdemeanor, and on training. My mom's reprimand grew fainter with the passing of each day.

I made the short trip from Port Elizabeth to Graaf-Reinet in my rusty Volkswagen Golf. Winter isn't a good time to camp, especially in the desert of the Karoo. But I was a student and any spare pocket money I had was ploughed into my passion. I set up my tent in the municipal campsite by torchlight. The race was starting early the next day from Aberdeen and finishing in Graaf-Reinet. I still had to make my way to the race start 60 miles away by early the next morning.

On the morning of the race I left the campsite with the bare minimum of clothing. Extra clothing equals extra weight. My arm warmers were the only cold weather gear that I brought along. After a few minutes of sprightly riding in the morning dew, the cold seeped through my morning warmth and I shuddered to a stop. I realized that my lack of clothing was a big mistake. I looked back in the direction of the campsite. My mind unpacked my bag to reveal a windbreaker. Just then the thought of returning to get my windbreaker was unceremoniously barged aside by the image of a red London double-decker bus.

The race poster, which I had in my back pocket, mentioned a bus: "Bus available for cyclists to get a lift from Graaf-Reinet to Aberdeen. Leaving at 6 A.M. from the Drostdy Hof hotel." I looked at my watch. Twelve minutes to six. I dashed off in the direction of the Drostdy. The bus would be an ideal opportunity for me to get warm and focus on the race. I surveyed my bike while I rode and smiled at the thought of my two wheels crowned in Campagnolo parts.

The 1804 Drostdy Hof is a historic hotel that once housed the regional court. The lime-washed walls and thatch roof were made grand by a Cape Dutch style gable, and the old slave bell in the courtyard was a reminder of a bygone era. I wasn't taking particular notice of any historical artifacts when I arrived at the Drostdy, though. My smile had pursed as my eyes searched for the double-decker bus and warmth. My body was in a chilled state, brought to life only by intermittent jerks of cold convulsions. I started to clasp my hands and puff between them. I chose to accompany my whistling with an ungainly dance for warmth.

While I was doing this shimmy-shake I noticed that a large truck was the only vehicle parked on this forsaken street. It was a farm truck full of Karoo sheep huddled together in the largest incontinent woolen ball in Africa—urine jettisoned out of the truck and dung spattered forth with an alarming din.

A barrel-chested farmer emerged from the truck. He gestured in my direction with his khaki-clad arm. I stopped dancing immediately, leaving my legs straddled in such a peculiar manner that I almost toppled over. He once again made an arc with his thick-fingered hand, beckoning me.

I gathered myself and my bike and made my way towards him. The farmer introduced himself curtly as Koos van der Merwe.

"*Ons moet nou gaan*," he stated in Afrikaans, the language of a lot of Dutch South Africans.

My frozen jaw creakingly enquired, "Is this the *bus* that is taking us to the race?"

"*Ja*," he growled, slightly irritated by my now-perplexed body language and his having to revert to an unfamiliar tongue. "Looks like you is the only one that need a lift," he said, peering up and down Church Street to see if other cyclists would be joining us.

This was the bus? I could hardly believe it. I briefly longed for my sleeping bag and my tent, but then I reminded myself about the training I had done, and I thought how Laurent Fignon's pride and determination would never have allowed him to give up. Hardship is part of cycling, I convinced myself. And the prize was waiting for me.

I made my way to the passenger side, only to see that it was already full with three farm-workers scrunched into a single bucket seat.

"They are also doing the race," Koos motioned with his head to the three workers of Khoi-San origin crammed in the front. "You must get on top."

Koos was using the trip to take his sheep to Aberdeen's Saturday market, which causes the human population, in search of farm fresh goods, to double. The flatbed truck had a makeshift pen for the sheep. An upper level was where I would be spending the trip to Aberdeen. Grudgingly, I walked to the back of the truck, avoiding sheep excrement at every step. My cleated shoes made their way up the hand-welded ladder. This tinkered wagon reminded me of an Afrikaans saying, "'*N boer maak 'n plan*." Directly translated: "A farmer always makes a plan." Not only did this adage help inspire Koos's alteration of his makeshift truck, but he was also saving on trips to Aberdeen by delivering both cyclists and sheep at the same time.

My bike and I joined the three farmworkers' bicycles on the roof. They were sturdy delivery bikes. The well-used frames were black and bulbous, topped with sheepskin saddles for comfort. Sitting on the unwelcoming thick cold metal roof made my skin feel like it was covered in bedsores. Every pressure point of my flesh that contacted the roof drove chilling sensations through my body.

The truck stammered to a start. The pace through town and to the outskirts was bearable. Once it picked up speed, though, I started to go numb.

I took up a position lying flat on the roof. The cold air rushed over my face and body leaving me senseless. A long time passed. I remember singing the old Cliff Richard pop song "Summer Holiday" over and over.

Eventually we arrived in Aberdeen. I shed tears of joy. It took my body a minute to come to life before I made my way down the ladder. I was like the Tin Man in *The Wizard of Oz* before Dorothy squeaked oil into his joints. Koos handed my bike down to me, the smirk on his face broadcasting his disdain for city dwellers, especially ones dressed in Lycra.

At least a hundred cyclists had gathered in the church square. I hobbled in their direction. My bike, like my body, was cold to the touch. I looked for the sunniest part of the courtyard. I found it and allowed the sun's rays and the heat rising from the sandstone to slowly warm my body.

One of the farmworkers who had ridden in the front with Koos joined me. He struck a match for his hand-rolled cigarette and introduced himself as Frikkie. His beard was coarse and his skin taut, which made it difficult to guess his age. His cotton cap was well-worn and his blue overalls torn at the knees.

"You sure look cold, *baas*," he said. "How did you enjoy the ride?" The Khoi-San people are notorious for their particular blend of Afrikaans and humorous, if not racy, wit.

"It was bloody cold. I hope I can warm up before the start," I replied.

I asked him if he and his friends were also racing. Frikkie told me there was separate prize money for farmworkers on fixed-cog bicycles. I now understood why there were about twenty rough-shod bicycles and their owners all heading toward the start, together with over a hundred shaven-legged racers.

"*Jislaaik*, I really need to win this," Frikkie spluttered between puffs of his cigarette. His breath reeked of plum brandy.

A lot of cyclists had now congregated at the start line. My poster ripping had been in vain. I inwardly felt relieved. I wished Frikkie luck, said farewell, and hastened to the start line.

## Campagnolo Dreaming

My normal regimen of warming up for twenty minutes and checking my equipment now seemed completely irrelevant. I had just learned the previous week during a lecture on Abraham Maslow's *Hierarchy of Needs* that mine were food, water, shelter, warmth, and sex. My need for sex was being satisfied, as Sandy the masseuse could attest to, but right now, my need for shelter and warmth were certainly not. And a more lofty need, Campagnolo components, seemed even further out of reach.

The mayoral garland shimmered in the winter sun. The stout, semi-baldheaded man raised a gun to start the race. Only a ten-minute microwave equivalent of "easy defrost" would ready me for the start. I was still frozen to the core. *Bang!*

I was surprised that the farm workers and the elite cyclists started together, but this was quickly forgotten as my racing instincts kicked in. A paceline formed instantly. I moved towards the arrowhead of the race. My "quawking" (the ability to position one's self in the peloton) skills allowed me to adroitly place myself in a vortex created by a big sprinter's bum in front of me. "Bill's Plumbing & Hardware" was embroidered on his bib shorts.

A few miles into the race a false flat (where I thought I reached the peak of a hill, but looked up to discover much more hill waiting) caused me to have a power outage. It was at this moment, my weakest moment, that I heard the sound of tires on gravel. The sound came from a pair of thick tires, not typical racing tires. The sound got louder. I dared not look around. All my senses were focused on riding through the painful cold. My peripheral vision first picked up the sight of his cotton beanie on my left. Slowly his unmistakable beard moved into view. It was Frikkie. His leather gloves were clasped to the brake hoods as his wool-covered Brooks saddle squeaked with every pedal rotation. He winked as he passed. But then the sound came again from behind me. His two farm worker friends were hooked to his back wheel. One had a thick basket of woven reed mounted to the front of his bicycle.

I stopped counting after the sixth farm worker passed me and moved to the front of the peloton. The speed picked up unpleasantly. I peered over the heads of the pack and caught site of the well-oiled motley crew of farmworkers traveling at over 25 miles an hour.

The early warning signs of system failure had already passed. I was in red-light-flashing mode. I thought I heard the distinctive sound of an air-raid siren. And it was just then that I melted down. A combination of being frozen, delivered on an icy truck, and unceremoniously spat out the back by farm workers was too much for me. I sheepishly dropped my head in capitulation. My Campagnolo groupset was now a distant dream. My dignity had taken a monster hit.

It took me a long time before I could truly process the defeat. My weary legs turned around in a metronomic zombie-like state. The Karoo desert was silent. The cavalcade had long since disappeared up the road. Eventually my day of despair unfolded in storybook fashion. I was trying to make sense of what had happened. Maybe cycling wasn't for me? Could this be payback for ripping off the race poster? Maybe I wasn't talented enough. I was at an all-time low, and still a long way from Graaf-Reinet.

Every few miles, I would look back down the road, watching intently for any signs of Koos's flatbed truck returning from the sheep market. Luckily, the day had warmed up some.

# Sabotage on the Tour de Femme

## JACQUES DEBELLE

### November 1996, Canberra, Australia

Every November women cyclists come to Canberra, my hometown, to ride in a 20-kilometer race known as the Tour de Femme. The race attracts a wide assortment of female cyclists, from top-tier professionals to those who treat it as a "fun run" on wheels. On this particular November day, the contestants had not just the road, the weather, and the other riders to contend with—they would also have me, looking for a date.

When I met up with my friend Mark a week before the event, we discussed the trouble I was having with the opposite sex. For example, I had recently gone out with a woman who, to my surprise, explained at the end of the date that she was a lesbian. When we parted ways, she suggested we should "stay friends." Canberra is regarded as somewhat of a socially cold city. And because I'm not the smoothest of cats, I find it difficult to meet women in the usual ways.

While talking to Mark in my time of desperation, I had the hair-brained idea that if we scattered thumbtacks along the course of the Tour de Femme, we could assist the riders with their subsequent flat tires and hopefully turn our charitable work into dates. I imagined dozens of beautiful, athletic, Lycra-clad women pulling to the side of the road with mysterious punctures. Mark and I would then come to their rescue, removing wheels and patching tubes. In return we'd receive kisses and hugs of gratification. Mark laughed off my idea as a product of depression or lunacy, but I persisted, and by the end of the conversation he agreed to give it a try.

I had just watched the documentary film on the Tour de France entitled *23 Days in July*. At one point the narrator of the film says that in bygone eras, the riders cheated by using invisible wires to get towed by their team cars, or by getting friends to scatter nails in strategic places along the route. Perhaps the film had inspired my idea. At any rate, I considered the plan genius. I should have looked back into my past, though, and reconsidered.

I have a history of sabotage. When I was 12, my friend organized a local race and I threw tacks down on the course. Some of the other kids discovered what I'd done and chased me, trying to bash my head in with a two-way radio. When I was 16, I covered a runner in chocolate milk as I rode by him. I was too fast to catch, but he caught my friend, who gave me the message that the man would soon find me and throw me in the lake. When I was 17, I poached a training ride and brought along a boom-box playing noises of dogs barking, and then of people having sex. I almost caused a full-pack crash. A soon-to-be road champion of Australia was on the ride and he yelled: "Stop this shit before someone has a serious accident." I have no criminal record from my teenage years, but I crossed the line numerous times.

Early on the morning of the race, I packed my bike in the car and headed down to the paper shop. At the counter I set down four boxes of thumbtacks, fifty to a box. The cashier didn't blink an eye, but I felt as though he was suspicious of the absurd quantity of thumbtacks I was purchasing.

I met Mark at roughly the halfway point of the course, where a lower road ran parallel to the road the race would take place on. When I brought out the boxes of tacks, Mark's eyes lit up. "You sure you've got enough?" he said as I began placing them strategically across the line I thought the women might take. After I had methodically placed around 25 tacks, points up, Mark said, "We'll be here all day—just scatter all of them and hope for the best." So I did.

Then we got on our bikes and headed towards the start. Our plan was to meet and ride with the peloton one kilometer into the race. We would pose as cyclists, perhaps husbands of two of the competitors, enthusiastically cheering on the racers.

We were running a little behind schedule, but were sure we would be able to catch and keep pace with the racers, as we both had been competitive cyclists in the early '90s. I rode in Category 1 and 2 events, while Mark, who never trained quite as hard as I did, competed in Category 3.

We rode at a furious pace until we found the peloton, 200 meters in front of us. I had dropped competitive cycling for weight lifting several years previously, so the riders' pace of 35 to 40 kph seemed really fast. Just as the peloton entered the "tacked-out" portion of the course, we veered onto the lower road so that we wouldn't sabotage our own tires. A race official, thinking we were participants yelled, "Wrong way, ladies!" At the time I was 24 and wore my hair shoulder-length, Fabio style, while Mark, a somewhat nerdy computer programmer, stood a mere 5' 3". With our helmets on, I suppose we might have looked like ladies. I yelled back in a girlie voice, "We're okay."

Back on the race route, parallel to us, I could see no more than half a dozen stranded racers looking confused as they inspected their tires. A couple more had already begun making the necessary repairs. Where, I wondered, was the mass of long-legged, bronze-skinned beauties in need of a ruggedly handsome mechanic? Of the six women with flats, only one actually caught my eye, an athletic blonde with attitude. She was hunched over her front wheel swearing at her bike when I approached.

"Need a hand?" I said.

"No, I'll be alright," she responded without even looking up. She pulled a tack from the front tire and flicked it in my direction.

"Unlucky," I said, trying to hold back a smile.

She muttered something under her breath and went to work removing her tire.

I looked at the other five women, looked at Mark, then clipped in and rode leisurely with him towards the finish. The amount of energy we'd expended just to catch the peloton had left us winded. We noticed a handful of other riders who were clearly victims of our high jinks, but they weren't really our types, either.

"That didn't go quite as I planned it," I said to Mark.

He laughed at me. We got a cup of coffee and then went back to the car.

At home later that evening, I watched the race highlights on the local news. During an interview with the race winner, she explained how lucky she was to complete the race with a tack stuck firmly in her front tire. "With about five kilometers to go I heard a noise, and realized something was lodged in my tire. I just kept hoping it would stay up till the end of the race."

*Unbelievable*, I thought looking at her blonde hair, amazing smile, and beautiful legs. *Unbelievable.*

"What about the luck of the winner?" said the reporter, with a smug look on his face. "Could it have been sabotage? Well, that's all from the Tour de Femme, until next year . . ."

I didn't hear the rest of the newsman's words, because I was lying on the floor in the fetal position, laughing myself into stitches. Then, when I realized I was still dateless, I slowly stopped laughing.

# Iron Riders

*The Buffalo Soldier Bicycle Corps*

## GEORGE NIELS SORENSEN

In the 1890s, visionaries saw the bicycle as a new instrument of personal freedom, allowing people to move about without the expenses associated with a horse, carriage, or train. The bicycle's potential for revolutionizing the way people lived appeared limitless, especially to Lieutenant James A. Moss, a young Army officer who had recently graduated at the bottom of his West Point class.

In his distant post in Fort Missoula, Montana, Moss read about the new safety bicycle that was rapidly making the penny-farthing bicycle obsolete. The safety bicycles were so named because they had two wheels of the same size as opposed to the penny-farthing which had a large direct pedal front wheel and a much smaller rear wheel. In addition to symmetrical wheels, the safety bicycle had a triangle-shaped frame with a center-mounted seat and a rear-wheel, chain-driven propulsion system. The design provided for a much lower center of gravity than the penny-farthing, thus making for a more stable and agile ride. The more compact frame and ease of riding contributed to the popularity of the safety bicycle, but it wasn't until John Dunlop's invention of the pneumatic tire in 1889 that the bicycle became an ideal form of transportation. The cushier wheels made it possible to cycle city streets and rutted country roads in relative comfort.

Although Moss had never ridden the safety bicycle, he theorized that soldiers on bicycles might supplement or replace the Army's Cavalry Corps.

He asked the Army for permission to create and test a bicycle corps, arguing that the bicycle could move troops faster and more economically than the horse. Additionally, he argued that a bicycle did not need to be trained, groomed, stabled, or fed; "they don't get sick, they don't die, and they are easy to replace," stated Moss in his proposal. Though Army commanders had little confidence that a bicycle corps would be a viable alternative to cavalry, the Army granted Moss his wish with one stipulation—Moss's experiment must not cost the government any money. Upon receiving word that he could proceed, Moss wrote to the Spalding Company in Chicago and asked to borrow twenty-five bicycles. A recent entrant into the bicycle market, and competing with 300 other manufacturers in the U.S., Albert Spalding was eager to get publicity for his product. Spalding shipped twenty-five of his top-of-the-line iron-frame, wood-rim bikes by train to Fort Missoula, where Lieutenant Moss commanded a unit of Buffalo Soldiers[1] involved in the post–Indian Wars task of "closing the American frontier." Upon receiving the bikes, Moss created the 25th Infantry Bicycle Corps.

On a scorching summer day in 1896, Moss assembled his men on Fort Missoula's dusty parade ground, and there he explained to them his vision of a bicycle cavalry that would revolutionize and modernize the Army. "Those who wish to volunteer for this unit step forward," Moss instructed. Without hesitation, man after man volunteered his services, until there were far more eager soldiers than there were bicycles. Moss selected a group of twenty men from the volunteers and began training immediately. None of the soldiers had ever ridden a bicycle; few had even seen one. After brief and inadequate instructions on how to maintain balance, pedal, and steer the men were commanded to form ranks and ride in columns, as though they were marching soldiers. Confusion prevailed; they tipped over, collided with one another, and were unable to stop and start in unison when Moss shouted the orders.

Moss's vision was to command a self-sufficient unit of bicycle soldiers. To this end he began training his men with long rides through the valleys

---

[1] The term "Buffalo Soldier" refers to African-American soldiers, who at the time were segregated and assigned to white commanders. The Indians had given the name Buffalo Soldiers to black American soldiers after fighting them on the battlefields of the Indian Wars. The name is said to have come from one of two sources: the Indians thought the soldiers' hair resembled the mane of the buffalo, or that the soldiers had attributes—ferocity, strength, and stamina—of the buffalo. The name was quickly adopted by the soldiers themselves.

Five members of the 25th Infantry Bicycle Corps pose at Lolo Hot Springs, Montana 1896. [BI. J-3, Elrod Collection] Archives & Special Collections, The University of Montana.

around Missoula, often leading them to streams and fences to work on techniques of fording and scaling while carrying a bicycle. Back at the base, he lectured his soldiers on the construction, maintenance, and subtle nuances of the safety bicycle. He trained them to be a cavalry-replacement unit, though he noted in his journal that his men did not train in the full sense of the word—they saw no need to regulate their diet or abstain from tobacco.

In the summer of 1896, Moss led two trips in preparation for a proposed continental crossing the next summer.

## Ride One: Missoula to Lake McDonald, July 1896

The men were responsible for packing all personal and group gear necessary for camping and cooking. Moss's reports detailed that a typical soldier's bicycle was weighed down with: clothes, a sleep blanket, rifle, pistol, knife, rounds of ammunition, tent, toilet paper, soap, mess kit, canteen, and food: extract of beef, salt, prunes, sugar, rice, flour, cans of beans, and other staples. The soldiers employed a specific system for loading a bicycle, which Moss created and described as such:

On the front of the bicycle was strapped the knapsack, and on top of it the blanket roll, containing one blanket, one shelter tent half, and tent poles. The haversack was carried either on the front of the knapsack or was secured to the horizontal bar, well to the front. The cup was fastened under the seat with a small leather strap, and protected from the dust and mud by a cloth bag. The canteen was carried on the body. Every soldier carried a rifle on his back and an ammunition belt with fifty rounds of shot around his waist. In the diamond of each bicycle was a canvas luggage case. The cooking utensils were carried in a large tin case, resting on the frame on the front of the bicycle and securely strapped to the handlebars. A cylindrical coffee pot fastened to the front of the handlebars was carried ... and ... blankets [were] stuffed into these pots. As little as possible was carried on the persons of the soldiers, for if placed on the body, in addition to carrying the actual weight of the object, the soldier would also experience more physical exhaustion from the weight bearing down on his body. Furthermore, one falling from a wheel with much weight secured to the body is much more likely to sustain an injury than a person whose limbs and body are entirely free and unhampered.

Moss, who kept meticulous records about every aspect of his Bicycle Corps program, weighed each man's bike before departure. He then calculated an average weight for the bikes once they were loaded with gear: 79.7 pounds.

In the wee hours of a cool July morning, Moss and the 25th Infantry Bicycle Corps rode north out of Fort Missoula toward Lake McDonald (the area that would later become Glacier National Park). Farmers stopped their work and stared open-mouthed at the sight of 20 black soldiers riding fully loaded bicycles in two neat columns. At the front, Moss set a measured but brisk pace, while making sure to greet each passerby with a kind "good morning."

The well maintained road out of Fort Missoula allowed the Bicycle Corps to make good time initially, but as they approached the canyons which led to the mountain passes, the road narrowed to little more than an overgrown trail, slowing their progress. During the heat of the day they stopped for lunch—a routine that included building a cooking fire, smoking pipes, blowing smoke rings, and napping. Lunch typically lasted three to four hours. A common meal consisted of biscuits, bacon, corn, coffee, condensed milk, freshly caught trout, and prunes. The prunes, with their purging effect, were an essential component of the otherwise dense meals.

Obsessed with calculating and bettering the Corps' average moving speed, Moss grew disheartened by the number of mechanical failures among his riders. When a tire went flat, the solider had to patch the tire as best he could, cement it back to the wooden rim and wait for the cement to dry; then the soldier had to catch up to the unit. When more serious breakdowns occurred, the men had to either push or carry their bicycles to the day's destination. The bicycles, not meant for off-road abuse, suffered broken wheels, bent forks, crushed bearings, snapped chains, flat tires, and other breakdowns, all of which combined to cause significant delays. Nonetheless, the Corps' average moving speed was still 5.9 mph; almost twice the average marching speed of about 3 mph.

When the Corps returned to Fort Missoula, Moss calculated that his troops had averaged roughly 56 miles per day, and the journey cost next to nothing. Ostensibly, the purpose of the excursion was to determine the possibilities and limitations of the bicycle, and thus of the 25th Infantry Bicycle Corps. But the trip, serving to stimulate Moss's inventive and revolutionary tendencies, convinced him that a bicycle corps—as a mobile troop—might be superior to the horse-reliant cavalry.

### Ride 2: Missoula to Yellowstone National Park, August 1896

For the long and rigorous ride to Yellowstone, the men carried additional blankets, clothing, extra food, and tools necessary for repairs. Moss also decided to carry a group first-aid kit which included bandages, slings, splints, Jamaican ginger extract, one box of C.C. pills (laxatives), one box of quinine pills (for malaria, leg cramps, and inflammation), one box of camphor pills (to treat cholera), and one bottle of something known as Squibb's mixture.

*August 15, 1896, Missoula to Flint Creek Hills.* At 6:05 A.M., the Corps rolled out of Fort Missoula heading to the famed geysers and hot springs of Yellowstone National Park. Moss planned to lead his troops along the roads that paralleled the rail lines. Not long into the ride, the 25th encountered roads taken over by deep sections of wet clay that had the consistency of bread dough. The soldiers pushed their pedals with all their might, but their wheels only spun a few rotations before the mud-laden tires quickly became so large that they couldn't fit through the bicycle's front forks or rear seat-stays. Worse yet, what mud didn't stick to their tires got jammed in the rear cogs, causing the bicycles to come to a complete standstill. Getting off the bike to carry it through the mud created more problems—the men's boots quickly attracted many pounds of the mud. All of the bikes in the Corps

The 25th Infantry Bicycle Corps at Fort Missoula, Montana. Lieutenant James Moss is pictured at left, 1896.

The Buffalo Soldiers Bicycle Corps walk the rail tracks to avoid a bad section of road. Montana, 1897. [Mss 672, Edward Boos Collection] Archives & Special Collections, The University of Montana

became stuck so firmly that the men were barely able to push them free of the mud's grip. A few men tried hoisting the 80-pound behemoths onto their shoulders, only to have the weight of the bikes cause them to topple over into thick goo. Others just abandoned their bikes and slowly trudged to dry ground, often losing their boots in the process. After some time and a few relaxing puffs on their pipes, the soldiers eventually teamed up to drag their bicycles from their first encounter with "gumbo mud."

Once out of the mud, some men attempted to clean it from their tires with knives. The mud stuck to their blades, requiring a dangerous fling of the knife to remove it. Most waited for the mud to dry so they could bang it off with a stick. During the encounter, Moss paid close attention to his men and later noted some of the many things they called out in frustration, such as: "There was no bicycle one hundred years ago; oh, how I wish I lived one hundred years ago!" And, "A mule! A mule! My kingdom for a mule!"

It was fairly common at the time for landowners to clear and maintain sections of road that crossed their property and then charge a toll for the road's use. However, Lt. Moss was under strict orders not to spend any money on his "cycling experiment." To avoid both the "gumbo mud" and the tolls, he directed his troops onto the adjacent railroad tracks where they had two options: Ride their iron bikes and get jarred senseless by the raised wooden ties, or walk and push their bikes down the desolate stretches of Montana railroad. No matter which option they choose, when the Corps finally set up camp their still shaking arms could barely hold their canteens to their lips. The men covered 42 miles the first day.

*August 16, 1896. Flint Creek Hills to Little Blackfoot Valley.* On the second day of cycling, one unfortunate soldier fell ill with cramps after eating wild fruit and drinking bad water. The group waited an hour for him to recover, but there were no signs of improvement. Finally, Moss forced him to ride, not wanting to be delayed any longer. When the Corps reached the small town of New Chicago, population 50, Moss treated his soldier with Epsom salts and ginger, a combination that amplified the soldier's cramps and dehydration. Frustrated by waiting, and wanting to make good time, Moss gave the soldier six dollars, with instructions to take the train ahead to Fort Harrison where the Corps would meet up with him.

The men pressed through the brutal heat in their standard-issue uniforms, long-sleeved wool shirts and wool pants. Over smooth and dry roads, they covered 47 miles before setting up camp in the Little Blackfoot Valley. At a nearby farmhouse, they traded flour for fresh milk, and hay to sleep on.

*August 17, 1896. Little Blackfoot Valley to Helena.* The oppressive heat continued, but morale remained high as the Bicycle Corps spun onward. Moss kept a riding journal in which he detailed a continuous stream of broken cyclometers, chains, worn-out bearings, and broken axles. The Corps averaged five punctured tires a day, as well as one or two that simply came unglued from their rims. Moss also noted that some of his men fell frequently, while others were more careful riders and rarely lost their balance. Regardless, each man gathered his own collection of bumps and bruises.

En route to Helena, the Corps crossed the Continental Divide. Moss wrote: "Reaching the summit at 4:20. For the first time in history, a body of armed cyclists had crossed the main divide of the Rockies."

*August 19, 1896. Townsend to Three Forks.* Four days into the trip, the men had grown tired of biscuits and bacon for every meal. From Lt. Moss's journal we glimpse one of possibly many attempts to supplement their diet: "While bounding along at a ten-mile rate, we ran upon a covey of chickens near the road. Halting and dismounting we formed as skirmishers and advanced on the chickens until the command was given: Squad halt; aim, fire! The command was executed with precision, but we had government bacon for supper, nonetheless."

*August 23-25, 1896. Bozeman to Yellowstone.* Outside of Bozeman, Moss's unit crossed paths with a Buffalo Soldier Army Cavalry unit based out of Fort Assiniboine. The soldiers on horseback looked on in disbelief as the 25th approached from behind, gained on them, and then wheeled past. The irony of the moment was not lost on Moss, who, in pride, noted that a mounted cavalry soldier said to one of his men, "Say, honey, is your feet muddy?"

To which a bicycle soldier replied, "Oh, Mr. Jones, can I come up and see you groom your horse this evening?" The Bicycle Corps laughed hard as they overtook the cavalry soldiers.

*August 25-31, 1896. Yellowstone.* Yellowstone tourists were more interested in the soldier's bicycles and gear than in the world's largest active thermal area. Aware of the attention, Moss commanded his men to engage in a wide array of drills. Before the growing audience, the Corps formed a single column of 20 riders, and with each order from Moss, the column would break in half: two columns of ten, then four columns of five, and finally merge into the earlier circular riding formation. In front of the clapping crowd, Moss barked one final command, at which his men flawlessly executed a figure-eight pattern, each rider meticulously threading gaps between the others without the slightest waver.

The Buffalo Soldier Bicycle Corps rode around Yellowstone in a grand six-day tour. In the mornings the men displayed their gear and skill, and posed for photos. In the afternoons they relaxed with visits to Old Faithful, the paint pots, pools of bubbling mud, and hot springs. In the evenings they caught trout and cooked them in the boiling pools along the banks of the Yellowstone River. On their final day in the park they rode over the Continental Divide again. Moss noted their rest break at the crossing in his journal:

> It seemed to amuse the soldiers very much to be able to stand with one foot on the Atlantic slope and one foot on the Pacific slope. We stopped about ten minutes for a rest, and as soon as I gave the command, "Fall out!" one half of the squad lined up on one side of the imaginary line between the two slopes and the other half on the other side, while they were all leaning over and shaking hands and crying out, "Well, old man, how's everything with you way down there on the Pacific slope?"
>
> "Oh, everything is fine with us! How are things getting along with you fellers way down there on the Atlantic slope?"

The return ride to Fort Missoula was fraught with pounding rain that soaked through the soldier's wool uniforms—the smell of which became gamey and later atrocious, as a rash of equipment malfunctions and breakdowns plagued them while going up and down the mountains. But while the mountain mud made for slow riding and plenty of crashes, the soldiers' morale remained high.

Encouraged by the success of his Bicycle Corps, Moss sent the Army a brief report concluding that a continental cycling trip was necessary to prove the bicycle as a viable and efficient means to transport troops over long distances. In the winter of 1897 Lt. Moss fine-tuned his plans for the cross-country trip. He returned the bikes to Spalding and asked for a new fleet with two specific modern modifications. The following spring Spalding sent 25 bikes with unconventional steel rims and cog covers.

### Ride 3: Missoula to St. Louis, June, 1897

On Monday, June 14, 1897, at 5:30 A.M., Moss and 20 members of the 25th Infantry Bicycle Corps headed southeast from Fort Missoula for St. Louis. The route would cover nearly 2,000 miles. Again, Moss had planned a route that paralleled train tracks; however, for this ride he coordinated with the Quartermaster's Department to send rations and spare parts ahead by rail. The department placed nineteen food-drops each at 100-mile intervals between Fort Missoula and St. Louis.

Dark, threatening clouds gathered over the first afternoon of riding, and soon the sky was ablaze with lightning. Moments later the heavens opened, drenching the Corps. The heavily rutted wagon trail they were traveling on turned into the dreaded "gumbo mud." Some soldiers managed to get their bikes buried in two feet of mud, while others pedaled off the road onto neighboring farm land, searching for an alternate route. As darkness fell, the men began firing pistol shots to locate each other. At half-past midnight, Moss finally managed to regroup his hypothermic troops.

For the next few days, the rain continued in torrents, slowing their pace considerably and forcing the Corps to eat through their rations faster than usual. Crossing the Continental Divide, the soldiers encountered a freak summer snowstorm. Unprepared for the cold, Moss led his men off their planned route and into the valleys, where the weather was more seasonably warm. The riders reverted to their old routine of resting, eating, and smoking during the hottest part of the day. In this fashion, they spun their 80 pounds apiece of bike and gear across the arid plains of South Dakota, where the only available "drinking" water was to be found in stagnant holes. Onward they mashed through the burning summer sands of Nebraska. And in each town they pedaled through, the press interviewed them, and then wrote and wired stories to the three newspapers in St. Louis and others around the country.

When the Corps finally crossed the Missouri River at St. Joseph, the *Kansas City Journal* reported the event on the front page of its Sunday edition, stating: "The men are in the best of condition, and are in good spirits on account of the comparatively short distance left to reach their destination."

By contrast, Moss described the Missouri roads and the condition of his men as the worst of the trip. They rode with saddle sores in furnace-like heat, lacking regular supplies of good water, and all were fatigued to the point of exhaustion. But their spirits were lifted when they arrived on the outskirts of St. Louis to a cheering crowd of pleasure-seekers, wheelmen, and mounted police, who offered a grand escort into the city.

The Corps pitched their tents in Forest Park in the heart of St. Louis. Hundreds of people came to see their encampment, meet the soldiers, listen to their stories, and look at their well-worn bicycles. Over the duration of their stay, the men performed their drills, participated in parades, and rode

The Buffalo Soldiers Bicycle Corps ford a stream. Montana, 1897. [Mss 672, Edward Boos Collection] Archives & Special Collections, The University of Montana

with local cycling clubs. The Corps took the train back to Montana to prepare for their next ride, Missoula to San Francisco. But the Bicycle Corps
never rode again after completing the St. Louis ride. When the battleship
*Maine* exploded in Havana Harbor, touching off the Spanish-American War,
Moss's troops were among the first sent to Cuba to fight.

These days, few people know of the Bicycle Corps and perhaps the only evidence of their legacy is to be found in small museums in Montana. Nonetheless, Moss and his men were in the vanguard of cycling. They prefigured
both road- and mountain-bike touring and blazed the first true crosscoun-
try cycling route.

  At the conclusion of his cycling experiment, Moss filed a complete report with the U.S. Army. The report, substantiated by extensive data and
Moss's scientific approach to cycling, strongly recommended the establishment of a bicycle corps for the express purposes of tasks that required
speed rather than numbers, such as couriering and scouting. Among his
observations he listed 14 points that he had learned about long-distance
group cycling. Some were perhaps too individualistic or self-reliant for his
military audience:

- It is impossible to keep any kind of formation while traveling over
  ordinary wagon roads—every man naturally picks the best way.
- No fixed rules can be adopted as to the method of riding. . . . [T]hese . . .
  are determined by the geography of the country and other matters.

Some points he made, however, are now among the basics of touring:

- A bicycle corps should have a good mechanic and a complete set of
  repairing tools.
- The wind is one of the worst and most discouraging things to contend with.
- The regulation [food] ration is not sufficient for a cyclist who does
  much riding.

Other observations prefigured inventions to come (suspension bikes and
the standardization of parts), and expressed a hope for some things we may
never see:

- Some handlebar device for taking up the vibration . . . is badly needed.
- The various parts [of the bikes] should be made interchangeable as far as possible, and the machines so constructed that a tandem could readily be made from two single wheels.
- One of the most important points to be solved in military cycling is the construction of a resilient, puncture-proof tire.

The Army, of course, regarded Moss's conclusions as irrelevant. But even if they had adopted his recommendations, the invention of the gas-powered motor would have quickly rendered the military's use of bicycles outdated, just as it did their use of horses.

Editor's note: *This story is based on the research and information presented in the book* Iron Riders: Story of the 1890s Fort Missoula Buffalo Soldiers Bicycle Corps, *by George Niels Sorensen (Pictorial Histories Publishing Co., Inc., Missoula, Montana, 2000).*

# The Need for Speed

DAVID MONNIG

Children who race road bikes are a strange breed; I know this, because I was one of them. As a prepubescent middle-school student, I shaved the peach fuzz from my legs, memorized the weight (in grams) of top-of-the-line bike components, watched old Tour de France videos, clothed myself in fluorescent spandex, and chose training over hanging out with girls.

My parents supported my hobby. My dad and I would take rides together, and my mom would patch my Lycra tights and local team jerseys when I ripped them. I remember watching the 1979 movie *Breaking Away* with my family, and feeling a strong connection to the main character, a road-bike-obsessed high-school boy. Unlike my parents, the boy's parents didn't support his cycling fantasies. But, much like the character in the movie, I kept it a secret that I would use my mom's razor to shave my legs in the shower, and that I would take after-school rides by myself to neighboring towns 15 miles away.

During eighth grade I trained six days a week, riding at times up to 125 miles a day with a local adult club. I was the youngest member by at least 10 years. Unlike most kids my age, I found pleasure in physical exhaustion, and I wasn't afraid to be perceived as a nerd by my peers. In addition to increasing my fitness, I constantly tinkered with my bike, trying to make it lighter and faster. I would take apart the hubs and replace the bearings more than necessary in attempt to have less rolling resistance, and re-greasing shift and brake cables was a favorite pastime. Drooling over bike components in catalogs was a daily activity, and during the summer I would mow lawns and then spend the money on mail-order bike parts. I used simple mathematics to determine my purchases; drop the most grams for the least amount of money. I remember the excitement when I found a titanium bike seat on sale for $30—roughly equal to three lawns' worth of work—and it dropped the weight of my bike by 100 grams, (about a fifth of a pound). What a deal!

Although I was fast for my age, the training, smooth legs, and obsession with lightweight parts still didn't give me the edge I was looking for. I decided to research aerodynamics.

I owned a pair of Scott Aerobars, the same bars that Greg LeMond used during his come-from-behind win in the 1989 Tour de France. Aerobars clip onto regular road-bike handlebars to give the rider a more aerodynamic stance. They are traditionally used during time-trials, in which riders are not allowed to draft behind each other, so wind resistance becomes the cyclist's biggest enemy and an aerodynamic stance is the rider's greatest friend. Aerobars, although great for time trials, are not permitted in road races because they compromise a rider's braking and steering ability.

I had been reading an article in *Bicycling* magazine about the recent developments in aerodynamic bicycle technology, and I figured I would try some developing of my own. I looked at my aerobars carefully and then decided to hacksaw them into two pieces. I then reattached the two pieces to my drop bars, near the stem, so that they faced the rider and tilted downward. Aerobars normally extend out and over the front wheel. My modification would put me in an aggressive, low, and efficient stance.

I noticed that it would be difficult to turn because the bars rubbed against the steer tube. Neither the poor steering nor the lack of turning radius bothered me. For time-trial purposes my setup seemed adequate.

The next day, I took my idea for a test ride. The riding position felt comfortable and fast. I was a little leery that I had left the sharp, sawed-off edges of the bars exposed, but I didn't plan on crashing. I figured I'd patch up the rough-cut ends when I got home. I barreled across the campus of the University of Montana, passing pedestrians in the way that makes pedestrians hate cyclists. Classes must have just finished, because there were college students everywhere. I treated them like slalom gates, weaving in and out as I cruised down the sidewalk. Yes, I was 13 years old and fearless, but I also had a fair amount of experience racing my bike at high speeds in close proximity to other riders, so I felt calm and in control. Eventually I came upon a larger group of students and needed to hop onto a lawn to get around them.

I did so, but carelessly lodged my front tire in the narrow groove between the sidewalk and the grass. Most avid cyclists have at one time or another flipped over the handlebars. There's a split second, just before it happens, when you try to make the best of the situation but usually nothing can be done. I braced myself for a hard landing, and soon I felt the all-too-familiar cold and gritty smack of the concrete.

I stood up immediately and looked at my palms, arms, and legs for road rash. I had crashed multiple times over the past few years and I was accustomed to road rash. Months earlier I had knocked out a front tooth when I flipped over the handlebars, after which my mom wrote her work number on the inside of my helmet. As I assessed the damage to my appendages, my breath stopped as my eyes focused on my right knee. What I saw horrified me. The entire width of my knee was sliced clean open, exposing the bone of my kneecap. I lay down again on the sidewalk, hoping that what I'd seen wasn't real, but knowing that it was.

I had never seen my own bones before, and I didn't want to see them now. How had this happened? Why didn't I just have normal road rash? I quickly realized that it was my new handlebars that had sliced me open, and that I was in no condition to pedal home. The cruel irony became clear to me: by trying to make my bike faster, I had prevented myself from riding at all. That's when I broke down and cried. The tears were 40 percent the result of excruciating pain, and 60 percent knowing this would put a damper on my training regimen.

The students who had forced me to jump off the sidewalk came rushing over. A fit young man in shorts and sandals ripped off his t-shirt and wrapped it around my knee, which I assumed was now bleeding profusely—I was still too distraught to look, In hindsight his actions were a bit extreme, but I could see the urgency in the faces of those around me as someone ran to call 911. I turned to the lady beside me and told her my mom's work number was written on the inside of my helmet; I was too upset to remember it myself.

"It's only my knee," I said through sobs as the paramedics strapped me to a backboard.

"It's just routine, son. We need to do this in case you have a neck injury." In the ambulance I squealed in pain with every bump we went over.

My mom met me at the hospital. She held my hand as the emergency-room doctor spent an entire hour scrubbing the dirt out of the wound before stitching it up. He told me I had been lucky to not slice any tendons or ligaments. Twenty-six stitches later, I was back at home, feeling sorry for myself.

The night that I had put the bars on, my parents had told me they were too dangerous and that I should take them off. I had dismissed their warnings. When I came home from the hospital I lied to my mom and dad and told them there had been a sharp rock on the sidewalk that had sliced my knee open. They seemed to believe me.

When I went to get my stitches removed, I was pleased to hear that the emergency-room doctor at St. Patrick's Hospital had given me the unofficial "Wound of the Month" award for October. I'd have been happier to have won *Bicycling*'s "Handlebar of the Month" award, but I was willing to settle.

# Outsourced

## STEVE PUCCI

On March 1, 2007, the company I work for, Profitsoft, distributed an alarming press release. The Boston-based software firm announced that it had outsourced its elite cycling team to India. CEO Barry Gerharz is quoted in the release: "It was a flash of brilliant business maneuvering. We cut costs, reduced liability, and gained exposure in India and the Asian market. The move adds up to a long-term benefit for our stockholders."

The ostensible reasons for the move didn't add up for me, so I began my own investigation of sorts. A friend in the human resources department told me there may have been another reason for the move. Several employees, who will not be named, had filed repeated complaints about the cycling team's behavior in the cafeteria. The most common complaint was that the team riders—along with their support crew of mechanics, trainers, and drivers—often ate multiple entrees in the corporate cafeteria after morning training rides. The complainants claimed the riders intentionally sat next to, or "targeted," employees on diets and then binged in front of them. Fearing a lawsuit on the grounds of gastronomical harassment, the company cut its ties to the team.

The new Profitsoft elite road-cycling team, based in Bangalore, caused some controversy even before taking its first training ride. In a revealing article, four of the riders—Jham Bhagger, Gehan Jhones, Jhan Grahn and Bharog Bhoyce—were interviewed by the *Bangalore Telegraph*.

Team Captain Bhagger said, "The carbon bikes and team jerseys are both made here in India. I do not understand why Pocketsoft [sic] has to ship them from the U.S. I argued for many hours about this with headquarters, but I lost. So now we will wait for eight weeks for our bicycles to arrive."

Gehan Jhones, the grandson of the last British Governor of India, declared that he was added to the team against his will, and that his house-boy, named Gohan, would ride the bike for him. But Jhones will keep all trophies and awards. He has also reportedly signed lucrative endorsement contracts with Hindutrans Motors and Wild Turban Vodka.

Jahn Grahn said, "I am grateful to all the people at Profitstock [sic] for this opportunity. I look forward to receiving my team uniform. I am going to have it tailored for my wife. She will look very appealing in it."

Lastly, Bharog Bhoyce claimed, "My bullocks will be astounded to see me traveling so fast. But I have promised not to sell them as my fortunes increase. Besides, you can't sell your bullocks and still have your cart drawn."

The news story went on to say that Bollywood has already begun talks about a movie that would chronicle the exploits of Team Profitsoft. A representative from the studio reportedly said, "We promise plenty of singing and dancing. The choreographed bike-dance scenes are sure to be sensational." It was also rumored that an undisclosed cable channel is creating a reality show in which the Profitsoft team lives together in a one-room house, working odd jobs while they await the arrival of their bicycles.

The *Bangalore Telegraph* story shook the ranks of Profitsoft management, who took two immediate steps to control the damage. First, the team was barred from speaking to the press. And second, Profitsoft hired a team of virtual immigration consultants to teach the team neutralized accents, pre-race posturing, podium poses, fixation upon component (and overall bicycle) weight, and idiomatic cycling expressions such as *gravity tattoo*, *powerbarf, dopey doctor* and *caught in the slinky*. Additionally, each team member was given an American name.

Professional cycling-team managers around the globe eagerly await the early-season results from Team Profitsoft. "If they are successful, we will have to rethink our whole approach," said Heinrich Wolfe, CEO of German telecommunications giant Wonder-Telecom. "Team Profitsoft could be responsible for a cycling revolution."

Responding to Wolfe's comments, Marc Richter, last year's Tour de Serbia winner and a member of Team Wonder-Telecom, said, "This is a terrible trend in cycling. I am embarrassed to participate in a sport that is now driven by shareholders and the bottom line. Where is the loyalty?" Richter went on to say that he has sold his multi-million-dollar house in the south of France, anticipating that Wonder-Telecom will indeed outsource.

On a recent Boston radio program, American Joel Turkawitz, former captain of the Profitsoft Elite Team, said, "I am now a side effect of globalization. First they took our call-center jobs, then our programming positions. Where will it end? Why was my job outsourced and not President Bush's job? I did mine well. I never understood the WTO protests until now."

About a month after Turkawitz was laid off, I saw him at a nearby bike shop working as a mechanic. He had gained weight, and the hair on his arms and legs was growing in thick. He wore a T-shirt that said, "Victim."

# Genius, Not-Genius

## GREG TAYLOR

Somebody had to try it, and if my buddy BK's experimental tire repair had worked, it would have been *huge*.

To be totally fair to BK, even I'll admit that sometimes there's a fine line between genius and its opposite—those alarming examples of inspiration that I call not-genius.

Approached properly, a genuinely bad idea can have the same look and feel as a brilliant one, right up to the point where things begin to go all wobbly. The hardest part, of course, is telling the two apart. What I'm talking about is the subtle difference between *It's just crazy enough to work* and *It's just crazy*. And like I said, if BK had pulled it off and actually fixed his bike tire with dental floss, I would have personally handed him the application form for Mensa.

Dental floss is pretty brilliant stuff. It doesn't involve complicated electric gizmos with vibrating brushes or miniature pumps blasting jets of water; it's just a hygienic, inexpensive, nylon thread that you run between your chompers to remove tooth barnacles and prevent gum disease. Simple. Elegant. Genius, really.

But its greatness doesn't end there. According to the Australian Broadcasting Corporation's Dr. Karl Kruszelnicki, when it comes to the topic of dental floss, human beings have shown the same dissatisfaction with the status quo that coaxed our prehistoric ancestors out of the trees and into cookie-cutter homes close to shopping malls and Starbucks. People have found many more uses for this humble cleaner of teeth than its inventors could ever have imagined. It can be used to slice cheese, remove biscuits from baking sheets, repair a backpack or tent or winter jacket, and—if you're really obsessive—to clean the crevices in the turned legs of your wooden furniture. Anesthetists sometimes use dental floss to secure the location of an endotracheal tube in a patient's mouth during surgery. And (again according to the good Dr. Karl) one Italian mafioso escaped from a Turin jail after sawing through the bars of his cell with strands of dental floss.

Just don't try to use the stuff to sew up a big ol' gash in the sidewall of a high-pressure racing tire.

BK said the idea came to him while he was brushing his teeth. He had woken to find that his brand new tire had suffered a rather horrific sidewall cut. Normally, you'd bin a tire like that and start fresh. Not BK. He is made of sterner stuff. Plus, he can be a cheap bastard. BK figured that rather than eat the thirty dollars—after all, it was a *brand new tire*—he'd repair it somehow.

Staring into the bathroom mirror, toothbrush in hand, BK reached for the roll of unwaxed dental floss that sat on the shelf above the sink. As he flossed, he mulled over the tire problem. He had never considered using floss for any purpose other than its traditional one of oral hygiene. Then he noticed that the floss was damned hard to break.

Lightbulbs snapped on, choruses of angels sang, and the floor rumbled as BK's now-febrile train of thought pulled out of the station, a high-speed express headed around the bend and straight for the washed-out bridge next to the dynamite factory. Before he could think, "My, what a remarkably bad idea," BK had found a large sewing needle, grabbed the wounded tire, and set to work, nimbly stitching up the tear with dental floss. For good measure, he completed his handiwork by smearing the area with Shoe Goo, a self-vulcanizing liquid rubber used to repair sneakers.

The finished product looked a lot like what you'd expect from a man sewing up a tire using a carpet needle and dental floss while sitting cross-legged on the floor of his bathroom. "Lumpy" pretty much captured it.

Flushed with the intoxicating but misplaced confidence that comes from a true flash of not-genius, BK showed up for our normal Sunday group ride, ready to rock with his Franken-tire mounted on his bike.

BK's handiwork was naturally the object of much interest among the guys gathered in the parking lot before the ride. BK is a federal agent; he responds to domestic threats from foreign terrorists, and he looks like an elite soldier—tall, broad-shouldered, clean-cut, with a square jaw and steely eyes.

On a group ride he's usually the strongest guy there, by a wide margin. There are days when you just hop on to BK's back wheel, cross yourself, and try to hang on for dear life. But this wasn't one of those days. Things were looking pretty good for about 15 miles, until someone noticed at a stop sign that BK's tire had been quietly amusing itself during the ride by doing its best Pamela Anderson impression. The dental-floss stitches BK had so carefully sewn into the sidewall were coming undone one by one in a slow, majestic, velo-striptease. We all circled around the back of BK's bike, transfixed as a pair of breasts began to emerge from the sidewall of his tire—a diminutive set of mammaries created by the distended inner tube poking out from between the stitches and Shoe Goo.

BK gingerly turned his bike around and headed home.

Despite this small setback, BK hasn't given up on bike repairs using dental floss. He's a true believer, a convert to the Dental Floss Way of Bike Repair. At last report, he had cleaned out the oral hygiene aisle at his local pharmacy so he could wrap his handlebars in strands of dental floss. If you are careful, he says, six rolls will do one handlebar.

And, you know, he may be on to something. Floss makes a dandy bar wrap, he claims. It's grippy, unaffected by rain or dampness, and—here's the part he's really excited about—if you use one of those fancy breath-freshening flosses, it leaves your riding gloves with a nice, minty smell.

Mint-scented handlebar tape? This could be *huge* . . .

# Bike Crash Photo Gallery

Prior to overturning the Relax Team car, the driver was shouting encouragement out his window at a rider leading Stage 2 of the Tour de Langkawi. Not paying close attention, the driver let the car go up an embankment, which caused the car to flip. The bicycle crushed underneath had been racked on the roof; it was not one of the passing riders. Tanah Rata, Malaysia—February 7th, 2004. Photo: Yuzuru Sunada/PhotoSport International

Kui Song of the China Merida team loses control as he takes refreshments from his team car during Stage 6 of Tour of Qinghai Lake, on July 20th, 2006. The front of his bicycle, his arm, and his shoulder are run over by the rear wheel of the team car. Miraculously Song escaped serious injury, though he did retire from the race. Photo: Mark Gunter/PhotoSport International

During the 2005 Paris-Roubaix cycling classic a strong tailwind kept the peloton in a high-speed, tight formation over the old Great War cart tracks of northern France. Here a lead rider falls after making it

though a mud puddle and the majority of the pack piles up in a mass crash. France—April 2005.
Photo: Peter Witek/PhotoSport International

**Above:** Lance Armstrong (right foreground) crashes during the finish of the 15th stage of the 2003 Tour de France. His handlebars snagged on a *mussette* bag held by a young boy, causing both him and Iban Mayo (behind Armstrong) to go down. **Below:** Jan Ullrich (behind the other two riders) slows and waits for Armstrong, the overall Tour leader, to remount and continue riding. Armstrong immediately got back on his bike and with a rush of adrenaline rode to win the stage, increasing his lead to 1:07. Photo: TdeF/PhotoSport International

Arjan Blaaw, of Holland, breaks the seat post and tacos the front wheel when he lands a jump from a rock formation, while participating in the Primal Wear Secret Summit event. Moab, Utah—April 2006. Photo: Jonathon Rasmussen (courtesy of Arjan Blaaw and Alann Boatright)

Chad Wassmer going over the handle bars during the 24 Hours of Moab race. Moab, Utah—October 18th, 2003. Photo: MoabActionShots.com

Czech rider, Michal Marosi abandons his bike after hucking off a 30 foot cliff top during the Red Bull Rampage 2003. Kolob Reservoir, Virgin, Utah—October 19, 2003. Photo: Christian Pondella

A 14-year-old rider crashes after taking a drop at the Eagle on the Hill Mountain Bike Park. Adelaide, Australia—November 5th, 2006. Photo: Charlie Lawrence

**Above:** Travis Healey goes airborne while competing in the ABA Great Salt Lake Nationals. West Jordan, Utah—August 4th, 2006. **Below:** Brock Hefron slips off his bike in turn three during the ABA Mile High Nationals. Dacona, Colorado—August 20th, 2006. Photos: Dan Mooney

Judy Tran-Ocondi racing for Adventure Cycling misses a log jump and goes over the bars while competing in the Super-D Race. Telluride, Colorado—July 29, 2006. Photo: Dominique Revelle

REUTERS/China Photos

Taking part in China's National Day celebration, Wang Jiaxiong, 30 years old, rode a BMX bicycle down a 240 foot ramp attempting to jump the Great Wall of China. As he left the top of the ramp, he was over 100 feet above the ground. Jiaxiong was the second of two riders attempting the stunt that day. The first rider cleared the wall without incident and touched ground safely in a special landing pen filled with large foam pads. Jiaxiong was not so lucky. On his attempt, he flew from the take off ramp and reached an apex of 138 feet high, clearing the wall with ease. But to the shock of hundreds of onlookers, he also cleared the foam landing area—a safety zone 250 feet long and 70 feet wide, providing enough coverage, the stunt coordinators had calculated, for any possible undershooting or overshooting of the wall. Jiaxiong let go of his

中国人寿保险

REUTERS/China Photos

bike in mid air, presumably in an attempt to land himself within the safety area. Instead, he landed headfirst in the shrubby, rocky hillside. Spectators and event officials dragged him out of the bushes. Jiaxiong died several hours later at a nearby hospital.

Organized by China's Great Wall Tourist Bureau, the stunt was part of a series of Great Wall "fly overs" that began in 1992. Previous to this bicycle attempt only cars and motorcycles had successfully cleared the wall—an act that most Chinese see as part idiotic, part unifying (in a Nationalist sense), and part shameless tourism promotion. Huangya Pass, Tianjin, China— October 2nd, 2002

**Above:** local rider Todd Glasgow gets familiar with the Wall Ride feature of Granny's Kitchen trail. **Below:** trail manager Troy Munsell demonstrates the proper technique for riding the wall. Black Rock Mountain Bike Area, Falls City, Oregon—March 2006. Photos: Joe Rykowski

Raymond Galang goes over the bars and then gets drenched in a stagnant pool of water during a recreational ride. Sedona, Arizona—Spring 2001. Photo: Pete Fagerlin

Bobbing for river rocks: An unidentified rider crashes face-first during a mountain bike race at Bonelli Park in San Dimas, California—April 2006. Photo: Paul "Ratt" Rudman

# The Jungle Is Hungry

*Exploratory Riding in Bolivia*

## AARON TEASDALE

*In the summer of 1999, I took a break from living in my Volkswagen van
and vagabonding around the American West. I went to Bolivia to ride with
a friend, Alistair Mathew, an unfailingly gung-ho New Zealander who had
recently turned his back on a successful career in the financial industry to
explore the mountains and jungle of this little-traveled South American
country. At the time, I was a twenty-something freelance writer and photographer with a knack for getting lost in remote places. Alistair had spent
the preceding year working in Bolivia as a mountaineering guide. When I
visited, he was seeking out rideable mountain-bike routes and in the process launching a mountain-biking guide service based in the capital city, La
Paz.*

*United by a masochistic love of exploring the unridden, we picked new
routes each day. Some we had heard about, others we found on maps. Seeking a true humdinger for our last ride together, we attempted a trail that was
not listed on any of my maps of the Andes. Alistair had found an ancient yel-
lowing topographical map that showed the locations of ancient Inca roads.
We decided on a ten-mile dotted line that appeared to wind down the side
of an uninhabited gorge on the back of the Andes, where the range plummets
into the Amazon basin.*

*We knew local maps were notoriously unreliable. We knew nothing
about the trail, nor could we find any locals who did. But with the blind con-*

*fidence of young mountain bikers drunk on adventure, we decided to ride it anyway.*

The day begins with great promise at eight A.M. with an hour-long, bike-on-shoulder hike up an overgrown trail of ancient cobblestone to a mossy, 12,000-foot-high saddle in the sky. The Inca webbed these mountains with an astoundingly extensive network of stone pathways in the centuries before the conquistadors arrived. In the weeks we've been exploring them, we've made many jaw-dropping discoveries—certainly there are no rides more spectacular anywhere on the planet. But unlike most of the other trails, whose existence we'd been able to confirm with trekkers, mountaineers, or local villagers, we weren't certain that this trail still existed in any meaningful way. This uncertainty should have scared us, or at least given us pause. Alas, no. It simply gave us cause for high-fives over too many rounds of cheap Bolivian beer the evening before.

When we reach the saddle, Alistair scampers up a grassy knob to gain a view of our impending descent. "Wow," he says quietly, with an unlikely measure of surprise for someone who's been exploring the Andes for over a year. "We are going *down*." I climb up to his vantage and my mouth falls open. I whisper, "Oh *shit*." Below us drops a landscape of 5,000-foot deep ravines choking under a million shades of steaming green cloud forest. The sheer depth and scale of the gorge before us, combined with the overwhelming density of the vegetation, renders us momentarily speechless. I break the silence: "As long as we make it, this ride will be a success," I tell Alistair, thereby surely jinxing us.

Pointing down several hundred feet to an open sliver in the shadowy verdure, Alistair says, "That's our trail." It's visible for a few hundred feet before disappearing into the mist. We look at each other and our mouths curl into smiles—the adventure potential here is off the charts. We put on arm and leg armor and drop in.

For two hours we plunge down cobblestone switchbacks and tunnel through thick, arcing vegetation. The human-skull-size cobblestones are fitted with miraculous precision into a rock-solid runway that makes for thrilling technical riding with headlong plunges down shockingly steep pitches. We hoot and high-five, drunk on endorphins born of adrenaline and the thrill of bringing life back to a forgotten trail. The further we descend, the more the vegetation crowds in on the trail. Occasional clearings reveal endless jungle-walled valleys with ridge after ridge of flora-packed, plummeting

Alistair Mathew attempts to ride the overgrown remains of an ancient Inca trail in the Bolivian cloudforest. Bolivia—August 1999. Photo: Aaron Teasdale

mountainside. There is no sign of humanity except the primeval trail.

We drop several thousand vertical feet in short order; the jungle gets more unruly as we descend. Things get ugly as our trail narrows into a rough dirt seam through the cloud forest. Rocks, roots and enormous *Little Shop of Horrors*-like plants force us off our bikes; we have to crawl through slippery clusters of fallen trees. The sheer drop alongside the trail grows treacherous as the angle of the gorge's wall increases. Several waterfall crossings force us into a delicate tip-toe shimmy across 6-inch-wide, water-slicked rock ledges. We get wet, but our spirits are undampened.

By early afternoon we've covered what feels like close to 10 miles. According to our map, the trail should deliver us to a village in two or three more miles. I don't mind this kind of riding. The tough jungle makes me feel like Indiana Jones on a bike. And the end of the trail is near, I believe.

The gorge wall soon turns vertical and the plant life is so thick and gnarled that the trail begins to cut across ledges of tangled vegetation, rather than resting on solid ground. Holes appear in the outgrown roots and branches beneath us, gaps in the ledge providing nerve-tingling views of treetops 40 feet below us. We're mainly carrying and pushing our bikes now, though we cling to the riding dream and continually try to pedal the rideable stretches, but they never last more than a minute or two. Roots, branches, and plants that probably haven't been named yet snag our bodies, pedals, and bars. Thin vines yank us by the nose, forehead, and neck. Huge leaves blanket our vision and conceal spear-size branches with dagger tips. One of these Inca death-traps catches me an inch below my right eye. Before I have a chance to feel sorry for myself, Alistair gets lanced in the crotch. All the while serrated leaves like Ginsu knives slice our fingers, forearms, and legs.

"Woohoo! This trail rocks," I yell to Alistair after my upper lip is virtually pulled back over my head by an unseen vine. The jungle may be taking our blood, but it can't take away our sarcasm.

"Hey Alistair!" I holler. "How much are you going to charge clients for this ride?"

"I think we'll save this for a honeymoon ride," he fires back. "The ride you'll never forget."

Even Alistair's wit can't hide the truth, however. What promised on paper to be a grand adventure is turning bad. We're beginning to realize that bikes belong in this jungle about as much as legless midgets belong in bobsleds.

"Hey Alistair, can I suck your nipple?" I ask with a grin. I've just checked my water bladder and it's empty. Alistair's is too, which means we're now completely out of water. My grin fades. We've been charging for a good five hours now. We'll need to find a water source or reach the village soon.

Up ahead I hear Alistair yelling, "Ready to do some rock climbing?" When I reach him, I look ahead, drop my bike from my shoulder and cry, "We're fucked. Totally fucked. There's no way to get down that and back up it."

In front of us, the deteriorated trail ends abruptly where another waterfall, now dry, has carved a deep gouge in the mountainside. Above us is a sheer rock wall; below, the once running falls have carved a twenty-foot-wide rock chute that drops precipitously into the jungle. Vast valley walls of jungle mayhem surround us.

A ledge in the chute below us could get us across, but climbing to and from it would be impossible with our bikes in hand. Alistair lets me finish explaining how screwed we are and then says, "Relax, I've got rope."

"You've got rope! Thank God. Why didn't you say so?" I say, as he pulls several inner tubes out of his pack and ties them together. "This'll do it," he says, smiling.

Alistair quickly finds some holds and climbs down to the ledge. I hook the inner tubes around the nose of his bike's seat and lower it down to him. After we cross the ledge, Alistair scales the far side. We use the same system to lift our bikes back up to the trail.

"Alistair's Mountain-Bike Rides, suitable for advanced beginners," I cry, while climbing up the last segment. "Some walking may be required."

Soon our greatest challenge becomes crossing landslides—wicked stretches of trail where the earth has broken loose and ripped downward leaving a swath of loose rock and uprooted trees. Our path often consists of footholds barely as wide as our shoes. We hand our bikes along to each other as we gingerly step across the impossible. We're able to ride a stretch of the barely visible path for a few moments, but it quickly devolves into a slow jungle slog.

"At least we're going down," Alistair said. "Eventually we've got to get to something—the village, another trail, something." We're starting to recognize that something is amiss. Either the map is wrong (very possible), or the trail isn't going where we thought (also very possible), or we have no idea whatsoever where we are and where the trail will take us, assuming it doesn't just disappear entirely leaving us stranded in the middle of nowhere (a perilous prospect that neither of us dares verbalize).

We come to a 100-foot wide avalanche of earth and uprooted trees. It appears impassable, but we try anyway. I step across slippery, steeply angled trees that lie like a jumbled pile of Tinkertoys across what I think is the trail, but even on the other side of the landslide there is no sign of a path. Alistair explores another potential crossing.

"Shit, mate, I don't see it anywhere," Alistair says.

I backtrack, but in front of me and behind me all I can see is dense jungle. Below drops an impenetrable vegetated gorge displaying a thousand hues of green. Now I can't even find the spot where we entered the landslide. Alistair yells, "Anything?"

"No. You?" I call back.

"Nothing."

Pangs of fear stab my gut. It can't just end, I tell myself. We're in far too deep to turn back. It would mean untold hours of hiking up what we'd just spent most of the day fighting our way down, only to reach a dark dirt road in the middle of Andean nowhere. And then what would we do?

The pesky mechanism in a man's brain that won't let him turn around—the mechanism that has shortened many a life—is always in control when I ride. In the hundred-odd exploratory rides I have taken in my riding career, I've scaled steep mountain peaks, been chased by angry bears, and been utterly and completely lost in some of the most remote places in North America, but never, ever have I turned around and backtracked.

As I debate whether to abandon hope and curl up under a tangle of roots, or continue to seek the elusive trail, Alistair miraculously finds it emerging vaguely from a clump of fallen trees. I replace my fear with grim determination to press on and make it out before nightfall.

Our cause brightens further when the jungle produces a small waterfall, a tall and slender cascade carving an elegant slit through the rock. Its clear waters will tumble down ravine and valley until it joins the slow brown flow of the Amazon. We pause to appreciate its beauty, then we fill our water bladders, add iodine, and cruise.

A debate arises over our limited food supplies. I'm of the eat-it-now-while-we're-hungry-to-keep-us-fueled-for-the-push opinion, while Alistair takes the go-hungry-now-and-have-a-Power-Gel-in-a-couple-hours-for-a-moral-boost view. Because he's carrying what little food we have, Alistair wins the debate.

The going is still painfully slow. I begin throwing my bike over the constant procession of obstacles in our path. "Looks like we may be spending the night out here, man," I say. "I don't even want to think about trying to do this in the dark."

"Not an option," Alistair says without slowing. We are at 9,000 feet, where nights are dangerously cold and wet flora doesn't permit a fire. "We don't have nearly enough clothes to do that. We keep hiking . . . all night if we have to."

I've been taking photographs of Alistair bashing along the trail, but now I stow my camera in my pack. We no longer have time for such a luxury. We put our heads down and plow forward. As darkness grows, so does our frustration. If this ride is a war of attrition, we're losing—physically and mentally. Alistair begins to scream at any plant that dares to oppose him. Sensing his fragile state, I offer to lead but fare little better. The trail keeps getting more difficult and there is still no sign of humanity. *Why aren't we getting anywhere? Where the hell are we?* Our pedals, bar ends, and every other conceivable catching point snag on branches and vines. I scream as I do full-strength power yanks—veins threatening to pop out of my forehead—in a brutish yet ineffective attempt to extricate myself from organic restraints.

"Take it easy there, mate." Alistair has grown calm again and chides me for my tantrum. "You're wasting a lot of energy."

I don't speak. My initial, internalized reaction is, "Fuck off, *mate*. Maybe I *want* to waste energy. Maybe I want to rip this whole jungle to pieces!" My mental health is nose-diving fast. *Aaarrgghh, Hulk no like jungle.* In the back of my mind lurks the unthinkable possibility of abandoning our bikes. Every snag and fall reminds me how much easier this hike would be without my damn bike. But I'd sooner become the subject of jungle-safety lectures ("Never explore forgotten Inca trails, or you'll end up like those sad mountain bikers who were never seen again . . .") than leave my faithful steed behind.

After several more minutes of stumbling and yelling through the brush, teetering on the brink of becoming completely unhinged, I begin to recognize Alistair's wisdom. Mellowing a bit, I adopt a savvier strategy. A step backward and a little untangling proves to be a superior jungle-maneuvering tactic. We dance an ungainly ballet through the almost impassable, as we continue to make our way, sometimes crawling on all fours under fallen trees, sometimes heaving our bikes over them. Any way we can, we drag our useless bikes and battered psyches through the barely penetrable madness, hoping that each new clearing will reveal in the distance the lights of the village at the trail's end.

Light ebbs from the sky and night's first stars appear. My faith in the map is long gone, as we've covered at least 15 miles thus far. Alistair no longer pretends to know anything about the trail, except that it is leading us into the heart of darkness. Ravenously hungry, we push on with our reserve strength in a single-minded effort born of desperation. We feel like hamsters on a spinning wheel—we never arrive anywhere. We're just getting deeper into this lost world of prehistoric gorges, Inca deathtraps, and never ending jungle.

And if we arrived somewhere, where would it be? I imagine unexplored mountaintops and lost Inca temples. Perhaps we're on an undiscovered trail that leads to undiscovered ruins, maybe even a lost colony of Incas. Maybe they will revere us as deities. Or maybe they'll skin us alive, mount our heads on spikes, and write "Screw Pizarro!" (in Quechua, of course) with our blood on giant stone slabs.

Shadows grow into night, and then, just as darkness truly falls, we arrive at the worst landslide yet. It's loose scree and don't-even-think-about-it steep. We can't see much. A fall here would be the end of us, but we have no choice but to cross it. Using my bike like an ice axe, I start climbing across. Stones pour down with every step, tinkling and clinking down the scree in small avalanches. Halfway across, both of my feet suddenly slide out from beneath me in a cascade of stones. Every muscle in my body stretches cat-like for the crumbling slope. As the chiming noises of the plummeting scree sound more distant, I realize my grip on the loose rocks is holding. I've never in my life held onto anything with more strength and desperation. Somehow I don't drop the bike.

Once we're across, we break out the headlamps as the jungle slips into blackness. Our already slow pace is made twice as slow; our universe is reduced to dim, yellow, bobbing circles of light. The headlamps throw shadows that trick our minds. Sticks turn to snakes, Incas crouch in the bushes, hungry, fanged animals watch from tree boughs.

"We've got to reach something, *anything*, just to know the world still exists," I say to no one in particular. Half the cloud forest—leaves, root systems, long fuzzy vines—is wrapped around our bikes. My right leg pad is nearly shredded. There is still no sign of humanity.

Then Alistair stops abruptly. "There's something here," he says.

Hurrying forward, I ask, "What is it?"

"A grave," he says.

And there, just off the trail, overgrown with plants, is a lone concrete grave marker. It is shaped like a miniature house, with a slanted roof and a hinged metal door. The door is open, the spirit out roaming the night. We are jubilant over the find—a grave is a sign of civilization, of other people . . . even if they're dead.

Though bone-tired and weak-kneed from hunger, we push on with renewed vigor. The trail widens and the vegetation pulls back, allowing us—finally, blissfully—to ride again. Low, overgrown walls of stone arise to our right, a mysterious sign of past human presence. We feel close, but to what, we can't say. Watching my headlight illuminate the walls and a scattering of graves that we pass, I'm suddenly clipped across the forehead and thrown from my bike by an archway made of interwoven branches and vines. It's a rude surprise, but the doorway is another good sign. We're somewhere.

But then, as we continue on, the walls disappear and the trail closes in again. The coldness of the night sinks under my skin. After another half hour of bushwhacking through thick jungle, I come unhinged again. "This can't be right!" I bellow. "We *were* somewhere. Now we're jungle bashing again. . . . We aren't getting out. Ever!"

Alistair says nothing.

The jungle wants us to stay. I can feel its will, and I begin to see it as one tremendously powerful ecological cycle of life, growth, death, and rebirth. It's a cycle we are soon to join. Suddenly a vision comes to me: I will join the Inca. I will sacrifice Alistair to show them I am on their side. I will turn his Lycra into a shimmering black headdress. They will worship me like a god!

A stomping sound along the trail snaps me back to reality. There are beasts ahead of us—giant asses! Our path smooths and we mount our bikes and begin riding slowly, staring into the jiggling brown behinds of two burros. Minutes later, we reach a small thatched house. A man with deep wrinkles and leathery brown skin walks out with his wife. "We've been expecting you," he says cryptically and invites us inside.

I want to hug him and his wife as they give us bowls of the best soup in the history of the world—all pasta, potatoes, and warmth. The old man helps me wrest the jungle from my useless cogset, which is snarled with plant matter. He says it's two more hours to the village where Alistair's Land Cruiser is waiting.

We shoot a cliff-side single-track road in near blackness to the village. It's somewhere in the early morning hours when we wake our driver Carlos, asleep in the front seat, by knocking on the window. He stares at us in groggy disbelief. Convinced we are ghosts, he refuses to unlock the doors. After several minutes, perhaps convinced by Alistair's un-ghostlike and sincere threats of horrible bodily maiming, he relents. We load the bikes and soon we're bouncing through the darkness in the Land Cruiser, comfortable and warm. Alistair and I slump in our seats like battered rag dolls. Carlos turns to us and says, "The people in the village say the trail you came on can't be ridden on a bicycle."

I turn slowly, eyebrows raised. My mouth opens, but I'm too exhausted to say, "Thank you, Carlos, for that extremely helpful piece of information."

Alistair, defiant to the end, simply lets out a long sigh and says, "No, it can be ridden. It's just crazy."

There's no sense in trying to explain the seductiveness of a map's dotted lines and the magic, irresistible lure of the unexplored. The only thing that matters now is that we've emerged alive. The jungle didn't consume us, warm food and more cheap beer awaits us in La Paz, and—most importantly—I don't have to wear Alistair's Lycra on my head.

# First Impressions

## MICHAEL FEE

In 1997, I applied to Stanford Business School. I was accepted, and based my decision to go there on the school's academic reputation—though there was also the matter of Stanford's cycling team having won the 1995 and 1996 national championships. Grad students can join collegiate cycling teams, I'd learned, and as a novice bike-racer and an athlete who never made it onto the playing field as an undergrad, I figured this was my big chance.

When I arrived on campus with my wife Karen, an elementary school teacher, I split my days between cycling and my accounting pre-work. The routes around Palo Alto are incredible: on a given weekday, packs of riders of every ability wheel along the roads of nearby Woodside and Portola Valley—and on the weekend, the cyclists outnumber the cars two to one.

Five days before classes began, I rode the Portola Loop for its wide shoulders and sparse traffic. I gently descended the only big drop, the broad and winding Highway 84, using plenty of caution coasting down Alpine Road's gradual descent back toward campus. At Zott's Beer Garden, I decided to turn off Alpine onto the potholed and cracked pavement of Arastradero Road to extend the ride. That is all I remember.

It's not that my memory is cloudy; it's gone. I have no idea how I crashed or who found me. I don't know if any cars swerved around me, and then kept driving; whether the Good Samaritan who did stop called on a big, black, early-generation cell phone, or ran to the nearest pay phone; if bystanders flailed their arms to flag down the ambulance, or shouted at the paramedics as they dropped from their seats—all of that I've imagined as possible, but I remember none of it.

It's my uneducated guess that amnesia comes in two forms: forgetting everything without knowing you've done so, and forgetting everything and being perfectly, sharply aware that you've done so. I've always thought that this latter form would be a tough condition to deal with, and that day, it definitely was: shortly after I'd arrived at the ER, someone saw my wedding ring, and asked me my wife's name. I hesitated—realized I couldn't remember it—and burst into tears.

Fortunately, my wife had printed up a label with my name and phone number and stuck it on the inside of my helmet, and after fifteen minutes of patient, emphatic questioning by a kind nurse ("That's okay, Michael. . . . It will all come back, Michael . . . Let's talk about your wife, Michael."), fragments of memory started to appear. The first, somehow, was the name of my wife's school. I remember feeling proud knowing this relatively arcane piece of information, compared to her name or my address, and before long they'd contacted her. Later she would tell me of the horribly uncoached manner in which the nurse broached the news: "Ms. Fee, we need you to come to the hospital to identify your husband . . ."

After cutting off my jersey—it was my only one, and I pleaded briefly for them to leave it intact—the doctors determined that my face had broken my fall. (Weeks later, in a typical act of thoughtfulness, my mother-in-law stitched the jersey back together, and I still sport it on days when I'm feeling particularly nostalgic.) I had not a scrape below my neck, X-rays revealed no worries beneath the surface, and apart from a vague soreness in my wrist, I felt no pain except in my face.

From the moment Karen arrived, she kept her composure remarkably well. The doctors reassured her that my CAT scan looked fine; then she looked me over, astounded at how localized the damage was. "You really don't feel any pain in your arms or legs? What about your ribs?" she asked. After the doctors assured her that my face would, eventually, heal completely, she delicately told me, "Honey, I can't look at you when you talk. When you move your mouth, that cut on your chin . . . moves, and it's just a little too much."

This raised my curiosity. In the bathroom mirror I was able to take stock of my physical condition: I had lost a layer of skin above my right eye, where gravel had worked its way under my cracked helmet as I slid across the pavement. A significant gash ran along my right cheekbone, and I had no skin to speak of on the right side of my face. But my attention was drawn to the laceration on my chin—the one that made Karen squeamish. I stared at the mirror, working my jaw with little pain, and watched the edges of the gash open and shut in tandem with my mouth. It looked like a small second mouth. And then I thought: *Holy shit. I start business school next week!*

For a brief moment the doctor and a nurse suggested that I might be able to go home with some nasty, but cosmetic, flesh wounds. Quickly, though, their attention turned to an x-ray and the fractured jaw it revealed. They hadn't noticed the fracture before because my jaw had broken to the left of my chin, opposite where the impact had happened. "That," the doctor said, seemingly impressed, "was a hell of a fall."

I would need to return to the hospital after 24 hours to have my jaw wired shut, the mandibular equivalent of immobilizing a broken wrist with a cast. The doctor presented me with a couple of options: they could wire me shut and leave me that way for six weeks, or they could surgically fix a plate over the fracture, then wire me shut and leave me that way for twenty days. I decided on the second option.

We stopped at Taco Bell on the way home. I was fairly certain I wouldn't be able to ingest even a heated flour tortilla after the surgery, so this was to be my last solid meal for the next three weeks. As I gingerly chewed my bean burrito, I thought I could feel my jawbone shimmy, however subtly. I found the prospect of the next day's surgery oddly reassuring.

When I awoke from surgery, the first thing I noticed was—wait for it—that I couldn't move my mouth. It was perfectly, totally, inarguably immobilized. I'd had casts on various limbs before, and they always afforded me a bit of wiggle room. But not a wired-shut jaw; I could no more open my mouth than lift a painted-shut window.

Karen walked in. Steady as always, she asked to see the wires. I bared my teeth, and—just perceptibly—she drew back. "Sheesh," she remarked, "that's kind of . . . medieval looking." It was an appropriate reaction and an accurate description; as I learned when a nurse brought me a small mirror, my mouth was all twisted metal. Looking at my reflection, I realized my jaw hadn't been wired together so much as it had been twist-tied. I didn't blame Karen for recoiling.

Wanting to maintain a bit of levity, though, I attempted a smile and took a shot at my first word: "Thanks," I tried to say.

"Shanshhh," I heard myself say.

Knowing that I'd need to speak up in class, though, I decided that I'd better keep working at it. For the next couple of days, at the hospital and back at the house, per my request, Karen asked discussion-starting questions. Thankful for the adult conversation after days of teaching second-graders, she indulged me, and even coached me. At first I was all spittle—so much so that Karen learned to stand back farther than usual when we were speaking. But I soon learned to speak at a low volume and with little emotion; any modulation of either resulted in Karen laughing, despite my frustration, at the salivary spray I'd emit.

While speaking was frustrating, eating proved excruciating, and largely futile. Before I left the hospital, a nurse had given me two parting gifts. The first was a pair of wire cutters. I looked at them, and then back at her, perplexed.

"In case you vomit. You don't want to suffocate," she said.

The other gift was a crude, elephantine syringe with a tapered rubber tube at the end. With my mouth clamped shut I couldn't chew, nor could I command enough suction power to take food in through a straw. I would have to force-feed myself one large syringeful at a time.

In short order I found that virtually all of the food I consumed with the syringe was sweet: Ensure, Boost, smoothies, instant breakfast; I tried them all. Consumption with an immobilized jaw was exhausting and far from varied. I tried squash soup—too hot for my still-healing gums—and a liquefied burrito that Karen's mom kindly cooked. The burrito-in-a-cup was mercifully savory, but left me with a mouthful of black bean skins and flecks of pepper and onion for days afterwards.

Once the discomfort from the initial trauma subsided, and the novelty of my mouth bound and looking like Jaws from *Goldfinger* dissipated, I found a wired jaw highly limiting and bothersome. For example, if I got a hair in my mouth, and couldn't extract it, I would spend an hour trying to ingest it, one gag-inducing swallow at a time.

Five days after getting my jaw wired shut I brought my bike into the repair shop to fix its tacoed front wheel (as with me, the damage to my bike seemed miraculously limited to the leading end).

I wasn't mentally ready to climb back on the bike (nor was I ready to subject Karen, or her mother, to that). So, with energy to burn off, I began jogging. I decided that running uphill would best mimic cycling. The old Stanford stadium proved perfect for a challenging workout: the continuous flight of benches became progressively steeper as the stairs rose. The day before class started, I spent 45 minutes running stadium stairs. It was, as I had imagined it would be, a rigorous and painful workout. Down and up I ran, thrilled at getting my first solid workout since before the accident. At the top of each flight I'd pause, hands on my knees, breathing wildly through my wires and teeth. Karen accompanied me, both to get her own workout but also to keep an eye on me. We met at the top of the steps, my cheeks madly blowing in and out, while I whistled saliva from behind the wires. "Jeez," Karen remarked.

The following morning, classes began and the pain in my calves was intense. I spent the entire first day of business school lumbering around campus stiff-legged, my awkward gait conspiring with my face to make me the class freak. Nonetheless, I maintained an insistence on talking in class, and informally with new classmates. To make myself heard, I had to project my voice—which resulted in the occasional spray of spit. Figuring that my professors, and at least a few of my kinder-hearted classmates, would appreciate my effort, I spoke up in every class but one: accounting.

My accounting professor, in her first week of her first year of teaching, hadn't developed an awareness of the class. She cold-called, demanding spontaneous contributions from students at random. On the third day of class, while describing an accounting table, she glanced briefly at my name card and asked, emphatically, "Mr. Fee. Would that go in the debits column, or the credits column?"

I froze, and said nothing. After a few seconds, she repeated, "*Mr. Fee*," and then raised her gaze and noticed my condition for the first time. Her jaw dropped (lucky her!), but before she could say anything I took a stab at it. "Credits," I proffered as loudly as I could, and what came out was a confident "Hezzhits." After another awkward bit of silence, she nodded and—with her eyes now fixed on my metal and scabs and probably a bit of drool on my chin—replied, "Exactly."

If my fifteen seconds of accounting-class fame didn't earn me the attention of my classmates, three other feats must have.

The first was "eating" at school, and the resulting effect on my body. Twice a day I pulled my syringe, a source of possible hygienic concern to my classmates, from my back pocket and went to work on a smoothie or can of Ensure. Over the next couple of weeks what little weight I had visibly dropped off my body. I'd always been skinny, but with this eating routine I became ghoulish looking, and before long my weight reached a low point I had never dreamed of: at 6' 1", I weighed 148 pounds.

The second was cycling to school. Most of my classmates knew who I was, and had heard about my accident. So when I arrived at school on my mountain bike, some were impressed and some aghast. Before long I was on the road bike as well, sporting Lycra shorts, and soon I discovered I was known as "Bike Mike." Whether this was a designation of respect, bemusement, or derision I'm not sure, but in a class of Wall Street savants, twenty-something entrepreneurs, and even a couple of Olympic athletes, I'd at least earned an identity.

The third feat was beer-drinking. It wasn't the quantity that was notable, it was my style. At the first Friday afternoon LPF (Liquidity Preference Function), I showed off. I tipped my head way back, and then—using a plastic beer cup squeezed into a chute—I poured beer through my barely open mouth. My classmates understood my plight well enough to know that if I didn't dribble, I'd achieved something.

As my Bike Mike identity spread, and as I sought to make a good first impression, I found myself shaking hands frequently, and I found these handshakes to be increasingly painful. I'd felt a slight twinge of discomfort in my right hand in the hospital, and now it became more noticeable. I found myself wincing every time I met another classmate. Soon I started to avoid handshakes, which proved challenging, as people began to seek me out: "Oh, you're Bike Mike, I've been meaning to meet you . . ."

My twenty days with an immobilized jaw seemed like an eternity. Figuring that getting the wires removed might be painful and that the recovery might prove equally uncomfortable, I wasn't looking forward to returning to the hospital. Still, I'd answered the question, "How long will you be wired shut?" enough times that I was more than ready for my first solid meal.

As it turned out, neither the removal nor the following weeks proved painful. The surgery was outpatient, and with the doctor's okay, I drove with Karen directly to Taco Bell. It was another couple of weeks before I would bite down on an apple or chew a bagel, but a warm bean burrito was like manna.

Within a month, I was not only chewing, but riding my bike on the open road. As my scars healed, I needed to reply less frequently to variations of the question, "What happened to you?" Soon I joined Stanford's cycling team. Later in the year, in fact, I managed to earn a spot on the time-trial team. In the spring, the entire cycling team traveled to the National Collegiate

Cycling Championships, where we placed second, on the strength of our women's performance (this is typical for Stanford).

At my final checkup with my plastic surgeon, she said, "Well, Mike, you've been through a lot, but you've come out clean." Then she shook my hand. Hers was no death grip, yet I winced when she grasped it. "What's wrong?" she asked.

An x-ray revealed a hairline fracture. She splinted my hand and wrist and advised me to avoid shaking hands. I left the hospital and climbed onto my bike, which I'd locked outside. As I went about testing how well I could apply my rear brake, I wondered how I would explain the splint to Karen and my classmates.

# A Derailleur Soaks in Gasoline

**BOB BURT**

*A body in motion tends to stay in motion unless acted upon by an outside force. Newton wrote an unwritten law. I break laws. All day, every day. A stop sign here. A red light there. I stay in motion because it's what I do. It's my job. I'm a modern-day Mercury. Two-wheeled instead of wing-heeled, I pedal whatever to whoever wherever.*

*But sometimes a bump in the road can put a bee in your bonnet and a dent in a helmet. She was a college student driving her boyfriend's Chevy. She chewed with her mouth open. She had a birthmark same as Marilyn Monroe's.*

*Right after she spit her gum out the window, I hit her harder than the flood hit Johnstown.*

"Sixteen," I bark. "Speak. Talk to me." My bite is saved for Vicodin. The doctor ordered bed rest, so I've traded the street for a seat. Dispatch is where broken messengers come to heal.

"Ten-four," he says.

"No. Not ten-four, Sixteen. Ten-four means good-bye. Say hello. Air time is money. Learn the lingo." Sixteen is a starry-eyed rookie, green as the backpack he pedaled in with. The country mouse come to stay with his urban rat cousins. He has left the nest with a borrowed U-lock, my spare Zo bag (the single-strap carrier custom-made for couriers), and a dream of knowing what I know: the flavor of every nook and cranny of Pittsburgh. He's never had to draft the dry wake of a snowplow, or climb Sycamore Street in the slap of a 40 mph wind at 10 below. He doesn't know humidity turns t-shirts into salt licks, that April showers lift oil slicks, or that an open car door equals a broken collarbone. He's never picked cinders out of his palms, or done a day in jail for running a red light. He is me seven years, eight wrecks, and a hundred thousand miles ago. Today he is my pawn. I move him around the city like I've been moved. It is as bitter as it is sweet.

"Are you clean, Sixteen?" If he's clean, he's delivered all the packages I assigned him.

"That's a big ten-four. Can I go home now?" One finger holds his radio on, and another blows his nose. It's music to my ears.

He's asking for a break, but I hear different. I hear someone's who's asking to make the bread without baking the bread.

"The only break I ever got was in my leg from a Ford Econoline, Sixteen. They put butter on it and gave me 15 minutes to walk it off."

My war stories have all become fish stories. I poke my freshest wounds. These day-olds, they sweat like glazed donuts in a plastic baggy.

"The fight always goes to the swiftest, Sixteen, and you are a thoroughbred. I see a stud fee in your future; your stones are worth money." I remember countless times cooling my heels in Market Square with the pigeons. I listened while other riders got handed deliveries that brought them money and miles. Waiting never guaranteed anything. "Go graze the pasture; you're fourth on my list." Fourth on my list means he might as well find a matinee. He should be first, but he's too new. He's staying in the stable. He just went from $22 an hour to making nothing. Bike messengers work on straight commission.

"Thirteen, Thirteen, Thirteen! Come in lucky number Thirteen! Press that microphone and sing!"

*From the far-right lane came tires squealing left. This was going to hurt. My crystal ball never looked so cloudy. 5th Avenue is a four-lane, one-way down hill. Its lights are timed for 22 mph. On a 28-pound bike with 21 speeds, 25 mph is easy.*

*Stopping is hard. The collision was inevitable. I knew my machine. I know when there's hope and when I'm fucked. I was fucked.*

*She looked right through me. Her hands were heavy with silver jewelry. They gripped the steering wheel at three and nine o'clock. She put the pedal to the metal and turned a Chevy Camaro into a moving roadblock.*

*I skidded an inch-wide strip of black right into her door. My wheel crumpled. I noticed the Diet Sprite squeezed between her knees just before I launched into an uncertain future. Under me, steel and glass cruised over concrete—the Holy Trinity of things not to hit headfirst.*

*Maybe I should have taken that job at Radio Shack like Dad wanted, I thought. My shadow was getting closer. The packages in my bag lost their importance. My goals, regrets, and responsibilities stole the freedom from my flight. No one would remember to feed my fish.*

*My hands planted briefly on the chalky roof of her Camaro before momentum moved me to the hood. My helmet hit the cursive "Chevy" in the tinted top of the windshield. The glass reflected buildings and wisps of the wild blue yonder. I grasped for reason. I clawed for a finger hold.*

*Roll with it, I told myself. Eventually you'll land on your feet. It had always worked in the past.*

*She never hit the brakes. Six cylinders roared. My career as a hood ornament ended. I tumbled ass-over-teakettle off the side of the hood.*

On a stack of map books my derailleur soaks in a cup of gasoline. A dozen drowned cigarette butts swim in the dregs of a Miller bottle. Over the keyboard stained with coffee, grease and nicotine, a storm of fruit flies rages. When they get too intense I will touch a flame to a can of WD-40 and incinerate their wings. They will crash onto a splayed copy of *Leg Show* or the *Collected Fiction of Albert Camus*.

"Nine, where are you? Please talk to me. Please. Pretty please with sugar on top."

"Elevator" his voice hushed for courtesy.

"Oooh, I'm sorry. I didn't know. To all you beautiful people sharing an elevator this morning with our favorite messenger Number Nine, a bit of advice: Do not—I repeat—*do not* let him get behind you. That's not toothpaste around his mouth. You are in the presence of a Level 3 sex offender. Grab your mace and douche his face. Those lips are blistered for a reason. If he tells you he only wants to be loved, shoot him. Call me outside, Nine."

"Thirteen? Enough with the silent treatment already. Are you alive? Come on, Thirteen. Fart. Burp. Do something."

My best friends at the moment are two space heaters. They blast summer at my feet. They don't complain: "I've got a flat tire," or "I can't find it," or "It won't fit in my bag." They breathe life into the maps on the wall and stir dust bunnies to stampede.

"Mr. Seven. Señor Siete, where are you? Please talk to me. Thirteen's left me feeling all alone, and now I have abandonment issues. You ready to write?"

"Go."

"Grab a TP on 42 at the X for 2 Gateway, two at Clapp and Ferrone for the Kossman, a Mellon on 12 for Reprographics, and Countrywide has five all dressed in ribbons and bows, call me holding nine." Initials, acronyms, and insults move messengers around the city. As the calls roll in, it is my job to put all the ducks in a row. Seven is the gull in my flock of vultures. The others can eat garbage without getting sick and ride the wind, but Seven is the wind. He has two Hefty bags for lungs and pistons for legs.

"Seven. Clear on nine." Clear means we're on the same wavelength. Nine is the number of packages he'll be holding.

It's a beautiful run I've woven; a quadruple jump in Checkers that nets three kings. Seven is well on his way to a two-hundred-dollar day. I gave it to him for two reasons; first, if he isn't pulling in at least twenty bucks an hour, he is more irritating than a four-inch hemorrhoid. He'll bitch and moan, call your mother a whore, throw a tantrum and threaten to quit. In the messenger world, the squeaky wheel gets the grease. Or it gets a beat run—a delivery that breaks the back, bank, and spirit. The second and real reason I bequeath it to him is he deserves it. Every day without fail he is ready to ride at dawn. Before the beggars, bakers, and trucks awake, he is gliding down alleys, hopping curbs, and slaloming traffic. There's something to be said for that in a world where half your workforce is dry-heaving or still asleep at 10 A.M.

I revere and envy Seven's fleetness.

For the past six months, I've been later than sooner to the office. I've been waiting for the elevator rather than running the stairs.

I'm slowing down.

I tell myself wisdom permits slack, but an ugly truth refutes that: I've lost my edge. I crush an aspirin in my teeth. Both are bitter to swallow.

*I sailed like a kite without a string until I bowled into a bus stop. Suits, skirts, and culinary students toppled into a seven-ten split. Headphones, purses, and backpacks cushioned my cartwheel across the sidewalk, and like a human tumbleweed I crashed through the front doors of Candy-Rama. I lay beneath bins of jelly beans and Jolly Ranchers. I could hear my dad's voice crooning a Bing Crosby song that he once used to taunt me, "Would you like to swing on a star? Carry moonbeams home in a jar? And be better off* than you are? Or would you rather be a mule?" *Children stared wide-eyed. I examined myself. No bones poked through the skin. No holes begged direct pressure. No numbness. I could breathe. I couldn't ask for more from blunt-force trauma.*

*Outside, people screamed and confusion reigned. She stomped on the gas so hard her tires repaved the street. Her four-barrel carburetor fueled 350 horsepower away from the scene. One of my cat lives escaped with it.*

"Thirteen, I'd like to have a summit. Do you read me? I want dialogue. I want a meaningful exchange of ideas, and I want it now." For three hours Thirteen has been maintaining radio silence. He's M.I.A. If it were anyone else, I'd be worried his head had been turned into pudding by a truck, but this is Thirteen, he's been in the game three years longer than me. Three years too many. "Communication requires two people, Thirteen, and you are not living up to your end of the bargain. There is no excuse for selfishness."

My red ear presses the phone to my shoulder. It's been ringing and blinking like a Christmas pageant for the last two hours. I adjust ice on my hip. "Do I know where your package is?" I parrot the caller's query. "I know you have a nice package, can you hold please?"

"Six, Six, Six," I scream into the radio, "where in the Antichrist are you, Six? I need some beta on the BBB and D to Gway Studios, stat. Pronto. Yesterday. Now. Call."

"Six here." My acronyms find a half-gloved hand wiping sweat from a brow. Cold burns the fingers on mornings like these. A jake brake hammers air in the background. "I'm drinking coffee on the South Side. Holding two."

My chair groans. "A picnic? That's so nice! I didn't RSVP because you didn't invite me. What's the estimated time of arrival on those stale little muffins you have tucked in your bag?"

"I dunno. Forty-five minutes. When I'm done smokin' a bowl."

None of the ten sets of ears that heard that pays it any mind. A drug test in the courier world consists of distinguishing oregano from cannabis. "Great. You just go on being that special person that you are. Keep spreading the joy, sharing the bliss. You've got my vote for Employee of the Month." Six is banned from three offices because he smells bad. His legs look like he grew up carrying a keg. He's got homemade tattoos, a front tooth gray as the Pittsburgh winter, and dreadlocks that resemble a third-grader's attempt at stuffing pork into sausage casing.

I chew a Vicodin. I never want to be Six. The day I need to get high to get through work will be my last. The pill bottle stares at me. I tuck it in a drawer before the vultures can pick it clean.

*No just deserts were going to be found in the candy store, so I ran to the gutter. My bike was wounded but not dead. With my knees and some jumping upon it, I reinvented the wheel the Camaro had disfigured. I saddled up and hit the road hell-bent on revenge.*

*Urban decay sprayed off my tire and up my back. I shot a stream of tail lights in a haze of belching tailpipes and saw red everywhere but in the traffic lights. "Nowhere to run to, baby, nowhere to hide." Martha and the Vandellas knew my mantra. Block by block, I clocked the watch. I know the city like the back of my windburned hands. "Come out, come out, wherever you are." My handlebars are cut to the width of my shoulders. My bike fits anywhere I do.*

*The potholes, sewer grates, and plates of steel that pock the streets are nothing but feathers in my cap. A car is governed by the rules of the road. Bikes move by a higher law. I grabbed the side of a cab and cruised up 2nd Ave. She won't get away. On Cherry Way I took to the sidewalk. It's only a matter of time. Going the wrong way down Smithfield Street, I hugged the curb. I could smell her. I cut through a parking lot up to Grant Street. She was in my cross-hairs.*

"Samantha? Yeah, sorry about that, thanks for holding. The all-knowing mother ship has located your missing documents. Both you and I know only snowflakes are perfect. The courier who promptly picked up your package and placed it securely on his person for transport has experienced 'technical difficulty.' He was riding down the street, legally, at a prudent speed, with the flow of traffic, and a man in a suit hit him in the head with a honey-baked ham. What? I can't believe it either. His helmet saved him. I'm just glad I don't have to call his mother. Yeah. So it's going to be a little late. Our new motto is not rain, snow, sleet, or the other white meat. Oh, while I have your ear, I was going through the bills, and I couldn't help but notice you're account is a tad more pink than black. Yeah. Those six letters we sent probably got lost in the mail. I understand. It's the damn controllers. I'm telling you, you think you've got the world on a string and a honey-baked ham hits you in the head. What? I'm not joking. Ham is serious. Oh by the way, I'm selling a kidney this weekend, just so this place can have toilet paper . . . So if you could cut us a check . . . what? Sure. I'll do my best. Have a nice day."

Samantha is like most of our clients; with the snap of her fingers she wants fax-machine speed at the old Pony Express prices. Samantha needs to learn *rush* service happens for a dollar more, not an extra phone call. Samantha needs to reprioritize her life. She needs to pay her bill.

*"I didn't do it!" Those emphatic words poured out of a back window shattered into a million tiny diamonds by my U-lock.*

*The roof was dented where my helmet hit. My sweat was speckled among the insects on the windshield.*

*"Lies hurt more than Chevys." I said.*

*I tore off the little door that covered her gas cap. I kicked her quarter-panel like I've always wanted to take my boots to the razor-burned executives who talk about downsizing while practicing their golf swing.*

*My lock pocked her hood. I couldn't stop. I was sick of the conditioned air. I was sick of the pools of smokers outside every damn building. The locked bathrooms. The security guards. The horns. The spit. I was sick of everything that my money could not buy. And I was sick of pretty girls who couldn't acknowledge me even after they'd run me over.*

*Two broken taillights and a turn signal later, I saw myself in her Jackie O sunglasses. I was being tackled to the ground.*

*She left me in the street for a second time.*

*I was wrapped in the less-than-loving arms of a stranger and dropped face first to the pavement.*

"Numero Uno! I'm lookin' for the head cheese, the Grand Poobah, El Presidente, Mama Pajama. Where are you, Big Daddy?"

Number One owns this freak show. His John Hancock is on the lease, insurance, permits, and paychecks. He hires and fires, sets the prices, and cleans the toilet. He has an Ivy League education, the social skills of an autistic wolverine, and it is he who usually captains the desk at which I sit.

"I hate you, Zero," he says—flowery candor is not his forte.

"Why so glum, chum? Do you need a hug?" The big guy has traded his seat for the street because he knows, after ten years of oiling them, that a chain is only as strong as its weakest link. He'll pull his weight on the road while I mend. In recent years his belt size has grown with his responsibilities. It seemed like a natural transition: being a messenger and then starting your own messenger service. There was only one problem. When the ante was upped, he was no longer of the city; he was part of it.

"Everyone," he says catching his breath, "Everyone in the world should be allowed to kill five people. Five: whomever, whenever, and for whatever reason. You get five and after that you're done. Tallies get tattooed on the forehead. Everyone knows where they stand."

Interesting, a universal system of checks and balances. I love him, but I wouldn't want to be him. King on an island of misfits.

I radio back to One, "Mr. Sunshine, how you doin'? Wanted to touch base, let you know I'm thinking about you. I just used your underwear to clean my bottom bracket, and now I'm eating your lunch. Judge Judy starts in ten minutes. This is hard work. I can understand why you whine all day. I vote we all kick you another five percent of our commission." I wash a Vicodin down with tap water the color of cola. "I'd tell you you're moving a little slow, but that's only compared to a glacier. Keep up the good work. Try to make it back by Thursday."

Yesterday I was him; avoiding broken glass, weaving among suits and skirts, silently cursing a society subjugated by General Motors. And then a car turned my bike into a piece of abstract art. Today I dispatch. Tomorrow? A cockroach falls from the ceiling onto my scabbing knee, and I forget all about tomorrow.

"I heard the cops charged the lady who left you in the gutter with littering," says One. "I'm on the North Side. Holding one for uptown."

*The cop's eyebrows were longer than any messenger's ponytail. "The vehicle's operator, can you describe her?" He was eating a donut. I swear on my mother's eyesight he was eating a donut.*

*"Here." I offered him the woman's driver's license and purse. And then I puked. The good Samaritan who tackled me had also punched me in the stomach. "I snatched the purse when she took off."*

*I should have known by the way those two caterpillars above his eyes collided, by the way he said "Hmmmmmm," when I handed him the license of the public menace, by the way he walked away from me as though his shoes stuck to the pavement. I should have known things can always get worse.*

*He sat in his car and squawked numbers and very few words into his radio. "Code Blue," he said in a hushed voice. I recognized that one from the time a cop car sideswiped me on 2nd Ave and left me lying in the dust. I called the police on the police. Code Blue means cops investigating cops. It's redundant. It's also a waste of time. Code Blue means you're shit out of luck.*

*"You want an ambulance?" he asked, handing me his official report.*
*Five hundred bucks for a five-block ride wasn't in my budget. "I'll walk."*
*"Suit yourself."*
*Waiting in the emergency room, I stared at the police report. It lacked a*
*case number. The officer had signed his name as Mickey Mouse.*
*"It's good to be the daughter of a cop," I told the guy in the seat next to*
*me. His ear was dripping. I crumpled the paper and tossed it in a bag labeled*
*Infectious Waste.*

"Thirteen here."

"Thirteen? Thirteen! What a pleasant surprise! How the Sam Hill are
you? What's it been? Three, four hours?"

Thirteen has forty-four Lou Reed albums and a lazy eye. He got the lazy
eye on a day when it was minus twenty-seven. He rode off the curb in front
of Heinz Hall and his front fork snapped. His face hit before his hands. He
rode four miles with three teeth dangling by their nerves.

Over the radio I hear a long exhale laced with smoke. Birds are chirping. Children giggle in the distance. "Dude," he says, "you ever think you're
getting a little long in the tooth for this shit?" He wipes his nose with the
shirt he's most likely been wearing for three days, and continues. "Nobody's
saying you got to swim in the mainstream, but there's gotta be something
better than being errand boy and getting run over every six months. Shit, I
ain't goin' nowhere but on a liver transplant list, but you . . . hell, you went to
school. You know how to drive. You can read. You can swing a hammer, and
make coffee."

I look out a filthy window at a dirty town. "Interesting point. I'll put it in
the minutes for the next meeting."

His words rub salt in my wounds. I limp over to continue harvesting
components off my dead bike. "Damn Thirteen," I mutter. I hate him. Only
because he's right.

I give up my salvage operation and stare at my worn and weathered bag,
my cracked helmet and my bloodstained socks. I look out the filthy window
at a dirty town and ponder my darkest fear—I've outgrown the scars, the
mileage, and the memories.

# It's All in the Name

## CARLA AXT-PILON

**Saturday, July 1, 2006.** "Get rid of the shoes! Get rid of the shoes!" my father yelled after I told him about my accident.

"Papa, everyone wears clipless shoes," I explained. "I would be laughed at if I didn't wear them. It would be like biking in blue jeans."

"There could have been traffic. You could have been injured, or worse!"

I thought he and my mom would get a kick out of my accident, and I had hoped, when I called, that their sense of humor would alleviate my humiliation.

*Well, that didn't go very well*, I thought as I hung up the phone. Not only was I still humiliated, but now I felt guilty for worrying my parents. I wondered if maybe road cycling was a foolish recreation for a 43-year old mother of two.

**Saturday, September 3, 2005.** On my initial ride with the Naperville Bike Club, Big John (the largest of the eight Johns in the club), asked me how many miles I put on in a year. I had never even thought of keeping track before. I looked down at my Trek 1000, and I calculated my handful of triathlon training rides, some of which were a whopping twelve miles long, then I tripled the actual total mileage that I came up with, "About two hundred or so."

"Oh," was his only response.

Baffled by the disappointment in his reply, I asked him how many miles he rode a year. He replied, "About two thousand." And then, as if I didn't feel green enough, he added, "Moo-Moo puts on around five thousand a year."

I gulped, and was glad I'd lied about my two hundred.

"Did you say Moo-Moo?" I asked.

"Oh, his name is Rick, but he wears a cow-spotted jersey when he rides. Nobody in this club goes by their real name."

At the end of my first ride with the club I vowed: 1) never to earn a club nickname, 2) never to complain on a ride, no matter how much I was hurting or how windy or cold it got, and 3) never to hold up the group. I didn't want to draw any attention to my inexperience. I upheld these vows for almost one year, until Saturday, July 1, 2006.

**Saturday, July 1, 2006.** We were one hour into our group ride and averaging 19 mph. The twelve of us (nine men and three women) were finally out of town, in the farmlands. Away from the congestion of city streets and traffic lights, we stretched out the pace line and broke into occasional sprints. My cycling confidence had grown with each ride, and I was especially pleased that, after ten months of riding with the group, I had not been given a ridiculous nickname.

Ahead of us, the country road was being resurfaced and widened to accommodate a new subdivision. As we approached the newly paved surface that was not yet open to cars, The Evangelical Vegan (Wally) was extolling the health benefits of his guacamole recipe. As we debated over the best ingredients to use, I noticed the riders ahead of us were darting through a small opening between two concrete barriers.

It looked like a bad situation. Normally, negotiating the barriers would not have been a problem, but a few months ago I'd purchased a new pair of clipless pedals and cycling shoes, and I had already fallen over twice, unable to disengage in time when I came to an abrupt stop. Luckily, in both instances I was riding by myself. After each fall I had made a mental note to loosen the release on my pedals, so I could get out of them more easily. But I never got around to it.

As I neared the gap between the barriers, I squeezed my brake lever hard while I attempted to release my left foot from the pedal. My bike wobbled, and I went down in full view of the entire group.

"Oh nooo!" I heard Wally say as I fell in slow motion. On the way down I laughed to cover my embarrassment, but when I hit the ground the impact of the fall was horrific. The edge of my bike seat hit me hard between the legs. I stood up quickly and tried to brush off my stupid mistake. I wanted to get back on my bike and continue riding as if nothing had happened, but the pain between my legs precluded the thought of sitting.

As I drew a few breaths leaning over my now upright bike, I filled the awkward moment by saying, "I'm sure glad I'm not a guy!" Laughter erupted from the riders behind me, who had stopped and were waiting patiently to move on.

"Okay," I said hoping the pain was about to subside, "I think I'm ready." I sighed, then I looked at my bike. I thought that I could continue riding without sitting, by keeping my weight on my legs.

"Okay, let's go!" encouraged Wally. "No broken bones, no blood."

"No broken bones, no blood," I repeated with a forced smile. No sooner did I say that then I felt a warm sensation in my bike shorts. I had only felt this sensation once previously when my water broke before the birth of my first daughter, nineteen years ago. *Oh my God!* I thought, *I've either wet myself, or I'm bleeding, bleeding a lot.* I discreetly brushed my fingers between my legs. As I lifted my hand, I was mortified to see blood.

"What?" said Wally in disbelief when he saw the amount of blood on my hand. "But where are you bleeding? I don't see where it's coming from?" he asked as he looked me over. "Where are you bleeding?" he repeated as Rev, Ace (also known as Tom the pilot), Rider X, Monk, Tucson, and Moo-Moo looked on dumbfounded.

I was speechless and absolutely unable to answer his questions. I could not bring myself to explain to these men that the blood was coming from between my legs!

"Where are you bleeding from?" Wally stammered a third time thoroughly confused. Then he got his answer as a bright red stream of blood ran down my right leg. It was soon followed by another stream trickling down my left leg.

"Um," I muttered to the speechless men, "I think I'll go home now. You guys go on. I'll just walk." We were a good sixteen miles from home. But I was so embarrassed that I wanted to walk home in my bike shoes rather than have to explain the situation to the other members of the group. I just wanted to disappear.

I turned my bike to leave, but Wally, being ever chivalrous, wouldn't have it. "I'll go with you." I don't know which made me feel worse, making Wally miss the rest of the ride on such a beautiful day or facing the disgrace of bleeding from my private parts in front of him.

"No, that's okay," I insisted, "I'll be fine, really." I felt I had held up the ride for too long.

"You can't walk home like that!" scolded Moo-Moo. The blood was now pooling in my bike shoes. "You should have your husband pick you up."

At that point, the riders who had cleared the road barrier were circling patiently fifty yards ahead. They were politely avoiding eye contact, so as not to embarrass me further than my novice fall already had. Cindy, a nurse, sensed there was a problem. She rode back through the barrier to where I stood. When she was close enough to see the blood, she shouted, "This woman doesn't need to call her husband! She needs to call an ambulance!" Cindy quickly dropped her bike, and grabbed my crotch, putting pressure on it to slow the bleeding. Then she asked me if I thought I'd cut my femoral artery.

I knew the femoral artery is located on the upper inner thigh, so I told her I didn't think so, but she hurriedly explained that arteries are in different locations on different people. I began to worry. Although I was pretty confident I hadn't cut an artery, I agreed to have someone call an ambulance. Moo-Moo, who conveniently had his phone out, volunteered to call 911. Later, I learned he had been taking pictures of Cindy holding my crotch.

Another rider produced a phone so I could call home. Cindy held my privates tightly as I dialed. I hoped my eleven-year-old daughter wouldn't answer. I didn't want to explain to her that I'd had an accident. Fortunately, my husband answered, and I described the situation. He responded in coded language to avoid upsetting our children.

Cindy made me sit down on the pavement, her bare hand still firmly in place as we waited for the ambulance. Wally donated his handkerchief to help sop up the blood.

The ambulance arrived quickly and out jumped two cute young paramedics. They rolled out a gurney and ordered me to lie down. "You really don't have to do that," I objected as they strapped me in.

"We do have to, Ma'am. It's standard procedure," responded the taller of the two paramedics.

"That's right, strap her down tight; she's a wild one," joked Ace.

The group decided to wait for my husband and daughters to pick up my bike. I shouted one last instruction before the paramedics closed the ambulance doors, "Don't tell my daughters I'm bleeding!"

"Let's have a look," the bald paramedic said, snapping on latex gloves.

"Do I have to?" I whined with my arm over my eyes to cover my embarrassment.

"Ma'am, you can either remove your shorts, or I can cut them off, which would you prefer?"

*You don't hear that every day,* I thought as I reluctantly pulled down my bike shorts. "These cost me sixty bucks," I said, trying to make light of the situation.

Quickly I turned my attention to the other paramedic who was wiring me up with all kinds of gadgets. "What are you doing?" I asked him.

"Just getting your vitals, ma'am. You know, your blood pressure, heart rate, and temperature."

"You want to know my heart rate?" I quipped, "I can tell you that." I looked at my heart-rate monitor, "It's 64. Wow!" I giggled with amazement. "64—I'm in decent shape."

The bald paramedic confirmed what I had suspected; I had cut my labia. He said I would probably need stitches, and off we went to the hospital.

At the emergency room, I was relieved to be greeted by a middle-aged nurse, who, unlike the paramedics, was very sympathetic. After a few initial questions, she drew the curtain and went to get the doctor.

Alone, and shielded from others, I relaxed a bit. I told myself that my ordeal would soon be over. Then I imagined my doctor—perhaps he would be an older man, a bit overweight with a beard, or maybe he would be a slender, balding Indian or Asian man wearing glasses; he might even have a mole or two. I about died when a fresh-out-of-medical school, blond-haired, blue-eyed doctor pulled back the curtain with a movie-star smile and introduced himself. This man should have had a romantic theme song prefigure his appearance. He was stunning, and I was just making a cameo appearance in the soap opera that I imagined his life to be. I wondered if I had actually died on the outskirts of Naperville, and this was the beginning of a perverse afterlife.

"Your injury is actually fairly common, especially for little girls," he explained as he stitched me up.

"You're kidding," I groaned. "How do they get hurt?"

"Usually by falling off a chair, or running into the corner of a piece of furniture or something sharp. Only we usually anesthetize little girls before giving them stitches. It is just too painful and traumatic an experience for them." Then making light of my situation he added, "But for you it's just painful."

"No," I disagreed, "it's not so much painful as humiliating."

**Sunday, July 2, 2006.** "How's your ... wound?" my mother asked timidly when she called me the day after the accident.

Her choice of words was slightly off; *injury* was the correct terminology. I responded callously to get revenge for her silence the day before. "My inner labia is resting comfortably."

Her reaction was dead silence.

*Oh no!* I thought. I've done it. I've finally pushed my white-haired, seventy-six-year-old Scotch Presbyterian mother over the edge. She may give me the silent treatment now for the rest of my life, or worse yet, she might lecture me. But before I could panic further, I heard a little "Tee hee hee," on the other end of the line, which built to uproarious laughter. My humiliation lifted.

In subsequent conversations, my parents no longer made mention of bike shoes or traffic. The only other time the accident came up was when I called them a few weeks later to tell them my new nickname in the club: Stitch.

# The Road Forbidden

**BOB NEUBAUER**

I've never been able to stick to the highways. The back roads are far more interesting. Roads that bear Bridge Out or Road Closed signs are natural magnets for me. This attraction has led me into some odd situations; perhaps the oddest occurred while I was a student at Penn State some years ago. I often took long weekend rides back then, ranging across the countryside on a quest to see new things. The farmland, woods, and mountains of central Pennsylvania were an endless source of wonder. As a kid from suburban Philadelphia, I'd had only subdivisions to ride through. Here I was free to lose myself in the relative solitude that the quiet back roads provided.

And lose myself I often did, wandering for miles down narrow roads with no idea where they were taking me. Far off the main roads, I would encounter small, sleepy villages, dilapidated cabins buried in the thicket, or an unexpected field filled with buffalo—captivating discoveries that would make me marvel.

One spring day in my senior year, I set out riding in a direction I had never taken before. Winter's chill was in fast retreat, and the warm weather coaxed me to ever faster speeds. It was in this jubilant state of mind, as I raced down a long hill alongside a winding river, that an old steel bridge, a relic from decades past, caught my eye.

I decided to cross it, but I had to quickly clench my brakes to avoid running into a waist-high wooden barricade blocking entry to the bridge. Perhaps the rusty span could no longer support traffic, I considered, as I hoisted my bike over the barrier. I stepped eagerly across the bridge. A dirt road, its edges lost in the tall grass, beckoned me onward, and I happily followed it, heading into the unknown.

The stress of homework and exams melted away with each push on the pedals, and I smiled as I took deep breaths of the fresh spring air. The road carried me into a beautiful meadow of tall, swaying grass and yellow wild-flowers, and I was pleasantly surprised that there was not a building to mar the landscape. I had found a secret passage back in time, I mused. My fantasy was abruptly shattered when I rounded a bend and came face to face with an old wooden fence, blocking the road. Maybe it was resentment that made me blaze a trail around it, not even glancing at the worn and tattered sign stapled to the wood. Perhaps it said No Trespassing, but I planned to disturb nothing and would leave behind no trace of my presence.

After a few more minutes of riding, I was annoyed to see another gate blocking my path. I skirted it just as easily, with just as little concern for its intended purpose.

It couldn't go on forever, and eventually my secret byway met up with a paved road, signaling my return to civilization. To underscore that, a couple of houses appeared over the next rise. I headed in their direction. As I ped-aled past them, I glanced over and saw a man standing on the front porch of one of houses, staring at me. I nodded at him in greeting.

"Hey, come here!" he shouted, waving his arms at me.

I stiffened.

"Get back here!" he screamed.

I quickened my pace. This prompted him to pull out a whistle and he began tooting at me with the shrill intensity of a lifeguard. What a freak! I pushed harder on my pedals, eager to put some distance between us.

Down the road I saw a barn and calmed a bit. More buildings meant more people. When I neared the barn, I noticed three men in front, digging trenches in the mud. They raised their heads to stare at me, blank looks on their bearded faces. I nodded and gave them a cheery "hello," but they didn't respond, they just stared, as if they had never seen a cyclist before. Odd, I thought. Lost in their work, I guess. Leaving them behind, I charged up a hill, passed a second barn and headed toward the sound of traffic ahead of me. Soon I could see cars rolling down a highway. The whistle weirdo wouldn't dare come after me now.

As I neared the highway, I discovered I had a slight problem. My road didn't actually connect with the highway. Between the highway and me was

a 10-foot fence topped with barbed wire. Why, I wondered, was this highway sealed off? Was it a toll road? I couldn't think of any toll roads passing through this area. Puzzled, I turned around and pedaled back toward
the barn. If I could scare up the farmer, perhaps I could ask him for directions, preferably along a different route. Perhaps the farmer would be a little
friendlier than the suspicious-looking farm hands. And then it hit me: what
if this was a private community—some sort of retro farming sect like the
Amish that didn't welcome visitors?

I was gripped by apprehension as I closed in on the barn, unsure what
kind of a reception I might get. If the farmer was holding a pitchfork or any
other sharp tool, I decided, I would just turn around and flee. There was
no farmer waiting for me; instead there were six burly men milling about
near the building. Great, more farm hands. One of them spotted me, and
they all turned to look with fixed glares that were more than a little creepy. I
dismounted and walked tentatively toward them. No pitchforks, I observed.
That was good. A couple of the men had their shirts off, revealing large, tattooed biceps. Their hair, long and matted with sweat, hung in wet strands
around their unshaven faces.

"Excuse me," I said as I neared them. "I think I'm lost. Is this private
property?"

"Yeah, you might say that," said a man with a long bushy beard, and they
all laughed. I smiled nervously. Then he spoke again and my smile faded. "It's
kinda like a prison," he said.

My heart stopped beating. Prison? Did he say prison? A chill passed
through my entire body.

With a sick feeling I recalled the gates I had passed, the signs I had ig-
nored. Somehow, using a forgotten back entrance, I had broken into the state
correctional institution's work farm. And even worse, I had fled from a guard
in the process! I was now fraternizing with a small group of murderers.

"Got any joints, man?" asked a scruffy blond guy with a scar near his eye.
The others moved in, hungrily awaiting my reply.

"Uh . . . no," I stumbled. "Sorry. I, uh . . . How do you get out of here?"

"You spend about ten years, then hope for parole," the bearded guy
laughed, scratching the skull tattoo on his arm.

A shiver ran down my spine. Suddenly the guy with the whistle didn't
seem so bad. I didn't know what was worse, hanging around with these fel-
ons or turning myself over to a guard for possible arrest. I spotted one about
20 feet away. He had his back to me and was directing some prisoners as they

lifted a heavy piece of equipment. Somehow, I had slipped up on this crew without him seeing me. Some guard.

"You gotta have a smoke on you," insisted the blond.

"No, sorry. I wish I did. Sorry," I stammered.

"Can I see your bike?" another one asked, with a ravenous look.

"No, I'm kind of . . . on it," I blubbered. I wanted to turn and flee, but I thought that exposing my fear would only make them pounce like leopards. The circle around me seemed to tighten.

"How did you get in here?" asked one of them.

"Good question," I stalled. "I guess I snuck in the back."

"And nobody saw you?"

I thought of the guard with the whistle, tooting furiously. "Not really," I said.

"I used to aim for bike riders with my truck," interjected another prisoner with a look that left no doubt about his sincerity.

"Ahhh," I said, stupidly. This was going downhill fast. "Um . . . " I tried again, "You sure there isn't a way out of here?"

"Back the way you came," one of them offered.

Then the bearded guy motioned me over. Maybe he pitied me or possibly underneath his imposing exterior there was a gentle soul. "Go left, then right, then under a bridge," he said, "and straight out through a gate. Simple." I mounted my bike. "Good luck," he laughed, as I pedaled away from the inmates.

I had my doubts about his directions, but to my surprise he was exactly right. There was not even a guard at the gate. I lifted my bike over a knee-high roadblock and I was out, free, pedaling down the road as fast as my quivering legs would take me, vowing never to leave campus again.

Since then, whenever I'm about to step around a barricade or ride down a private road in search of adventure, I've made it a point to actually read the accompanying signs—even if I do then disregard their warnings.

# Enlightened in Laos

## DAVE STAMBOULIS

The most frequent question people ask me about my seven-year, around-the-world bicycle journey is this: "What is the most important thing you learned?"

My answer is always the same, unequivocally obvious and unhesitating: I would never carry the same amount of gear anywhere, ever again. For the record, the weight of the gear that I hauled around the world was about 80 pounds, strapped upon a 20-plus-pound Trek Single Track bike. Traveling across Tibet and over the Himalayas, I carried spare freewheels and derailleurs, trekking boots, and other items equivalent to the proverbial kitchen sink. When my seven-year journey concluded in San Francisco on New Year's Day, 2000, I didn't ever want to come near a bicycle with a pannier or luggage rack on it.

Several years later I found myself working as a writer in Bangkok, and longing to get back on a bike. Memories of hardship fade with time, and sedentary life starts to beg for its opposite. I began looking at maps of Laos, and plotting a dream bike trip—the one I'd long envisioned involved a single pannier containing little more than the essentials.

Tourism had just begun to trickle into the sleepy People's Democratic Republic of Laos, so it seemed like the ideal place to head for an off-the-beaten track, lightweight journey. My guidebook said that Laos was one of the "last quiet countries left on earth," which sounded like music to my ears, compared to the daily barrage of trucks, trains, and construction going on outside my Bangkok apartment. What's more, the Lao people consider sleeping to be a national pastime. I found this intriguing—and one more reason to pack light.

I drew up a plan to cycle along the banks of the Mekong River for a week and then make my way over the Annamite Mountains and meet up with the Ho Chi Minh Trail. This would take me into Vietnam, where I would finish the trip with a pleasant week-long ride along the coast of the South China Sea. I would be traveling in December, so the temperature in Laos would be a balmy 80 to 90 degrees, with minimal rain—the "cool" season in this part of the world. Vietnam, with its proximity to the ocean, would be a few degrees warmer.

My guidebook informed me that hotels in Laos would cost less than $10 a day, and most meals less than a few dollars. Cheap hotels and meals meant no tent, no stove, no sleeping bag, and of course no winter clothes, boots, or any of the other silly gear that had weighed me down on my round-the-world trip. I was grinning just thinking about it.

I made the decision to go with one pannier for the whole trip. I packed a swimsuit, a towel, some toiletries, one change of clothing, camera, film, and a blank journal. I had recently shaved my head like a monk, so the brush, comb, gel, and blow dryer were abandoned. (Yes, I had packed a blow dryer on previous journeys.) The bag wasn't even half-filled yet. I thought about using the extra space for a Tolstoy novel, but instead I choose my Gore-Tex rain jacket—I'll take comfort over a good read. Lastly, I threw in my pump, patch kit, a handful of spare spokes, and two tiny tools—a spoke wrench and a freewheel remover.

I caught the night train from Bangkok to Nong Khai. The following morning I pedaled across the Friendship Bridge into Vientiane, Laos's tiny capital, built on a crescent-shaped bend in the Mekong River. I sat in one of the parasol-covered cafés and sipped a cup of strong Lao coffee (made densely sweet with scoops of sugar and a large pour of condensed milk), while enjoying the view of the world flowing languidly by in the streets and on the river. Later I took a leisurely ride through neighborhoods of picturesque, decaying colonial mansions.

That evening I returned to the same café and enjoyed the sunset and a meal of grilled river catfish, sticky rice, and *tam som* (spicy papaya salad), the Lao national dish, washed down with many glasses of *Beer Lao*, the extremely tasty national beverage.

For a few days I relaxed, explored, drank coffee, and ate amazing meals in Vientiane, before I got on my bike and headed down Highway 13, the road that parallels the Mekong River into the Lao countryside. I was astonished at how fast I could move carrying only 7 pounds of gear, as opposed to my customary 80 pounds worth. Just out of town, I passed a few soldiers snoring away at a roadside checkpoint, hammock included. An empty whiskey bottle lay at their feet (a scene I would grow accustomed to; the Lao appear to have a fondness for whiskey). There was virtually no traffic on the road except an occasional bus and a few small motorbikes, usually ridden by a family of four carrying a pig or a crate of ducks.

As I passed through the tiny hamlets scattered along Highway 13, children would emerge from the nooks and crannies of stores and homes, all of them smiling and screaming *Sabai dee* (hello) at the top of their lungs. In the town of Paksong, when one small boy spied me wheeling along, he ran after me at full speed, yelling, *Meh, Meh, falang maa laew*! (Mother, the foreigner has arrived!).

Most of the children were slightly shy, but their curiosity always got the better of them, and whenever I stopped, they would inch slowly towards my bike and soon they would be crowded around, jostling each other for a good

Lao schoolgirls in their uniforms ride home from class. Savannakhet Province, Laos — 2003
Photo: Dave Stamboulis

look at me, as though I were an alien. I was dirty, sweating, tall, hairy (except for my head), and big-nosed, everything the Lao are not.

Rather than a bell on my bike, I had a soft rubber pig, which honked whenever its snout was squeezed. The children caught on to it quickly, and each stop usually resulted in a hundred small hands reaching in, wanting their own personal honk. The children shrieked in merriment at each squeeze. Needless to say, the pig expired before I even left the Mekong.

Several times a day, schools let the children return home for lunch and other breaks. The children either walked or bicycled home. Often the empty road I rode on was suddenly filled with grinning Lao boys wearing button-down white shirts and short pants, and smiling girls wearing the traditional Lao sarong, called *pha nung*. The children in Laos struck me as the happiest kids on the planet.

The kids on bicycles would usually ride along with me, yelling out the ubiquitous *Sabai dee*, as they rode, playfully circling around me, like dolphins frolicking around a small boat. I recalled places like Indus Kohistan in Pakistan, where children had stoned me as I tried to escape their taunts on my overloaded bike, and decided that Laos was paradise on wheels.

Several days into my ride, I reached the provincial capital of Savanna-khet, a major bastion of French trade during their rule over Indochina. Un-attended French colonial villas sat in silence along tree-lined boulevards. Today, the city is a crossroads for Thai and Vietnamese trade, but it retains a languid atmosphere.

I spent a few days relaxing in Savannakhet. On my first day, I hung out in the local park where old men sipped flasks of whiskey and slowly played *pétanque*, the outdoor bowling game inherited from the French. The next day was Christmas Eve, and I was invited to mass at St. Theresa's Catholic Church. I sat in the pews with the congregation of local and Vietnamese Catholics, sweating profusely in the humid air. I did what the rest of the congregation did, which included eating handfuls of *larb pet* (spicy duck salad) while listening to an interesting version of "O Little Town of Bethlehem."

That evening, back in my hotel, I joined a game of cards with several ladies of the night. They occupied most of the rooms in the otherwise empty hotel. The evening didn't strike me as incongruous at all—it was simply part of the pace and flow of discovery on a road trip. I had no real plans, so the unexpected and unorthodox became the norm rather than the exception. To attend a tropical Christmas mass in a Buddhist country, then play poker with local hookers, was part of the whims and winds of the open road. All

I could think of as I lay under my slowly rotating ceiling fan on December 24, was that traveling light in a warm climate, going from town to town and hotel to hotel, was truly an amazing way to take a bicycle vacation.

The following morning, I left the Mekong, and headed up Highway 9 into the Annamite Mountains. A traveler I had run into in Savannakhet told me that he had taken the bus down the road I was going up, and that the road's condition was nothing short of atrocious. I didn't put much stock in his remarks. After cycling through seas of deep mud and roads more akin to rivers in places like India, Tibet, and China, nothing could be that bad. Besides, the sun was shining and I had little weight on my bicycle to slow me down. I was traveling light.

The first 15 kilometers out of town I rode on sparkling new tarmac, which eventually narrowed into an area where work was still being done. I took the new lane (closed to vehicles), while the infrequent buses and cars had to negotiate a rather disagreeable-looking track. I congratulated myself on my luck, thinking I was certainly going to enjoy this ride into the mountains. And then the new lane abruptly ended, and I was faced with a rutted track of boulders, uneven washboard, and potholes the size of Volkswagens. I swerved right and left, avoiding the holes and rocks, while my bike pitched up and down the ruts. After 20 minutes of extremely rough riding, I heard a loud ping. Something felt odd in the steering. I looked down to discover one of the spokes in the rear wheel had popped. The wheel wasn't wobbling too badly, and there wasn't much I could do repair-wise, so I continued on.

Ten minutes later, another ping; spoke number two had sprung loose. Another 20 minutes of wobbling along and two more spokes were claimed by Highway 9. With four missing spokes the wheel was so out of whack that I had to release the rear brake to continue riding. Fortunately, the small village of Atsaphangthong appeared just ahead. The garage next to the hamlet's only noodle shop had several large wrenches, a refrigerator full of cold *Beer Lao*, and a mechanic lying in a hammock, an empty bottle of whiskey by his side. I gave the soused mechanic four new spokes, and went in search of a room for the night.

There was no accommodation available. The locals recommended a guesthouse in the next village on my map, but they cautioned me about the long steep climb ahead. I figured there was still enough light to do the 30-odd kilometers, so I went back to the garage, and dropped a grand total of 70 cents into the hands of the mechanic who was now back in his hammock, fast asleep. When he had found time to fix my wheel I'm not sure, but the

Cyclist's paradise: The road out of Laos and into Vietnam winds east with little traffic and amazing views. Lao Bao, Vietnam—2003. Photo: Dave Stamboulis

spokes seemed tight and the wheel was true.

I got about ten kilometers into the climb—a steep, horrid track, indeed—when another two spokes broke. At the top of the pass I assessed the damage and reckoned I could stand up off the saddle and just coast down toward my accommodations for the night.

The descent was joyous, but at the bottom of the hill there was no sign of a village. The road again rose abruptly, even steeper and more rutted than before. As I dismounted, I cursed the engineers who built this road. Even with a light load, pedaling was nearly impossible. I walked the bike uphill for ten kilometers until I saw lights. Dirty, fatigued, and not at all happy, I arrived well after dark in a small town atop a mountain. I noticed later that the town's name was Phu Khao, which I knew meant mountain in Lao, and I cursed my failure to recognize it on my map.

Phu Khao's one and only guesthouse was squalid. A set of rickety wooden stairs led up to several filthy rooms that smelled of unwashed truckers and fermented fish paste. A young boy, who appeared to be in charge, feigned sleep when I came to the reception desk. When he did acknowledge my presence, he informed me that the hotel was closed.

Too tired to try and speak Thai (the Lao could understand my Thai due to the languages' similarities, although I usually failed to understand them), I berated him in English, telling him that I was tired, hungry, and couldn't possibly go anywhere else, since my spokes were broken. My tantrum worked, and he begrudgingly unlocked a shabby room on the second floor.

The town's few eateries had shut for the night, but I found two cold, greasy pieces of fried chicken at a sidewalk vendor's stand. I bought a warm bottle of *Beer Lao*, and retreated to my room, where I spent most of the night awake shivering, as the blankets provided, along with my raincoat, weren't nearly enough to keep out the chilly mountain air.

In the morning, I gave a local mechanic the last of my spare spokes. He was so friendly and so enthralled by my freewheel removal tool (local freewheel removal was done with just a piece of flat metal and a hammer) that I offered it to him as a parting gift.

The road into the mountains picked up exactly where it had left off—full of ruts, holes, rocks, and absolutely nothing worth cheering about. My rear wheel agreed with this assessment, and my journal entry for the afternoon read, "This sucks . . . big time!"

One day and four more broken spokes later, I reached the town of Sepon, truly not in a good mood. Yet I suppose things could have been worse. If I'd arrived in Sepon 30 years earlier, I might have disappeared and later been classified as "missing in action."

Sepon, now a tiny, nondescript village near the Vietnam border, was smack in the middle of the famous Ho Chi Minh Trail, a series of paths, jungle tracks, and caves that served as a major supply route for the Viet Cong and North Vietnam's People's Army during the Vietnam War.

Between 1964 and 1973, the US attempted to prevent the influence of

North Vietnam's Communist government from taking root in Laos. Did we attempt to win the Lao over by building schools and hospitals? No, we employed a secret division of the US Air Force, the Ravens, to drop two million tons of ordnance on the country—that is one bomb every eight minutes, twenty-four hours a day for nine years. US taxpayers spent $6.5 billion dollars (or two million dollars a day over that nine-year period) to give Laos the distinction of being the most bombed nation in human history. To this day, unexploded ordnance remains in the area where the Ho Chi Minh Trail meets the Vietnam border—exactly the area where I was cycling.

Despite B-52 bombers dropping their loads to the tune of some 1000 sorties per day, the Trail was never shut down. The Viet Cong and the People's Army hauled tanks, trucks, and provisions the length of the country to keep their troops supplied and fortified. Stories abound about bizarre American attempts to disrupt the supply chain along the Trail. For example, some pilots dropped detergent bombs to make the trail too slippery to travel on, while others dropped hundreds of cases of Budweiser "bombs" in attempts to intoxicate the enemy.

The local bike mechanic did not have any spokes that fit my wheel. His were all too long or too short. I was out of spares and out of luck. I thought to myself just how random one's wheel of fortune could be in life. On my trip around the world, I traveled seven years and over 25,000 miles on some of the worst roads on the planet and never broke a single spoke, and here in Laos, in the space of a few days, I had broken nearly every spoke on my rear wheel.

Present day Sepon, I discovered, was still a rather grim spot—I spent a day wandering about, and later hired a motorbike driver to take me to an area just outside the city limits where rusting tanks sat half buried in the jungle, relics and reminders of a tragic past. Local schoolboys showed me some large bomb craters nearby, and piles of scrap metal and other debris that defiled the forest floor. At that point it occurred to me that I had a fairly large piece of scrap metal sitting back in my hotel room as well.

Exactly one week later, I was lounging in a rented beach chair on China Beach, just outside of Danang in Vietnam. A pretty Vietnamese woman wearing the traditional *ao yai* silk dress suit approached me. She spoke English well and said that I looked like a highly relaxed person with much travel experience. I asked her what gave her that impression, and she answered that other travelers she saw arriving in this area had huge backpacks and suitcases, and that they usually looked weary and unnerved. I, however, had simply arrived with a water bottle and a plastic bag of toiletries.

I laughed and replied, "I am David," extending my hand.

"I'm My Linh," she said.

"I used to be like the other tourists here," I said, "hauling too much luggage, and going from place to place with my guidebooks. But the road sometimes rises to meet us in strange ways."

"What do you mean by that?"

"Well, if you go to Sepon some day to visit the Ho Chi Minh Trail, look around at the tanks that got bombed and were left in the jungle; look some more and you might come across the rusting frame of a bicycle, sitting next to some tank parts. That's my luggage. I left it there. It's now a relic, perhaps a metaphor."

I reflected on the fact that when I rode around the world, I planned for everything that could possibly go wrong, and I carried the baggage that accompanied that planning for seven years and 25,000 miles. In the end, I did indeed reach the finish line, but I was so weary, both physically and mentally, that my arrival back home was rather anticlimactic. All I could think of was that I needed a holiday, a *real* holiday.

Here in Laos, I had planned for nothing, taken nothing with me, and had seen everything possible go wrong. I failed to reach the finish line, and I no longer even had my bike. Yet, lounging on a beach on the South China Sea, with nothing more than my toiletries and a water bottle, I was as happy as a lark. Perhaps "finishing" had nothing to do with enjoying the journey.

# Lost and Found in Boise, Idaho

**ADRIAN KIEN**

*If a sparrow come before my window I take part in its existence*
*and pick about the gravel.*
—John Keats, Letter to Benjamin Bailey, 22 November 1817.

Last week I was riding my bike past the cemetery near my house when I looked down and noticed something long and purple. I didn't think much about it as I rode past—just another piece of trash. It looked like a plastic grape juice bottle, the kind I used to get with my lunch as a kid, but then I thought, *What else looks like a grape juice bottle?* I turned my bike around to take another look, and sure enough it was an eight-inch long vibrator—right there on the sidewalk between the Warm Springs Cemetery and the junior high school. I picked it up delicately, as you would any prosthetic device, and took it home. What made this discovery special was that the previous week I had been riding in the foothills when I came across a life-like clip-on ear and a wax finger. Soon, I might have enough parts to make an artificial human.

Before I learned how to ride a bike (which wasn't until I was ten), I liked to collect junk. My grandfather and I would spend hours digging through the trash at the landfill near my family's cabin in Ashton, Idaho. The "cabin" was actually the farmhouse of an old barley farm. Also on the property were some old outbuildings and a small dump, which was actively used by the neighbors. In addition to the usual kitchen trash, it contained a variety of old farm equipment, water heaters and automobile parts—tetanus in all its pretty blades. While my grandfather was looking for usable parts, I believed I was uncovering the skeletons of robots and the hulks of spaceships. This was my heaven—a heaven that was greasy, rusty, sharp, rotting, and squirming with maggots—filled with the mystery of abandoned items from people's lives.

At night my parents would practice the old national-park pastime of spotlighting black bears that fed on the very same junk that my grandfather and I played in during the day.

A lot has changed in the last twenty years. I learned how to ride a bicycle. My family sold the cabin. My grandfather died. I now recycle. But as the poet Brenda Coultas says, "There is a shit load [of garbage] in this world," and that garbage is becoming more interesting every day. So it should come as no surprise that when I started mountain biking as a teenager in Missoula, Montana, it was more because of its potential for discovering artifacts left in the ditches of logging roads than for its adrenaline rushes. Though the two sometimes overlapped, like when was 15 and found a full bottle of Jim Beam.

It was August 1994. I was listening to Soundgarden on my Walkman while I rode along Hayes Creek through a cedar grove. I decided the trees would make a great place to stop and take a nap. So I wandered off the trail into the trees and found an old camp next to the creek. I kicked through a spent fire pit and some piles of trash, hoping to find someone's lost pocket knife or set of dentures, and then my foot connected with a bottle, a full bottle of bourbon! I took a large swig, put the lid back on, and buried the bottle beneath some bark. My nap was more pleasant than I expected. That summer I took about a dozen rides up Hayes Creek, and the routine was the same. I dug out the bourbon stash, took a swig, and then drifted off.

I now live in Boise, where I teach writing at the university while working towards my master's degree in poetry. When I'm not feeling inspired to write, I find myself riding a certain loop in the foothills above town. The loop starts by going up a gravel road that leads directly out of downtown and through what is known as Rocky Canyon. After following the road for about four miles, the loop branches off to some single-track trails, with all their inherent thrills and natural beauty. However, for me the real fun comes from slogging up the road through the canyon. After reading postmodernist theory all day, riding up this road is like meditating. It provides time for me to just breathe, sweat, ingest the landscape, and find trash and inspiration.

If you are not familiar with roads like Rocky Canyon in Boise, which so immediately link town and wilderness, their charm is similar to those moments between waking and sleeping that John Keats explores in "Ode to a Nightingale." Like Keats, I've found that valuable experiences happen at the thresholds of different environments. The road up Rocky Canyon permits the use of firearms, motorcycles, off-road vehicles, all-terrain vehicles, hunting, hiking, and bicycling. As a cyclist, I stand in wonder at this estuary of sorts, where people with radically different priorities are forced to merge, and, if not encounter each other, than at least see the evidence of each other's existence. For example, the car thieves who dump stolen cars along the road might have to look at stray water bottles and energy bar wrappers left by cyclists. While cyclists might find distraction in the fragrant blue smoke of two-stroke-engine vehicles or the sparkle of the beer bottles that the riders of those vehicles toss on the hillside. And the two-stroke-engine riders might have to encounter the evidence of unknown artists, who spray paint rock-canyon walls with obscenities, depictions of genitalia, and other failed communications.

"The others," as I call the non-hiking, non-cycling users of the wilderness, leave behind trash—and lots of it. And this is what I come to investigate. A few years ago while riding in the foot hills, I came across a note that said:

*To who finds my body,*

*Use this cell phone to call for help. Please also contact my family at XXX-XXXX. Tell them it concerns H_____ Foster, talk to M_____ Sanborn if you can. Thank you for your help and I'm sorry to inconviencience you. Sorry my spelling sucks.*

*Sincerily,*

*H_____ O'Casey Foster* [1]

With my head whirling up death scenarios, I went in search of the dead man rotting in the bushes. I have always wanted to own a human skull, but I couldn't imagine riding back into town holding a head. I left my bike by the trail and hiked through shrubs and up and over the ridge above me, looking for clues—a backpack or a cell phone. But I found nothing, not even an

---

[1] The actual names in this note have been changed.

empty cigarette pack or an old *Playboy*. All I had to go on was the note flapping in my hand.

I suddenly realized the responsibility I now had to the Foster family.

I said to myself, "Sorry Mr. Foster. Because of your spelling I cannot rescue you. I will just have to confiscate your note."

It was a cold and windy November day, so I put the note in my pocket and continued along my way. Besides, I had to keep my cardio going. When I got back to my office on campus, I decided to delay my responsibility to call the Fosters. I tacked the note to the corkboard above my desk, alongside another note that I had found while riding on campus, which referred to an unnamed man who "should be considered armed and dangerous." I looked at the Mr. Foster note every day for months, but I never had an urge to make the call and unravel what was still unknown to me. Though I was unaware of it at the time, my colleagues called the number on the note often but no one ever picked up.

On another ride, I found more remnants of "the others"—an abandoned Mercury Sable. The car's windshield was smashed to pieces, its doors were ripped nearly off their hinges, and trash oozed out of the car and onto the road. Among plastic bags of clothes, diapers, cookie wrappers, and mascara kits, I found a collection of letters addressed to a certain "Baby Boy."

Baby Boy, the letters revealed, was once a high-school stud, but now he was a 24-year-old working at the Albertsons flagship store in Boise, and apparently not destined for much more than that. The letters were written by the mother of his toddler, a woman for whom his interest drifted from hot to cold. The tone of the letters made me feel uncomfortable, because they forced me to remember all the love notes I used to want to send to girls in my math class in high school, when I thought love was some celestial fruit all dripping and juicy with nectar. In the pages of the letters scattered around the car, I saw an idealized sort of worship that any person would have a hard time living up to. Picking through the stuff on the ground and in the bushes, I was a detective-voyeur. I kept one ear open all the while, in case someone came up the road. Not that I was doing anything wrong, but I felt these letters made anybody who read them guilty of the crime of judging love.

I shoved the entire collection of letters between the back of my pants and my skin. I knew that if this was my disaster, I would want somebody to find it and at least share it with someone else. I hold onto the belief that the world will continue without me. That's why I always turn to marvel at my ski tracks and at the mountain on which I've just been riding. I want to imagine myself living the experience again.

When I got home I looked more closely at the collection of letters. Her desperate sparkle ink formed bubbly letters and simply constructed sentences: "I'm trying to make it like it was." And "Things, Baby Boy wants . . ." And "When you go off playing at night in the middle of nowhere, and leave me and the kids alone . . . I start to have panic attacks."

He wrote no return letters, but she did save his accounting notes: a list of all the items he had pawned, how much he got for each, and how much "intressed" he would have to pay to reclaim the items.

This collection of unsigned letters sat waiting for an author to sign them all, or perhaps to edit and shape the collection. And with lines like "I can honestly say I can't find anything to complain or even bitch about when it comes to you," and, "I'm trying very hard right now to impress you and be the girl and look good for you like I did when we first met," they needed an editor. But I edit and correct seventy essays a week written by my freshmen students. I had no intention of spending my time on this collection, so I brought the letters into class, and assigned my students the exercise of writing greeting cards using a line from the letters. The cards came out remarkably Hallmarkish.

After teaching one day, I decided to take another ride to lose myself in the canyon. Once there, I passed the spot where the Mercury, long since towed, had once been parked. The only sign of its existence was the dried trace of an oil leak leading to the creek. I pulled to the side of the road to adjust my seat height for the strenuous climb. As I tightened the seat collar it occurred to me that Baby Boy and Mr. Foster might in fact have been the same person.

At my feet lay the usual assortment of shredded underpants and empty Keystone Light cans, but there was also a damp notebook. On the cover was scribbled "Keep Out! Privit!" I felt guilty about opening it. Should I be looking at this, I wondered? Yes, I concluded—if not for my own pleasure, then as a sociologist. Its pages contained cutouts from porno magazines, poetry and erotic stories about underage drinking, marijuana, and a girl having an affair with her mom's boyfriend. The wild nights, the sex, the drinking, the drugs, the liberated libido—it was all meticulously detailed. Unpunctuated and misspelled, but detailed. Who among us has not secretly wished to have our lives exposed to a stranger? Finally, I had a document that explained how "the others" lived their lives in direct language, not in the coded, duplicitous, masking language of love that the "Baby Boy" letters were written in.

A collage of some of the author's finds—the Baby Boy Letters and artificial appendages.
Collage: Adrian Kien

I gave up any expectations about getting in a good ride and retreated further into the bushes so that I might study the journal more carefully. I pulled my bike with me, so I would be invisible to any casual passersby. The bushes bore a faint scent of urine. Was this marked territory? I sat directly on the ground anyway. Alone and hidden, I read about "My mom's boyfriend Curtis . . . an old hippie who always had bomb weed." Reading through the journal was like peering into the window of another person's life. Are these the stories that future anthropologists will cite to explain our civilization? I wondered.

At this point I heard a car groaning up the canyon. I quickly crammed the journal into my pocket, reminding myself not to put my fingers in my mouth until I'd washed them. The car was getting closer. I could hear "Every Rose Has Its Thorn" blaring from its tinny speakers as it slowed and then stopped just a few yards away. I was concealed in the bushes so I just sat there as quietly as I could while I heard someone get out. There was the sound of someone peeing, the smell of cigarette smoke. Somebody swore. I couldn't make out much from my hiding spot but the car had a familiar baby blue finish. Then the squeal of a loose belt and the car pulled away. I let out a gasp, waited a minute longer and then made my way back to the road, careful to avoid the fresh puddle. On the ground, new trash—an empty gallon milk jug and a *Playboy* from 1984.

Because I find so much on my rides and leave so little for others to find, I thought of a way to give back to *all* the people who use the wilderness area. I now ride my mountain bike wearing a shirt and tie whenever I venture into the Boise foothills. This way when I pass people on the trail they have something to discover as well. And like my discoveries, which usually leave me mystified and wondering about other people's lives, I hope to impart similar feelings to those who encounter me. "What an odd man," they will say. "Is he a lost Mormon missionary?"

No, I am on a mission to give the compelling mystery I find in your garbage back to you.

# Cycling in a New World

## STAN GREEN, JR.

Today the sky is clear and blue, the air sharp in a way that is rare in this damp, nearly tropical clime. I have insisted on taking a bike ride as a means to assert that all is not insanity, that the chaos and darkness of these last months are not absolute and all-pervasive. Cycling is a piece of the life I once knew, and I am determined to begin reclaiming that life today.

In the prolonged chaos and unrelenting darkness that followed Hurricane Katrina, the wish to ride my bike was driven not by fear of loss of form, nor by a physiological pining for missing endorphins, nor even by the aching memory of the sweet sensation of a smooth, tight machine beneath me. The wish to ride my bike was driven by my need to take hold of any small piece of the life that existed before that fearsome day when an unprecedented surge from the Gulf of Mexico inundated 80 percent of the city in which I was born.

My bike has hung untouched in the garage for almost six months. The brake calipers and down tube show the road tar I picked up on my last ride in early August. I'd foregone cleaning the bike that day because it hadn't been important; my father's precipitous decline in health had rearranged my priorities. Hurricane Katrina was pushing its way north through the Gulf of Mexico, two days from impact, when my dad relinquished his too-tenacious grip on life, his heart at last granting him peace from the malignancy that had wrapped its strangling tendrils around his spine. Tending to my father's needs in his last days, along with the growing need to plan for Katrina's imminent arrival, had relegated a tarnished bike to insignificance.

Now, I take the bike down from its hook and restore some air pressure to the tires. I slip a couple of bottles into the cages and roll down the driveway, clipping feet to pedals with little thought. Just over a year ago, my wife and daughters had surprised me on Christmas morning with this titanium-framed wonder, and I'd sat dumbstruck before the hearth with a holiday fire at my back and uncharacteristic wetness in my eyes while, contrary to all reason, snow began to drift from the gray December sky on the city of New Orleans.

My house stands in Metairie, a suburb just west of the city. Most of this area escaped the devastation, but house flooding to depths of half a foot and more was common. Construction materials and contractors are so difficult to come by that even six months after the flooding, many of my neighbors have not returned to their homes, residing instead in small trailers provided by the Federal Emergency Management Agency (FEMA). I spent the first weeks after the storm in Baton Rouge, serving as a liaison between the Corps of Engineers and FEMA during the mission to remove floodwater from the drowned city. However, the Corps' New Orleans District, where I've spent a quarter of a century as a civil engineer and project manager, soon called me home to assist in a special project. I lived in my damaged house during those dark days, sometimes not leaving the office until 3 A.M., making my tentative and occasionally fearful way through the eerie city for a short respite under my own roof, only to be back at my desk before the sun began to lighten the eastern sky. The demands of my work and this ruined city have only now let up enough to allow me time for a bike ride.

My bike glides down the driveway into the street, and I turn north out of old habit. Within five minutes of leaving the house I'm crossing into New Orleans over the 17th Street Canal, the waterway whose east-side floodwall failure inundated one of the city's most prosperous neighborhoods. The repaired breach is to my right as I coast down the bridge that makes a low arch over the canal. On my left proceeds the non-stop effort to construct giant sluice gates across the canal's mouth, to bar any future storm surge from entering the waterway. The homes that once stood near the failed portion of the floodwall were destroyed or forced from their foundations when the sea's massive push displaced both the wall and the levee in which it was founded, allowing water to fall like a sledgehammer on the neighborhood. I have a recurring vision of what it must have been like to witness the failure, to hear the first warning sounds from overstressed concrete and steel, to realize with sudden and consuming horror that failure was both inevitable and imminent, to see floodwall and levee pushed back, yielding to a flood that was instantly unstoppable.

As a quest for normalcy, this ride is already largely a failure, I quickly realize. Nothing is right. The pedestrian bridge on which I ordinarily cross the canal is gone, demolished to facilitate access for crews repairing the breached floodwall; as a consequence, I've been forced to deviate from my usual route. The avenue before me is lined with houses, but these are nightmare visions. Ugly brown lines mark various levels at which the water sat as it was slowly pumped out of the city and back into Lake Pontchartrain. In most cases, the highest line is at the eaves of single-story structures. Cars are covered in a grey film of sediment. Most of the cars have a window broken, a sign of the recovery teams who apparently searched every vehicle that succumbed to the flood. The houses, too, carry the searchers' sign, a painted "X" in whose quadrants are identified the organization that accomplished the search, the day on which they performed it, and what the results of that search were in terms of people rescued or bodies recovered.

I pedal along a street I've ridden countless times, but my surroundings offer no familiarity. The desolation is unspeakable. The quiet is unbearable. There is no one here to animate this place. And that odor lingers, compounded of many things but consisting chiefly of all-encompassing mold, punctuated with the occasional taint of rot, of something once living but now dead, returning by slow and measured degrees to its elemental form.

My route takes me to the New Orleans lakefront, the southern shore of Lake Pontchartrain. The traffic signals that control the intersection at which I turn left onto Lakeshore Drive are still not functional; there are more important tasks for a desperate city than repairing traffic lights in areas with few inhabitants and no commerce. I ride north toward the lake along the New Basin Canal, and just across that waterway I can see the sailboats that the storm surge tore loose from their moorings in the yacht harbor and tossed about as though they were children's toys, leaving them stacked in ungainly piles on docks and in streets, wherever they happened to come to rest when the dark waters receded. Ahead lies the old Coast Guard station, a lakefront fixture I've known since childhood, now canted crazily toward the water, the lighthouse that constituted its upper level neatly decapitated.

The road curves to my right, and I pedal east along Lakeshore Drive, a pleasant, four-lane parkway that meanders for five miles along the southern fringe of Lake Pontchartrain. To my left, the placid lake stretches to the horizon and beyond, merging seamlessly with the sky; in the distance, I can barely detect a portion of the Lake Pontchartrain Causeway, the 24-mile-long bridge that connects southern and northern shores.

The stepped seawall that fronts the lake has been undermined by the storm's power, and the street on which I ride has similarly suffered. Barricades have been erected to prevent motorists from inadvertently dropping their cars into one of the sinkholes that disfigure the pavement.

On my right, the old shelter house that offered protection from summer sun and afternoon thunderstorms for picnics and crawfish boils stands in near ruin, battered by winds and waves. On weekend mornings, the parking lot that serves the shelter ordinarily sports a fair number of vehicles that deliver bikes and their riders to the starting point for the Giro, an intense, 45-mile-long training ride that for years has served as the basis for many local cyclists' training programs. I have not ridden the Giro since August, and I long for the camaraderie of the group, for the physical, physiological, and mental demands of a high-speed paceline; I long for a Saturday morning devoted to a pursuit so ordinary as riding my bike with friends.

I've ridden countless miles on Lakeshore Drive, in summer heat, spring rains, and brutal winter winds that swept down on the occasional arctic blast; it is as familiar to me as any area in this city. However, there is little I find comforting now in this place of uprooted trees, bent streetlight standards, and cratered road surfaces. I've been on the lakefront for less than a mile when I turn south at Canal Boulevard, the street ramping up and over the hurricane-protection levee before dropping down into some prime New Orleans real estate.

One of the storm's ironies is that the properties nearest the lake generally suffered little. They are on the rim of the bowl in which the city lies. The flooding came not in a frontal attack over the lakefront levees; rather, it penetrated the interior by defeating the defenses along two of the major outfall canals through which the city is drained of rainfall. The water poured through the breaches and immediately sought the lowest ground in the center of the bowl, and in the days it took to fill that bowl, the storm waters receded from Lake Pontchartrain, emptying back through the tidal passes into the gulf. When equilibrium was reached between the water inside the city and that in the lake, the lake was many feet lower than it had been at the storm's height, and the city's highest ground, located mostly along either Lake Pontchartrain or the Mississippi River, was spared from the flood. Still, I'm less than a quarter of a mile from the lake when the houses again show signs of high water.

I continue pedaling to the south, crossing Robert E. Lee Boulevard. A few blocks to the west is Mount Carmel Academy, the high school from which my wife and all three of our daughters graduated, now a beacon of light in this darkened neighborhood. The nuns galvanized students, parents, and alumnae, who collectively scrubbed the place clean and made it ready within a few months to resume its mission, despite its having been steeped for many days in more than ten feet of black water. Before the storm, this area was prized for the convenience of its location and the appeal of its shady, tree-lined streets. Now, many houses are being offered for sale, but not so many are being sold. An uncommon valor is required to invest one's life in such uncertainty. The steadfast Carmelite nuns, however, will not give up their faith—neither in their God nor, apparently, in their darkened city.

I turn east at Harrison Avenue. Here two churches succumbed to the flood, although there are indications that they will return. From where, I wonder, will they draw their congregations? I pedal past coffee shops and restaurants and grocery stores in this area that had undergone a startling rejuvenation in the last few years. All is quiet, all is stained brown. No one is here.

Not far to the east I find myself in City Park, an immense tract of urban green space, home to golf courses and tennis courts and a small amusement park and perfectly wondrous gardens that include an extraordinary collection of ancient oaks, their limbs spread wide and often resting upon the ground. The park is going wild now, with no one to tend its hundreds of acres and no revenue to pay for the needed maintenance. I pass through the park and head north on Wisner Boulevard toward the lake along the west bank of Bayou St. John. For thirty-five years I have cycled to and from work along this boulevard. With the park on one side and the bayou on the other, there is no development for miles; Wisner is one of the most bicycle-friendly routes in the New Orleans area. There is something comforting about being here on my bike, on this avenue I've ridden so many times. When Annie, my middle daughter, began to ride, she'd sometimes call me before I left my office near the Mississippi River, and we'd arrange to meet at the end of Wisner, where it intersects Lakeshore Drive, so that together we might do an out-and-back lap of the lakefront before dinner. When, I wonder, will we ever do that again?

I leave Wisner Boulevard, arcing into a right turn onto Filmore Avenue, cruising over the bridge that crosses the bayou, into the neighborhood in which I was raised. Most of these homes have brick-veneer construction, and the bricks, for some reason, often do not show a water line. The water was eight feet deep in places, maybe deeper. Some of these homes have been gutted—stripped of every interior feature save the wooden framing. Gutting is an awful thing, an ugly word to describe an ugly process. Ruined furniture is carted out and dumped on the curb—desks warped, sofas grown gray with mold, dressers spilling their contents. Carpets are cut into pieces, rolled up, and discarded with the furniture. Sheetrock is torn from the walls and added to the pile, and streets subsequently assume a coating of white from the dust. Cabinets are pulled free from kitchens and bathrooms; plumbing fixtures are ripped from their pipes. Clothes fouled by soaking for weeks in an awful stew of salt water, sewage, pesticides, gasoline, cleaning chemicals, and who knows what are cast onto the growing pile. Children's toys and dolls and boxed board games, the accumulated wealth of Christmases and birthdays, are toted to the curb. A family's entire life is laid out for public inspection. In this Gentilly neighborhood I see no such piles today, though. I pass near the old home of a boyhood friend, and I remember the times Jim and I would trundle his wooden skiff along Filmore Avenue to the bayou, where we'd fish for the occasional bass. The house is now a ruin, of course.

I turn left onto Paris Avenue and head north once more, approaching the destination to which I suppose I've been subconsciously drawn since gliding down my driveway miles ago. A couple of blocks ahead, I see rising high into the sky the slender, graceful spire of St. Frances Cabrini church, the cross at its top crazily awry. The church is a modern architectural wonder. The four legs on which the spire stands rise from the church's interior, joining in arches high above the floor, forming a golden dome above the altar. My father, working with many of the other men of the parish, had helped apply gold leaf to the underside of that spectacular dome.

Adjacent to the church is the elementary school I attended. As a child, I had watched from various classrooms as the church was being built, brick by brick. In that sanctuary I had worshipped my God as an altar boy, serving at Masses and weddings and funerals. Nearly thirty years ago, on a cold December night, Patti and I had been married there, standing beneath that golden dome, before an altar resplendent in Christmas poinsettias. But there will be no more marriages in this church, I think, no more baptisms, no more funerals; never again will that magnificent pipe organ fill a Christmas Eve with its profound and wondrous sounds, nor will the solemnity of an Easter vigil service celebrate the glorious mystery of the risen Christ.

And there, across the street from the school, is the house—the house in which I lived for almost a quarter of a century, the house in which my father mercifully died two days before Katrina unleashed her fury on the south-eastern United States. Like so many other brick structures, it carries no mark on its face. The once beautiful lawn, the lawn I tended with such diligence and pride in my youth, is set with scraggly weeds, struggling with one another for dominance now that the grass is gone. The sidewalks and driveway are covered with sediment deposited by the flood, caked and cracking now like a dry lake bed beneath a summer sun. On the roof, at the spot where a rescue boat landed while the flood still lapped at the eaves, is painted a symbol denoting that no one had been found taking refuge in the attic of this house. Two of the windows that face the street are broken out; a curtain hangs in one of them. The other served as the point of entrance when my brother Kenny, our sister Kathy, and I made salvage expeditions. The front door, its hardware corroded and its panels swollen by immersion in salt water, could be opened only with an axe. We'd avoided that method of entrance, having no wish to facilitate access to the house until we'd recovered whatever we might. There are, after all, looters who don't hesitate to enter homes at random and take away whatever of value they might find. The thieves have no fear of being apprehended. No one lives here. The streets are empty.

I lean my bike on the porch and climb through the window. Inside, it's as though a giant hand had ripped the house from its foundations and given it a thorough shake. Nothing is upright; nothing is where it ought to be. Furniture floated for more than two weeks in this flood, and my father's orderly interior design was rearranged in the most haphazard manner imaginable. The smell of mold is still strong; its splotchy patterns cover the walls like an abstract wallpaper. I'm standing in the living room, where, on my first post-Katrina trip into the house, I had found my parents' wedding album. It had been submerged in the flood, but by some miracle only the photos on the first and last pages were ruined. The rest remain pristine. There was something surreal about the photographs of the young bride and groom—the beautiful piano teacher who'd fallen in love with her student; the handsome airman who, having parachuted from his flaming aircraft as it plummeted from the skies above occupied France, made good his escape from a German prison camp and returned safely home, and who, on a whim, thought he'd have a try at learning to play the piano.

We've made no effort to clean up, given no thought to gutting this house. The refrigerator lies on its back in the kitchen, still filled with the rotting remnants of the few things that had been in it on that Saturday morning when Dad died. Refrigerators came to have a special place in the lives of New

Orleans area residents after Katrina, for there are few experiences quite so memorable as opening a box full of perishable food that has not been cooled in days, weeks, or even months. Many refrigerators, wrapped with duct tape to seal them shut and placed curbside with the fervent hope they'd soon be carted away, were painted with slogans. One on Kenny's street had read, "The horror, the horror," Kurtz's dying words (in Conrad's *Heart of Darkness*) as he considered the consequences of his misspent life, but in this case simply an accurate description of the box's terrible contents—and of the city itself. The kitchen table is upended, and I wonder if beneath it, pressed into the dried sediment, I might find the log we'd kept of Dad's last weeks, listing dosages of medicines administered, noting times of wakefulness and sleep, as if the maintaining of meticulous records might somehow lend an insight that could change the inexorable progress of decline.

I make my way to his bedroom, treading clumsily on cleated shoes, clambering over what was once furniture but is now nondescript rubbish. The door is blocked by Dad's heavy bureau, lying on its back, wood warped and splitting. One day we'll have to search this room thoroughly, sifting through the debris for whatever mementos we might hold precious. A few days before the storm, we'd removed from the house the portrait of Mom that had stood on Dad's bureau for as long as I could remember, along with the photograph of Dad that had been on Mom's dresser until her death in 1993; the latter Kenny had located after a long and diligent search while Dad lay comatose, unable to advise us that his picture lay hidden at the bottom of his sock drawer. The bed in which he died is scarcely recognizable as such, and I brush away a tear as I think of him lying there, awakening only when the pain drove him to consciousness, chest barely rising and falling with his shallow breaths, his heart futilely beating its relentless rhythm. His heart was strong, and it would not stop. It just would not stop.

I turn away and return to the living room so that I can climb back out onto the porch; after the fetid air within the house, my lungs are crying for the cool, fresh January air. A few blocks away, my sister Kathy's house stands in decay, and a half mile on from there our brother Robert's house is similarly devastated. Life has lately presented Robert with an array of challenges. The storm broke down the frail defences that had kept his emotional demons at bay, and we don't know whether he'll ever be able to live on his own again. Still, the sun ascends the crystalline, winter-blue sky with utter unconcern for those on whom it shines. In a few months, I think, spring will come. The season of new life, of reborn hope, will come even to this desolate city, and ravaged trees will present to a forlorn world their tender leaf buds, and sweet-scented flowers will fill gardens with brilliant, careless color.

I wonder if the coming spring will carry with it the season's customary promise of hope. I long for that hope in a way that I cannot easily express. Hope was once easy and natural; now, in the face of a devastation so widespread and so complete as to strain one's ability to comprehend, it requires an unprecedented act of faith. What once was normal never will be normal again. A bike ride through New Orleans can never be what it was before August 29, 2005. Something else lies ahead, something undetectable, something unknowable—a new normal.

# The Gowda and His Bicycle

**SHASHI KADAPA**

In my village, Aminabhavi (in the Dharwad district of southwest India), we have two community wells, one for the upper castes and one for the lower. Most of the houses are built of mud and are without piped water or electricity. The village is famous for its ancient temple of the Yellama deity, which stands just above the square on a small hill. The caste system, village, and temple are the same today as they were 1,000 years ago. There is one major difference between now and then: bicycles have taken over from the bullock[1] cart as the main form of transportation.

I rode a bicycle until I completed graduate school. Once I began working as a computer programmer, at the age of 30, I was able to buy a car. I have not touched my bicycle since then. Yesterday, as I drove down the hill that leads to the square, I saw an old man sitting under the banyan tree on his *charpoy* (wooden cot), smoking tobacco from a hookah. The old man reminded me of my great-grandfather, Ajja. He used to sit under that tree, resting on his *charpoy* with a pot of *arrack* (homemade liquor), and tell stories to the children. The majestic branches of the old banyan tree have presided over 300 years of daily storytelling sessions. It is in these sessions

---

[1] Hindu Indians regard cows as the sacred incarnation of the goddess Kamadhenu. They are used for milk, but are not eaten or otherwise harmed. Bullocks (bulls) are also regarded as holy and not eaten. They are used to pull carts and to till much of the farmland across India.

The common bullock cart has not changed in hundreds of years of use, and is still one of India's main forms of transportation, along with bicycles, cars, and trains. Aminabhavi, Dharwad District, India—January 2007. Photo: Shashi Kadapa

that the local history is passed down.

My favorite story Ajja told was about how our village got its first bicycle. The events took place in 1923, just after Ajja returned from service in World War I. I am presenting his story exactly as he told it to me.

The Gowda[2] was a massive, big-bellied, hard-headed feudal landlord. He was also head of the *panchayat* (the village council). His election term was due to expire soon, and he was looking for a good publicity stunt to capture the imagination of the villagers so he could get re-elected with ease.

One day he ran into Ajja in the *arrack* shop which was (and still is) the center for men's social exchanges. Ajja told him, "Gowda, bring a bicycle to the village and you will win the election."

"What is that?" the Gowda asked.

"It is a new *yantra* (machine) used by the British to move around. You have not seen it, because no one around here has ever seen one or even heard of one."

---

[2] Gowda is a common nickname or surname extension for feudal landlords in India. Typically, the name is given to those who are hot-tempered and bull-headed, yet naïve, large-hearted, honest, and easily manipulated.

The Gowda, who had a fiery temperament, went directly to the post office and sent a money order to the postmaster of Dharwad Town Fort with instructions to purchase a bicycle and deliver it to him.

When the bicycle arrived, the Gowda issued a diktat to the village farmers and those of the surrounding hamlets, requesting their presence at a special presentation. The farmers, a dirty, tattered lot, gathered around in the square, waiting and watching as a bullock cart wound down the hill carrying an odd shaped-gunnysack. The bullocks heaved to a halt, snorting and panting, at the crowd's edge. The crowd leaned and pushed forward as the Gowda's henchmen offloaded the sack.

Just as the Gowda went to open the sack, his wife screamed "Evil eyes![3] The Yellama deity must be propitiated before the sack is opened. We must go to the temple." The Gowda was angry with his wife for interrupting his publicity stunt. Nonetheless, he led the crowd up the hill to the temple. The priest, known to take hefty *dakshina* (offerings), said he could only perform the ceremony if he was given the proper items. So the Gowda sent his henchmen to nearby vendors to purchase six coconuts, a block of *jaggery* (raw sugar), and three measure of *paddy* (raw, unhusked rice). The priest took the offering—or the payment, as the Gowda saw it—and then performed a purification ceremony.

The *kirtankar* (a religious singer who has taken a vow of poverty) began beating a drum and soon the villagers erupted into song. As was their habit, each set his or her own pace and pitch and soon the mass of voices sounded like a herd of pigs being slaughtered. The noise alarmed the bullocks, and they began to snort and stomp their feet in the dust.

With the hidden *yantra* in the gunnysack now purified, the Gowda's henchmen slowly removed it. The crowd leaned and pushed and chattered among themselves as they jostled for a good view. The contraption had two wheels that looked somewhat like small bullock cartwheels. They were joined to each other by two shiny gun barrels. The contraption also had two arms coming from its bottom section and a handle to hold on to. And, most strangely to the onlookers, it had a small horse's saddle.

The Gowda ripped off a small piece of paper attached to the bicycle

---

[3] Evil Eyes is an expression for a Hindu belief that once a person acquires a valuable, useful, or beautiful possession, jealous people will yearn for it. The jealousy, in turn, can bring bad luck and the eventual destruction of the possession. Temple priests often perform rites to ward off the Evil Eye.

frame. He looked at it and then summoned the schoolmaster, who was the only one in the village who could read.

The schoolmaster took the paper, adjusted his glasses, and asked for a glass of hot water. When it was brought, he sipped it, cleared his throat self-importantly, and began reading. "Raleigh Bicycle. Important parts of the bicycle are handlebars, wheel, pedal, brake, and seat. To ride, climb on the seat and push pedals. To stop, press brakes."

The crowd started talking among themselves.

"How do you climb on?

"What happens if you cannot climb down?"

"Why has god given us legs and bullock carts?"

"It's a trick! The Britishers are trying to kill us with this contraption!"

"Why do you blame the Britishers? Blame the Gowda for bringing it to our village!"

The machine perplexed the Gowda. His total ignorance of how to ride it, and his fear held him immobile for a moment. Yet he knew he had to ride it in front of the people; his reelection was contingent on that.

My great-grandfather Ajja, just 22 years old at that time, told the Gowda that the *yantra* was to be ridden like a horse. The Gowda touched the ma-

The *panchayat* (the elected local council) meets to discuss village concerns. In the 1920s, it met under the banyan tree in the square of Aminabhavi, but now it meets in front of the wrestling gym. The walls of the gym are painted with images of Hanuman the monkey god; notice the door, built intentionally small to force wrestlers to bend low when entering, as an act of submission to Hanuman. Dharwad District, India—January 2007. Photo: Shashi Kadapa

A market vendor sells fresh garden herbs in the main square of Aminabhavi. Dharwad District, India—January 2007. Photo: Shashi Kadapa

chine, and seeing that it did not bite or kick, gestured to his two henchman to steady it. Then he raised one massive leg and placed his ample bottom on the seat.

The crowd roared in appreciation of this feat. Yelling and encouragement filled the air. The Gowda beamed with pride. He moved the handlebars this way and that way and noticed that the front wheel also moved.

Someone in the crowd compared him to a royal prince who had killed a tiger while riding a horse. Just as the cheers began to subside, the Gowda, by chance or instinct, pressed the bell. Again the crowd responded with hoots and hollers. The bell sounded like the small cymbals the *kirtankars* use. But soon the crowd grew tired of the spectacle of Gowda twisting the handlebars and ringing the bell. Their cheers fizzled to a mumble.

The Gowda asked Ajja for instruction on how to ride. But Ajja had only seen a bicycle being ridden. He had never even touched one himself. So Ajja told him to do what the instructions said: "Press down on the pedals."

The Gowda obliged and pressed down with all his might on both the pedals at the same time. When it would not budge he yelled to Ajja, "The cursed machine is broken." The Gowda stomped down again, but to no avail.

"Let the priest ring the bell to summon the goddess!" shouted a villager. So the priest rang the bicycle bell, while the Gowda pressed for a third time with all his might on both the pedals. The bicycle didn't move an inch.

Then Ajja was struck with an idea. He had seen the British soldiers glide down inclines without pushing the pedals. The temple was built on a small hill, with an incline that allowed the temple chariot to be wheeled down with ease during festivals. Ajja explained the solution to Gowda, and together they wheeled the bicycle to the incline.

When the Gowda looked down the steep hill, his stomach churned with uneasiness, and he began cursing Ajja for suggesting this idea. His fear of heights and the terror of falling clashed with his desire to become the local hero. With the entire village and his numerous cowherds watching, the Gowda was determined not to give up and risk being called a coward.

While choice curses escaped his lips, inwardly he prepared for certain death. He scowled at Ajja. "Whatever injury I receive from this, you shall receive threefold!"

The priest and the henchmen gave the Gowda a mighty shove and the bicycle began rolling down the slope. The Gowda sat tight for a few feet. Electricity ran through the crowd. The villagers could sense that something great was happening. But as the bicycle picked up speed, the Gowda felt the first pangs of falling. The machine began to tilt to one side. The Gowda clutched the handlebars and pulled them in the opposite direction of the fall. But the action did not get him back into a vertical position.

Ajja shouted, "Apply the brake! Apply the brake!" But, the Gowda did not know what the brake was, where it was, or what it was supposed to do.

The Gowda screamed as he attempted to jump off the machine, but his *dhoti* (the traditional garment of a rectangular cloth wrapped around the legs and knotted at the waist) got caught in the chain. He and the bicycle went crashing into the crowd and the people screamed and stampeded in all directions. The *yantra* flipped abruptly to the ground. The Gowda rolled over three times down the remainder of the hill, until he landed face-down in a fresh pile of cow dung. The cacophony of the shouting crowds was too much for the nervous bullocks. Their normally placid expressions turned wild as they released great snorts and broke their tethers. They charged into the bright colors of the crowd.

Among those rammed by horns were the Gowda's portly wife and the equally plump priest. The bullocks next ran helter-skelter at the vendors of the market, destroying stalls and overturning baskets of fruit and goods.

The schoolmaster showed remarkable agility as he shimmied up the flagpole and surveyed the scene. In the marketplace, some hens broke free

To this day, the practice of two people gliding a cyclist along still survives in the village of Aminabhavi. Dharwad District, India—January 2007. Photo: Shashi Kadapa

of their destroyed cages, and the village layabouts were quick to catch them, wring their necks, remove their tail feathers and stuff the birds under their turbans. Urchins pocketed soap bars, sweets, and anything they could pick up, while the vendors beat them with broom handles.

At last the bullocks calmed down and order returned. The Gowda, thought to be dead, moved one thick leg and began cursing for water. The cow dung was washed from his face. His right leg had massive bruises and scrapes, while blood oozed from cuts in his scalp.

The Gowda ordered his henchmen to find his bullocks and prepare the cart. His wife, who lay nearby, screamed, "I have been gored by the bullocks! What about me?"

The Gowda's attempt to ride the *yantra* was, however, not over. His shame at his poor performance possessed him to keep trying until he learned to ride. Furthermore, he still needed to prove to the villagers that he could ride the machine. Now and then, loud noises, crashes, and earthy expletives could be heard from the inner courtyard of the Gowda's house. As he devoted many hours to the bicycle, he became more obsessed and forgot his threats to Ajja.

And each time the Gowda appeared in public, he had a different set of bruis-es. The local quack visited his house regularly.

A few months passed, and one day, while the market place was bustling, a loud blast from a conch shell, along with frenetic beating of cymbals and drums, announced that someone important was coming. As one, the vil-lagers in the street turned towards the sound. They saw the Gowda on his bicycle, flanked by his two henchmen, who held the handlebars firmly and glided the *yantra* onward. The Gowda's wife was seated precariously on the rear carrier rack as she clutched his massive waist. The Gowda wore a brand new *dhoti*, a pressed shirt, and an enormous turban that almost covered the bruises on his temple. His moustache was twirled to a fine point, and he reeked of liquor. The henchmen had been threatened with a sound beating if they let go of the bicycle. His petrified wife had been warned that she would be sent back to her father's house if she refused to sit on the carrier rack.

The all-important concept of maintaining one's balance while riding the bicycle was unknown to the Gowda. He had improvised the best he could. And because no one in the village had ever seen a bicycle being ridden, they thought that this was the proper way to ride one. The villagers applauded at the heartening sight of the victorious Gowda. And he was re-elected as the head of the *panchayat*.

Soon others in the village placed orders for bicycles, and they too hired henchmen to glide them around on their new *yantras*. The bullocks snorted, stomped, and acted erratically when the machines came near them. But as more *yantras* came into the village, the bullocks became accustomed to the sight of them. Soon the bullocks merely gazed at the wheeled contraptions with blank expressions while they chewed their cud. We don't know exactly what a bullock thinks, but perhaps these bullocks were thankful that people were now pushing each other around on carts. And perhaps the sweating henchmen pushing the bicycles wondered why they had been hired to do the work of a bullock.

# Bicycles and Bagpipes

## ERIC PINDER

I decide to slow the pace a bit. Even now, my bicycle slides across the black-top as smoothly as a puck on ice; gravity has forgotten me. As I ride out of the shadows on Little Station Road and pedal across U.S. Route 9, the temperature jumps a degree or two—a small but remarkable difference. Under a roof of maple leaves, the chillier breezes of morning linger on back roads all day long, while the naked sun and the fumes of cars blast Route 9 with the intense heat of summer.

I wait for a gap in the line of traffic, then kick back at the gravel, gliding across the road. A horn honks. Briefly, the whining engines drown the grumbles of the wind. The roar of traffic rises sharply in pitch to the south, then sinks into a growl as cars, pickup trucks, and semis streak past me—a classic example of the Doppler effect. Quickly, I click up a gear and reenter the quiet, shady forest on the other side. The road narrows to a dimly lit tunnel of trees.

Today, sweating under the hot sun, on the outskirts of Amherst, Massachusetts, I have sought shady back roads as an alternative to busy Route 9. There's no hurry. As I ride along, kernels of weathered gray pavement crunch under my tires. The ground is a blur.

Breezes mutter wordless phrases in the leaves. A squirrel, startled by the swift, silent appearance of my bicycle, drops his acorns at the side of the road and leaps, panicked, into a maple tree. He pauses halfway up the trunk and watches me with tiny black eyes.

Up, up, up. I stand and grind my way up the hill, swerving into the center of the road. The pedals no longer turn smoothly, but stop and start, crank and grind. My legs must work each step, like a hiker advancing up a steep stretch of mountain.

At the top of the hill, the road levels off and the ride becomes easy and pleasant. A soft breeze pushes against my back like a strong, invisible hand coasting me effortlessly along; I feel as if I could coast uphill. Soon the branches spread apart over the road, opening again for the sun.

Summer heat dissolves the breeze, and the push at my back falters; I must pedal. On a wide, empty stretch of road ahead, there is a dark shimmer like a pool of water—a common mirage. It soon fades. What looks like water is just a reflection of the sky, bounced toward our eyes by a thin layer of warm air above the asphalt.

That mirage, like the Doppler shift of car engines on Route 9, belongs to the realm of physics. A stint as a weather observer at the Mount Washington Observatory trained me in such details. The physicist Ernest Rutherford once remarked that everything is divided into two categories: "physics and stamp collecting." So cycling is a branch of physics, too, I suppose, unless you happen to be riding to the post office.

Now on a flat stretch, I just pedal one rotation and glide, pedal and glide, resting after the mile-and-a-half climb. Then in the distance, I hear . . . bagpipes? The strains of music drift closer. There is a clearing not far ahead, where strong wind skims across a pond, kicking up tiny waves. On the crest of each inch-high ripple gleams a golden flicker of sunlight; a million tiny suns dance on the water. This natural phenomenon does not normally produce bagpipe music. What is going on here?

The lake sweeps around the road on both sides. Bullfrogs clear their throats in the tall grass along the shore. A man sits there with his back against a tree, his eyes hidden in the shade of a Red Sox cap. He is throwing clumps of sandwich to some ducks who have waddled away from the pond in search of tastier food. The ducks shuffle comically on their feet in front of the man, their eyes focused on the scrap of bread in his hand. He tosses it, and the flock scurries back to snatch it off the ground. They quack for more, but the shriek of bagpipes overwhelms them.

On a hill above the pond stands a tall, brown-haired man in a kilt, piping the strains of a highland bagpipe waltz, "Skye Boat." I recognize the tune. Far from southern New England, I have ridden, quite unexpectedly, straight into the hills of Scotland. What happened to the ocean along the way, I wonder?

Is this Brigadoon, come alive for a day? The bagpipes soon fade note by note behind me.

I'm almost home, pedaling up the last small hill when a German shepherd darts out from behind a parked minivan, teeth bared, barking ferociously.

I've met this dog before. Whether he smells me coming or hears the whir of bike tires on the pavement I don't know, but he's always ready to serenade me with the usual canine pleasantries. "Rowr! Rowr! Rowr!" The German shepherd growls and snarls. It runs at me full-bore, ears flat, until at the last moment the metal chain leash stops him short with a violent jerk.

Wolf blood runs in this dog's veins. He's a predator. I always half-expect him to have the strength to pull the garage he's tethered to right out into the street.

Today's attempted attack starts no differently from all the rest. "Rowr! Rowr! Rowr! Rowr ... then *ping!*"

*Ping?*

A second later, the beast's jaws clamp shut around my leg. "Hey!" I yell. "No!"

The dog's owner sits on the porch. Hearing my voice, he glances up to see his pet beast chewing on my femur. He frowns, then calls out helpfully, "Okay, who let Rusty loose?"

"The dog let himself loose, pal," I want to say, but my teeth are clenched. The dog's lunge ripped the leash's metal ring right out of the garage wall.

"Hey!" I manage to say again.

"Rowr?" says Rusty. What a name for a pet wolf. Remind me to get a tetanus shot. Having caught me at last, Rusty doesn't seem to know what to do next and releases me. One bite is all he takes. I increase my cadence and pedal home. I wheel my bike up my driveway past my car, which has grass growing through the bumper gaps. Inside, I pull up my pant leg. The wound feels worse than it looks.

For years, that hilly street where Rusty prowls has been a favorite place to end my daily ride, with a scenic view at the top and then a relaxing down-hill coast to my front door. But the dark purple bruise on my leg will remind me to find an alternate route.

Such encounters are why I'd rather ride in woods and on rural back roads. Fewer cars and trucks, no barking dogs. But even there, a bicyclist is not necessarily safe. The shade of the New England forest hides creatures with sharper teeth and bigger appetites than any German shepherd.

One afternoon, while riding outside the village of Gorham, New Hampshire, close to the Maine state line, I cycled straight into five hundred snarling pounds of fur, fang, and claw. The bear towered over me, glaring down with black eyes, and I could tell there was just one thing on its mind: lunch.

Well, okay, I'm exaggerating a little. I was tired that day, riding slow, and my gaze was fixed on the pavement. It's true that the bear was only a few feet away, almost close enough to touch. But before I noticed the animal, it had already turned and started to run. All I saw was its furry back vanishing into the trees. The animal heard me coming and fled. The whole encounter lasted three seconds. End of story.

Statistics show that the familiar black bear, *Ursus americanus*, weighs eight ounces at birth, up to five hundred pounds as an adult, and commonly grows to unrealistic, elephantine proportions once a storyteller gets hold of him.

I still prefer to ride my bike rather than drive, when time and weather allow. Why shouldn't I? Bears fear me. Dogs don't like how I taste. And toothy animals aside, the experience sure beats sitting in traffic staring through the frame of a windshield at the bumper of the next car in line.

I know it's easier to tap a gas pedal in a car than to pedal up a hill. And perhaps, if I wanted to exercise merely for the sake of exercise, a stationary bicycle would be more convenient. But this is what I'd miss—the wind, the trees, the unexpected. No indoor fitness regimen has ever provided ducks, bears, bagpipes, and the woods of New England to supplement push-ups and sit-ups. For now, so long as I must suffer to stay in shape, this is how I prefer to pay the piper.

# Contributors

**HEATHER ANDERSEN** is a bicycle-tour leader and a writer. She is currently working on a book about her experience cycling in southern Africa, a trip she embarked on after serving as a Peace Corps volunteer in the tiny country of Lesotho. She has worked for bicycle-advocacy groups in Washington, D.C. on both the national and local levels and has never owned a car. A traveler at heart, she has lived on three continents and cycled on five. She has cycled more than 100,000 miles, including more than 13,000 leading and working on tours.

**CARLA AXT-PILON** is a middle-school teacher living in Naperville, Illinois, with her husband, two daughters, two cats, and three bikes. She has competed in triathlons since 1999. When not training or racing, she gardens, and monitors amphibians for the Springbrook Prairie Forest Preserve. This summer she hopes to complete six triathlons, including her first half Ironman . . . with loosened releases on her pedals!

**LUKE BAUER** is a 25-year-old part-time college student, part-time traveler, and full-time writer/photographer. He currently lives in Madison, Wisconsin, but tries to get out of Madison as much as possible to ice climb, rock climb, ride his bicycle long distances, and generally enjoy the outdoors.

**BOB BURT** took on nine cars and lost every time in his seven-year bike-messenger career in Pittsburgh and Seattle. He put an untold number of auto mechanics' children through school by working his way around the lower 48 living in a '78 van, trying to sell photographs to people who didn't want to buy. Then he went to Alaska, where seven fishing seasons in the Bering Sea yielded more casts and stitches. Now he's changing diapers in the Pacific Northwest, working as a sub-par unlicensed, unbonded, uninsured contractor, and wondering why his back hurts.

**JACQUES DEBELLE** suffers from severe ADHD, which has inevitably led him to commit a number of mischievous acts. He grew up in Canberra, Australia. He has a four-year-old son named Oliver. He has road-raced on and off for the past 20 years. He is currently unemployed and seeking work in the fitness industry. His knee requires major reconstruction after a soccer incident 10 years ago; hence he no longer participates in any competitive sports. After his operation Jacques hopes to play social tennis, go running, and cycle recreationally.

**EUGÉNE ETSEBETH** is a recently married 37-year-old business analyst from Johannesburg, South Africa. He started riding his bike competitively at the University of Port Elizabeth when he was 19. Now, he enjoys the occasional cycle-touring holiday in Europe. He writes for *Bicycling South Africa* and other publications. While cycling, he has been shot at with a BB gun, hit with palm fronds, attacked by a drunken Dane, swerved at by a bus, and mugged. He has also broken a hip in a crash, but he wouldn't stop riding his bike for anything.

**MICHAEL FEE**'s final business-school project was writing a business plan for a bike-touring company with Greg LeMond. In the course of developing the plan, Michael and Greg worked closely together, including following the Tour de France for ten days. So while Michael started business school on a rough note, he completed it by riding the route to Sestrieres in advance of Lance Armstrong and the peloton (and without a crash)! Since then, Michael has worked with various education programs, and today runs a small company that teaches foreign languages to children. He lives in Oakland, California, with Karen and his three kids, and manages to struggle through Category 3 road races from time to time.

**ROLAND GOITY**'s stories have been published or are forthcoming in *Fiction International*, the *Bryant Literary Review* and the *Talking River Review*. He is currently editing a literary anthology on rock music and culture, and teaching writing workshops in Menlo Park, California. He received an MFA in Creative Writing from San Diego State University.

**STAN GREEN, JR.** is a native of New Orleans and a lifelong resident of the area. He and his wife Patti have three daughters, whom he characterizes as the scientist-adventurer, the nurse-cyclist, and the artist-runner. He has degrees in English, biology, and engineering, and has worked for 26 years as a project manager for the U.S. Army Corps of Engineers in New Orleans. Stan has been an avid cyclist for more than 35 years, although in the wake of Hurricane Katrina the exigencies of his job have left little time for his bicycle.

**MIKE HAINSWORTH** began cycling in the rural lowlands of eastern North Carolina with the encouragement of his cousin, who owned Right Bros Bike Shop in Greenville. After a summer of interval-training induced by dogs chasing him on farm roads, he won the North Carolina junior state road race championships in 1985. He raced for several amateur teams in the early 1990s, including the Tulsa Cyclones, which put him in the National Cycling League, a dangerous, no-rules criterium series developed specifically for ESPN. However, he gave up a chance at going professional to take care of his cancer-stricken mother. Recently, he has won several Category 1 and Pro Category races in Washington State, and he rides for the Dewar's Scotch team based in Santa Rosa, California. He lives in Seattle where he bangs nails as a contractor.

**SHASHI KADAPA** was born and raised in a small village in the Dharwad district of India. His earliest childhood memories include long bicycle rides perched on the handlebars next to his older brother, while his father pedaled and his mother and sister sat on the rear carrier rack. The bicycle was his family's only means of transportation, and they rode like this (all on one bicycle) to country fairs, the cinema, or wherever else they wanted to go. The revered family heirloom was handed down from grandfather to father to elder brother and then to Shashi (much to the envy of his friends). He rode the bicycle through rain and mud, through harvests and droughts, through mango orchards and rice fields, to and from school, and then to university, where he earned an engineering degree and later an MBA. He has worked as a production and design engineer, marketing manager, journalist, lead guitarist in a rock band, sadhu (an ascetic holy man), researcher, writer, animator, programmer, and knowledge management consultant. He is currently the CEO of activemuse.com, which offers services and consultancy to leading Indian software companies.

**ADRIAN KIEN** teaches poetry at Boise State University. He recently had to undergo an antibiotic treatment for a mysterious rash he had developed on his mouth. He rides a Diamond Back Axis TR circa 1995 with a single-speed conversion.

**AUSTIN KING** has been racing since he was 13. He lives in sunny Phoenix, Arizona, and currently races road bikes professionally in the U.S. for the Jittery Joe's team. He spent the best part of five years racing as an amateur in Europe with the U.S. National Team and the Cycling Center. In 2004, Austin was one of the main characters in a Belgian prime-time reality television show called *Man Bijt Hond* (*Man Bites Dog*). Off the bike, he spends as much time as he can with his girlfriend, Suzanne. Currently he is enrolled in a local community college (which is no place for a professional cyclist), chipping away at a business degree. He also runs a popular personal web site: www.AKingsLife.com.

**MICHAEL McCANN** has a near-unhealthy passion for pedaling. His solo travels on a second-hand, thirty-pound mountain bike have taken him across the United States on a number of different routes, as well as across the Arctic Circle—twice. Much of this riding was done in board shorts and flip-flops. Mike currently lives in Washington State, where he teaches in a Seattle public school program for homeless youth. He is a long-time volunteer/executive for the Seattle chapter of the Surfrider Foundation, as well as the founder and coordinator of their Snowrider Project. Many of his cycling adventures are documented at www.mikelikebike.com.

**BOB MINA** is 35 years old, and lives in West Chester, Pennsylvania. He was the fat kid in his high school band, but in 1988 he discovered the bicycle. Soon he lost 65 pounds and was racing. After a USCF racing career in which he maxed out as a Category 3 (total career earnings: one $25 prime, one T-shirt, one Power Bar), he was struck by a car on a training ride in April 1995. During his rehab, he saw an Ironman Triathlon on TV, and turned to triathlon training to complete his recovery. Since then he's raced in 45 triathlons of all distances, including 6 Ironman Triathlons. He's finished 26 marathons, including 10 Philadelphia Marathons in a row. He will race in anything he can find until they close the lid on him. Lately he's been messing around in Dragon Boats. Bob is married with a 15-month-old daughter and a cat.

**DAVID MONNIG** taught middle school in Portland for four years before moving to La Grande, Oregon where he attends Eastern Oregon University with his girlfriend. A passion for mountain-biking has replaced his childhood devotion to road-biking, and early morning rides in the woods near town are a daily activity. David still enjoys tinkering with bikes. Currently, he is building a tall bike—one bicycle welded on top of another.

**BOB NEUBAUER** has bicycled solo from Maine to Florida. His adventures from that trip are chronicled in his book *Two Wheels and a Map*. He has also published numerous travel stories in newspapers including: the *Philadelphia Inquirer, Los Angeles Times, Boston Globe* and *San Francisco Examiner*. When he's not riding, he serves as editor of a national trade magazine called *In-Plant Graphics*.

**AMY NEVALA** began her cycling career in 1999 by pedaling 3,254 miles across the United States to file reports on a group of bicyclists raising money for the American Lung Association. On an 88-mile day in Montana, a tall cyclist shared his peanut butter sandwich with her; she married him in 2004 on a Cape Cod farm. Amy and her husband live and bicycle in Massachusetts, where Amy works as a science writer at the Woods Hole Oceanographic Institution.

**CLAUS PALLE** is a 37-year-old father of one, living with his fiancée. He holds a law degree and works as a legal adviser at the University of Aarhus in Denmark. He played competitive soccer and basketball, while his bike was only a means of transportation. Eventually he discovered a passion for endurance sports, and began competing as a long-distance runner. At some point he was drawn towards road-racing, but still wanted to run, so he turned to triathlons. This in turn introduced him to adventure racing. Parenthood means an inevitable decrease in his sporting activities. He loves bikes for their pollution-free ability to get him out to the forest or countryside, far away from the city. He owns four bikes, but no car as yet.

**ERIC PINDER** is the author of three books about mountains, weather, and the outdoors: *North to Katahdin, Tying Down the Wind,* and *Life at the Top.* For many years, he lived and worked at the weather observatory on top of New Hampshire's Mount Washington ("the highest paying job in New England") and as a guide and instructor for the Appalachian Mountain Club. He teaches nature writing at Chester College of New England and lives in Berlin, New Hampshire.

**STEVE PUCCI** is a 57-year-old active cyclist. He lives in West Newbury, Massachusetts (35 miles north of Boston), with his wife, Jeanne. He has two daughters, Jennifer and Molly. He is the team manager of the regional powerhouse cycling team CCB/Volkswagen, for which he also races occasionally (five to six times a season). He has coached several successful bike racers, including Tyler Hamilton and Tim Johnson.

**GEORGE NIELS SORENSEN** has been a bicycle rider since the 1950s, when it was popular to clothespin playing cards to the wheels to annoy the neighbors. For the better part of 30 years, he has been a professional writer and marketing communications director in the corporate world. Author of several books, George has an eclectic background and set of interests. His undergraduate degree is in Theater Arts and he also holds an MA in Theology. He became interested in the Iron Riders when he wandered into a museum and saw a photo of them on the wall.

**DAVE STAMBOULIS** is a freelance photographer and writer based in Bangkok, specializing in off-the-beaten-track adventure travel around the world. He has written for many magazines and newspapers in Asia, and is the author of *Odysseus' Last Stand: Chronicles of a Bicycle Nomad*, which won the Society of American Travel Writers' Silver Medal for travel book of the year in 2006.

**RANDALL STAFFORD** has been an avid bicyclist since he was 10, when he talked his parents into buying a bright-yellow-and-white Falcon 10-speed for $200. Kidney disease and too much schooling have frequently threatened to interfere with his cycling. Stafford, his wife, and their two daughters live in Palo Alto, California, where he is a professor at the Stanford University School of Medicine. As Director of their Program on Prevention Outcomes and Practices, his focus is research on the prevention of heart disease. He is committed to helping individual patients reduce their risk of heart disease and to advocating for policy changes to confront the growing social problems created by obesity, physical inactivity, and poor nutrition. He is the author of nearly a hundred scientific papers and a handful of bicycling and kayaking travelogues. A successful masters racer and diligent bicycle commuter, his most memorable (and problematic) cycling experiences have been multi-day solo bicycle tours.

**GREG TAYLOR** is a native of Alexandria, Virginia. Identified by name in over one-third of the world's creation myths, he is a middling cyclist and a world-class smart aleck. While everything he says should be taken with a grain of salt, Mr. Taylor really did beat Miguel Indurain over a mountain stage of the Tour de France. He commutes to his job as a litigation attorney by bicycle, much to the bemusement of his colleagues. When the mood hits him, Mr. Taylor sends articles and stories to Cyclingnews.com.

"There's just something about bikes," says longtime velo-adventurer **AARON TEASDALE**, "that gets me in trouble again and again. They're such perfect vehicles for exploration—and, let's face it, true high-grade exploration leads to trouble more often than not." Teasdale has been writing about and photographing his exploits—being chased by spear-wielding Masai warriors in Tanzania, battling man-eating bogs in Newfoundland, getting utterly lost in Newark ghettos, and finding decaying mummies in the salt flats of Bolivia, to name a few—in various national magazines for the last 10 years. Currently Deputy Editor of *Adventure Cyclist* magazine, he lives in Missoula, Montana, with his wife and two young sons.

# Editors

**PAUL DIAMOND** grew up in Washington, D.C. He worked as a photojournalist for United Press International in Pittsburgh, and later taught writing at Ohio University and Tulane University. He now lives in San Diego and works as a writer and editor. When the ocean is flat—when there are absolutely no waves to surf—he takes his road bike out and rides along the coast in a t-shirt and board shorts.

**ERICH SCHWEIKHER** has always preferred wheels—his earliest memory is of being pulled around the neighborhood in a Radio Flyer wagon. A BMX bike replaced the wagon and the obsession began. While he has only one competitive race under his belt (he finished dead last due to a disqualification), he rides every chance he can get, mostly commuting to and from work in Portland, OR, where he teaches composition at Portland Community College. When not on the bike or in the classroom, he spends his downtime writing poems, a number of which have been published in national literary journals.

# Bibliography

Mina, Bob. "Spin Cycle." xtri.com, November 2002. (This story has been edited and revised since its original appearance.)

Neubauer, Bob. "The Road Forbidden." Portions of this story were originally published in Bob Neubauer, *Two Wheels and a Map*, Outdoor Action Publishing, 1998.

Nevala, Amy. "Riding Tandem with Rodent." Originally published as "Urban Jungle." *Adventure Cyclist*, March 2003. (This story has been edited and revised since its original appearance.)

Pinder, Eric. "Bicycles and Bagpipes." This story is based on and revised from material originally published in Eric Pinder, *North to Katahdin*, Milkweed Editions, 2005.

Sorensen, George Niels. "Iron Riders." This story is based upon information presented in George Niels Sorensen, *Iron Riders: Story of the 1890s Fort Missoula Buffalo Soldiers Bicycle Corps*, Missoula, Montana: Pictorial Histories Publishing Co., Inc., 2000.

Taylor, Greg. "The Day I Beat Miguel Indurain." Originally published as "Tall Tales, Taller Mountains and Statistics or The Day I Beat Miguel Indurain." Cyclingnews.com, 2003. (This story has been edited and revised since its original appearance.)

Taylor, Greg. "Genius—Not Genius." Originally published as "Genius, Not-Genius, and the Dental Floss Way of Bike Repair." Cyclingnews.com, 2005. (This story has been edited and revised since its original appearance.)

Teasdale, Aaron. "The Jungle is Hungry." Originally published as "The Jungle is Hungry." *Bike,* August 2001, 56-59. (This story has been edited and revised since its original appearance.)

# Rights

# Acknowledgements

Thanks to Tempe Bicycle for allowing me to walk their aisles for hours without ever buying a thing; Dominic's Cyclery in Tempe, Arizona for making a scrawny 15-year-old an honorary member of their mountain bike racing team; and George's Cycles and Fitness in Boise, Idaho, whose determined staff forced me to become a better mechanic.

Thanks to Mike Suarez, aka "Tank Ass," aka "Sore Ass," my good friend and occasional riding partner in Portland, Oregon, who continually proved to me that I wasn't nearly the cyclist I thought I was, but never rubbed it in, at least not verbally.

Thanks to my parents, Mary and Paul Schweikher, who bought me my first real bike, a bright blue Diamondback Topanga, and supported my cycling obsession even when I returned home broken and bruised.

And finally, thanks to Abbie Chandler, for having the patience over the last four years to put up with my expletive-packed rants when a simple repair turns into a full-scale nightmare.

For information on submitting a story to the next volume of this book,
visit www.casagrandepress.com